PHILOCTETES AND THE FALL OF TROY

FIGURE 1. Philoctetes on Lemnos. Painting on aryballos (oil flask). Fourth century B.C. *From L. A. Milani,* Il mito di Filottete, *1879*

Oscar Mandel

PHILOCTETES
AND THE FALL
OF TROY

Plays, Documents, Iconography, Interpretations

Including Versions by Sophocles, André Gide,
Oscar Mandel, and Heiner Müller

UNIVERSITY OF NEBRASKA PRESS
LINCOLN AND LONDON

Library of Congress Cataloging in Publication Data

Mandel, Oscar.
    Philoctetes and the fall of Troy.

    Bibliography: p. 251
    1. Philoctetes (Legendary character)   2. Drama—History and criti-
cism.   I.   Title.
PN57.P488Md   809.2'927   80–28524
ISBN 0–8032–3063–X

Contents

Maps

Figures

Plates

Preface

The centerpiece of this book is the *Philoctetes* of Sophocles. This can be read elsewhere, of course, in a variety of editions and translations; but here, for the first time in any language, the play has become part of a Philoctetes omnibus with the following specific innovations:

1. A collection of nearly all surviving allusions to Philoctetes from Homer to the ninth century A.D. A coherent arrangement and comments are supplied.
2. An account of the fortunes of the Philoctetes legends from the Renaissance to our own century.
3. The beginnings of a Philoctetes iconography for that same period.
4. An anthology of three modern Philoctetes plays, one of them translated especially for this volume.

The reader will also find a critical essay following Sophocles' play in which some fresh thoughts, useful or otherwise, are ventured. The commentaries on the three modern plays are—as I believe they should be—much briefer; and they address themselves exclusively to the major theses which can, in my opinion, be extracted from the drama. I make no apology for excavating all four plays for major thematic statements about our human realities. All four strike me as determined to make such statements and optimistic about the ability of literary works to communicate them. But they are also plays, they are works of art, and as such I have left them to fend for themselves. All in all, I hope that the grouping of these plays, and their grouping in the presence of the ancient documents and the later history of the Philoctetes legend, can give rise to an abundance of lively ideas, both philosophical (with my comments, perhaps, as points of departure) and aesthetic.

A less studious enjoyment can be recommended too, for I have sought to make this a pleasant book to read, and kept in mind not only specialists and university students but the general educated reader. I realize that casting such a large net upon the waters can be hazardous. On one page the general reader may gasp for air. On another the Hellenist may shrug his shoulders with impatience. I can only beg each group to make good-natured accommodations in favor of the others, and agree to live and let live.

A word about the genesis of this book. At the time I was writing my own play in the year 1959, I knew nothing about its hero beyond what Sophocles chooses to tell. I had probably forgotten that Homer mentions him, and would have been startled to hear that Euripides had thought of a *Trojan* attempt to enlist Philoctetes twenty-four centuries before me. Such ignorance is of inestimable value to an artist, and I doubt whether Gide and Müller knew much more about Philoctetes when they composed their own versions. It was only in the summer of 1978 that the scholarly project which resulted in this volume entered my mind. I was translating my play into French, and for good measure revising the English original and—after twenty years—rereading Sophocles' text. Thereupon I fell into a candid sort of enchantment, as if no one had ever admired Sophocles before. "La plus belle chose du monde," Émile Faguet had called *Philoctetes* at the beginning of our century. And so I thought it too. For if *Oedipus* is the more gorgeous vessel, it is a gorgeous vessel full of leaks. *Philoctetes* instead is not only sound, and grandly passionate, but it also speaks to us, I am convinced, of issues far denser with meaning for us today than those of *Oedipus*. Be that as it may—to each his favorite—this blessed delight, and then a growing curiosity about the Philoctetes legends as such (even though I recognized that Sophocles had shifted the center of gravity from Philoctetes to Neoptolemus), and finally a desire, I hope forgivable, to bring out my own revised version, all combined to energize me. I was able to set to work while residing with my wife at the Casa de Velazquez in Madrid, and I take this opportunity to thank M. Guérin, its chief librarian, and the other members of the staff, for their many courtesies.

Later that same summer, in a chance conversation with Professor Sigrid Kupsch-Losereit at Cerisy-la-Salle in Normandy, I heard for the first time of Heiner Müller and his *Philoktet*. Reading the play after my return to California, I recognized in it the wing I required to make the structure complete and harmonious. I met Mr. Müller briefly in early 1979, when he was in Berkeley for the opening of another play of his, and obtained his permission to translate and introduce his *Philoctetes* to the English-speaking world. The translation was made from the

Suhrkamp Verlag text in "dialectical" consultation with a basic English version by Maria Feder, who also carefully reviewed and corrected my work at the end. Valuable advice on certain knotty passages was given me by Professor Kupsch-Losereit, Norbert Alcer, and Klara Carmely, while Professor Marc Silberman was good enough to read the final text and make it even *more* final for me.

I have had much help from others, from timely hints to a wealth of materials. Some of those to whom I am obliged are named at the appropriate points in the text. Here I wish to name them all, and do so simply in alphabetical order: Madeleine Aubrun, Stephen Bailey (J. Paul Getty Museum), Michèle Beaulieu (Louvre), William M. Calder III (University of Colorado), Ruby Cohn (University of California at Davis), Philipp Fehl (University of Illinois at Urbana), Jacques Foucart (Louvre), Suzanne Gutwirth, H. W. Janson (New York University), Jenijoy La Belle (California Institute of Technology), Antoinette Le Normand (Musée d'Orsay, Paris), Jennifer Montagu (Warburg Institute), George W. Pigman III (California Institute of Technology), Anne Pingeot (Musée d'Orsay, Paris), Sir John Pope-Hennessy (Metropolitan Museum of New York), Aimée Brown Price (California Institute of Technology), Robert Torrance (University of California at Davis), Ann Wagner (Metropolitan Museum of New York).

I also want to thank Professor Torrance for taking the trouble to send me a number of revisions to his already published translation of Sophocles. It is by a fortunate accident that I came upon his version on the library shelf. I liked it at once because it succeeds, I think, in keeping a consistently noble manner within the terrible constraints of modern American English, and happily avoids the sudden drops into vulgarity that jolt the flight of other contemporary versions.

For all the busy work that goes into the making of a book—and particularly a collection like this one—I am vastly obliged to the skills, the loyalty, and the goodwill of Mary Ellis Arnett, who has, indeed, made many a crooked thing straight for me for nearly two decades.

The reader has already surmised that this book is not the work of a normally ordained classical scholar. Undaunted by this failure of unction, I have leaped headlong into the Sophoclean hot spots of meaning and intention where scholars and critics are waging courteous battle. My debt alike to those I have agreed with and those with whom I am sorry to disagree is enormous. Its full extent is to be gleaned from the bibliography—beyond, that is, the scholars I have named in the text itself as occasion demanded. I hope that many of them will continue to instruct me after this text has joined the common stream.

POSTSCRIPT

As the manuscript for this book was nearing completion, I heard from the University of Nebraska Press that *my* editor, Virginia Faulkner, had died ("suddenly and peacefully") the night of 15 September 1980. Many years before, Virginia Faulkner had been midwife and tutor to our book on Don Juan. Peremptorily intelligent, ebullient, learned, tough, kind, witty, loyal to the last dot, she orchestrated an unforgettable experience for me. When I approached the same Press with my notion of a work on Philoctetes, it was largely in order to enjoy another splendid time with VF. And so it turned out. Same ardor, same crackle and wise-crackle of ideas, same fidelity: all was as it had been. VF was already halfway retired, and *Philoctetes* would be among her last books for the Press. And last they came to be all too literally. Now I can make but a mournful pass at consolation by recalling that what I have said here about Virginia Faulkner, I made plentifully known to her when she was still in harness.

Her last note to me is dated 1 May 1980. It concludes: "Consider that I am placing a May basket on your doorstep." Let this then be an autumn basket, leaning against another door.

19 September 1980

Part I

PHILOCTETES
IN ANTIQUITY

A NOTE ON NAMES

Mythological figures often have Latin names which differ markedly from the Greek. As I have imposed no standardization on the texts I cite, the reader will encounter, besides the basic Zeus / Jupiter and Hera / Juno doublets, such equivalents as Heracles / Hercules, Athena / Minerva, Hephaistos / Vulcan, Odysseus / Ulysses, Neoptolemus / Pyrrhus, and Alexander / Paris. Variations in English spellings of certain names (for examples, Poeias / Poias) are minor and present no difficulties. Achaean, Argive, and Danaan are equivalents for Greek; Dardanian for Trojan; and Pergamon and Ilium for Troy. Two accentuations should be noted: Philoc*te*tes and Neop*to*lemus.

The Tradition

PHILOCTETES. In Greek mythology, son of Poias. He acquired, by gift, the bow and arrow of Hercules by lighting the pyre on which the hero was consumed alive. On his way to the Trojan War, Philoctetes was bitten by a snake. Because the smell of his wound and his cries made him offensive, his companions left him on the desolate island of Lemnos. When an oracle declared that Troy could not be taken without the weapons of Hercules, Philoctetes was brought to Troy by Neoptolemus (or Diomedes) and Odysseus. He was healed of his wound and helped conquer Troy by killing Paris.

The New Columbia Encyclopedia

1. In March 409 B.C., the *Philoctetes* of Sophocles won the prize at the Great Dionysia, Athens' yearly Competitive Spring Festival of Drama, as we might call it today. The playwright was nearing his ninetieth year. If we try to picture him at work on the play during the months preceding the festival, and sifting through memories of a long life of literary creation, what stories and notions concerning Philoctetes can we plausibly imagine wandering through his mind—episodes and ideas for him to imitate, reshape, perhaps contradict, and possibly transcend? No one doubts that he was familiar with the *Philoctetes* of Aeschylus, produced in or around the year 475 but surely not forgotten, and with the more recent version by Euripides, performed in 431. He knew the few words which Homer devotes to Philoctetes, and surely also the longer passages, lost to us, in several other epic poems concerning the Trojan War. We can suppose him

3

to have heard and seen several other Philoctetes plays, the names of whose authors, along with a few fragments, are all that remains today. He was probably acquainted with a passage in one of Pindar's odes relating to Philoctetes. And beyond this, we must imagine him as having had access to numerous allusions, retellings, and rewritings which time has utterly erased from our view, besides a fair number of visual representations, some of which have happily survived in fact or in report.[1] For even though the great archer had never achieved the stature or currency of the primary heroes of the Trojan War, he was nevertheless a figure known to all men, and perennially available for comment or allusion.

We are about to glance at most of what remains to us from this storehouse of materials. In so doing, we shall elaborate a sort of legendary biography of Philoctetes, and at the same time make visible the fictive landscape in which a Greek audience would, by and large, perceive a new play about Philoctetes. It is true that most of the extant texts and allusions postdate Sophocles. One of the most precious, for instance, reaches us through the words of a patriarch of Constantinople who lived late in the ninth century after Christ![2] Saint Photius compiled a learned reference work, in which he quoted from another learned reference work compiled four or as many as seven centuries before him, which in turn summarized the work of still other learned compilers, thus providing us, among other things, with a capsule account of several epic poems almost as venerable as Homer's. I give this example to justify the enlisting of Photius and many others who wrote after Sophocles. They are reporters, however late, of traditions which Sophocles *may* or *must* have known, for when they wrote, they certainly, or probably, or possibly, took their inspiration directly or indirectly from sources which were accessible to him. In short, we can almost never lower the gavel and declare

---

1. L. A. Milani, *Nuovi monumenti di Filottete,* enumerates sixty-three surviving visual representations from the fifth century B.C. to the second or third century A.D.

2. See the Register of Sources following this chapter. For place-names in this and other sections of the book, refer to the maps.

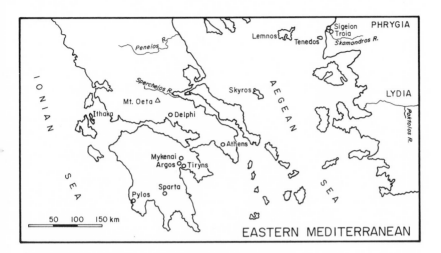

that any given episode concerning Philoctetes, narrated
after 409 B.C., was demonstrably unknown to Sophocles.

2. Our tale is launched by Homer, who names Philoctetes in his catalogue of Greek warriors:

They who lived about Thaumakia and Methone,   *Iliad* 2. 716–33
they who held Meliboia and rugged Olizon,
of their seven ships the leader was Philoktetes
skilled in the bow's work, and aboard each vessel were fifty
oarsmen, each well skilled in the strength of the bow in battle.
Yet he himself lay apart in the island, suffering strong pains,
in Lemnos the sacrosanct, where the sons of the Achaians had
    left him
in agony from the sore bite of the wicked water snake.
There he lay apart in his pain; yet soon the Argives
beside their ships were to remember lord Philoktetes.
Yet these, longing as they did for their leader, did not go
    leaderless,
but Medon, the bastard son of Oïleus, set them in order,
whom Rhene bore to Oïleus the sacker of cities.
    They who held Trikke and the terraced place of Ithome,
and Oichalia, the city of Oichalian Eurytos,
of these in turn the leaders were two sons of Asklepios,
good healers both themselves, Podaleirios and Machaon.
In their command were marshalled thirty hollow vessels.

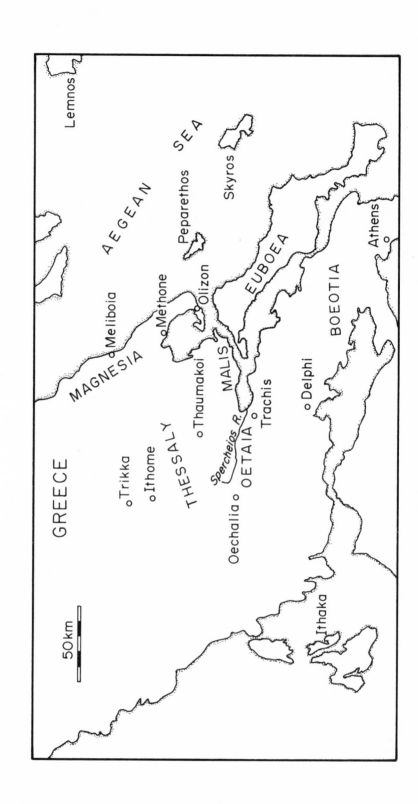

The warning that the Greeks will soon be remembering their need of Philoctetes is just possibly a late addition to the Homeric text. So Zenodotus, head of the Alexandrian library in the third century B.C., believed; but the question is in dispute; and even if the passage is an addition, was it added before or after Sophocles' time? We are safe enough in believing that Sophocles' Homer suggested, without stating it in so many words, that Troy could not be taken without Philoctetes. But it is noteworthy too that a hint suffices—an explanation to the audience seems superfluous—indicating that Homer's listeners were on intimate terms with a basic Philoctetes fable long before Sophocles wrote. However, Homer quickly drops him, for the essentials of Philoctetes' story occur during stretches of time covered by neither the *Iliad* nor the *Odyssey*.

Scholia Graeca in Homeri Iliadem 2. 724

For the purposes of his catalogue, Homer is clearly more interested in situating Philoctetes on the map and entering his contribution to the war effort than he is in his adventures. He places Philoctetes in Magnesia with such an abundance of detail that it becomes something of a minor puzzle why Sophocles turned him into a prince of Malis.[3] Modern scholarship answers: in order to bring him closer to Heracles in the region of Mount Oeta. As Homer does not connect these two heroes at all, it is argued that only those who do affiliate them want to see them in closer geographical proximity. This is undoubtedly *a* reason, but it strikes me as a weak one. Is Magnesia so far from Oeta that all ties between the two heroes become unthinkable? Hardly. For that matter, Thaumakia, one of the Magnesian towns Homer mentions, lies at no great distance from Heracles' resting place. Furthermore, a curious passage in Pausanias also suggests that the true Philoctetes had nothing to do with Malis. Pausanias notes that the bow and arrows were fairly alien to the Greeks in what we call their classical period:

Neither indeed did the Malians continue the practice of the

---

3. "In its original form, the story of Poeas and his son must have belonged, like that of Jason, to the legends of the Myniae who dwelt on the eastern coasts of Thessaly" (R. C. Jebb, ed. and trans., *Sophocles: The Plays and Fragments*, pt. 4, *The Philoctetes*, p. ix).

Pausanias *De-
scription of
Greece* 1. 32.4
bow; in fact, I believe they did not know it before the time of
Philoctetes, and gave it up soon after.

A reasonable inference is that they had never used the
bow to begin with and that Philoctetes was simply not one
of their native heroes. The truth is that we do not know
why Sophocles or one of his predecessors deprived Magnesia of its prince and settled him in Malis instead.

Homer seems to propose that Philoctetes was not only
abandoned, but also bitten on the island of Lemnos. Most
later writers, as we shall see, preferred to have him injured on a nearby island and removed *to* Lemnos. Furthermore, Homer tells us nothing about the occasion or
reason for the snakebite. He makes the Greeks in general
and not Odysseus in particular responsible for abandoning the Magnesian chief on Lemnos, yet without at-
taching any blame to them. He does not suggest that
Philoctetes is all alone on Lemnos. He does not speak of
an oracle urging that Philoctetes be recalled. He does not
hint that Philoctetes is angry and will resist the summons
of the Greeks. In sum, a number of elements vital to
Sophocles are absent from the *Iliad*—and from the
Odyssey—either because Homer is not acquainted with
them, or because they are irrelevant to the march of his
story. What we do get, however, is the strong coloring,
though in few strokes, of the wretched man in an agony
of pain. I will be returning in a while to this highly
pathetic feature of the legend.

Finally, we are informed that the modest forces of
Philoctetes are not leaderless before Troy. This concludes the chapter on Philoctetes in the *Iliad*. Homer goes
on to introduce the two sons of Asclepius. One or the
other—or even Asclepius himself—is destined to cure
Philoctetes of his wound.

3. In the *Cypria,* a shorter epic poem probably composed after the *Iliad*, but based on the same ancient mass
of orally transmitted tales and songs, a couple of gaps are
filled, and we move a little closer to Sophocles. All that
remains, unfortunately, is a sentence of summary from
Proclus as given by the patriarch already named:

Thereafter they [the Greeks] land on Tenedos. During a banquet, Philoctetes is bitten by a water-snake. Because a disgusting stench emanates from his wound, he is abandoned on Lemnos.

Cypria

Here at any rate is a precise statement of where Philoctetes came to grief. While Tenedos will be exchanged for other places by some later writers, and while some will even have Philoctetes wounded (if not bitten) before Troy itself, the notion of a small, inhospitable island not far from Lemnos will be generally favored.

The *Cypria* also tells us that Philoctetes was bitten during a banquet. Apparently the poet was content to regard the business as an accident of the kind that can occur at a picnic. The gods do not seem to be involved. As for the bare pain mentioned by Homer, it is now accompanied by an intolerable stench. This detail will acquire enormous importance in other accounts. In Homer we find nothing beyond a sick or injured warrior left behind in a perfectly normal manner; and a number of later writers will insist that Philoctetes was taken to Lemnos simply so that he might be treated there (a Lemnian earth or stone is sometimes specified), much as one would take an injured fellow-officer today from a barren island to a center boasting a well-equipped hospital. By contrast, the *Cypria* suggests that the Greeks shook off their companion because he stank. The possibility of an *offended* Philoctetes, and of a set of *blameworthy* Greeks, has been created.

4. Another summary by Photius quoting Proclus is even more useful. Once more we are allowed a tantalizing look at a post-Homeric poem, the *Little Iliad:*

And afterwards Ulysses took Helenus prisoner by a ruse. Helenus having foretold the final destruction of Troy, Diomedes fetched Philoctetes from Lemnos by ship. Philoctetes was cured by Machaon, and having met Alexander in single combat, killed him.[4] The latter's corpse, after being abused by

Little Iliad

---

4. Alexander, otherwise known as Paris, was the son of Priam who had abducted Helen and thus occasioned the Trojan War. Menelaus was the offended husband. Both Helenus and Deiphobus were brothers of Paris. Neoptolemus was the son of Achilles, and dwelled on the island of Scyros at the time his father was killed by Paris.

Menelaus, was carried away and buried by the Trojans. Thereafter Deiphobus took Helen in marriage. And Ulysses gave
Neoptolemus, who had been brought from Scyros, his father's
armor.[5]

For the first time we hear of the fateful prophecy. What
was its content in the *Little Iliad*? The summary, par-
simonious as it is, leaves no room for doubt: Helenus has
declared that both Philoctetes and Neoptolemus are *indispensable* for the destruction of Troy. Since neither is
present, both must be summoned to battle. Diomedes sets
sail for Lemnos; and while the summary does not say who
was sent to Scyros, it may well be that even in the *Little
Iliad* the emissary was already Odysseus himself.

For the first time, too, a specific action, namely killing
Paris, is ascribed to Philoctetes. But there is no hint that
the arrow which despatched the Trojan seducer had once
belonged to Heracles. The faint voices that reach us from
the eighth- and seventh-century epic tradition suggest
that the linking of Philoctetes to Heracles was to occur at a
later date.

5. By the time the *Little Iliad* was composed, we can
guess that an impasse had been reached concerning the
role Philoctetes was to play in the concluding phase of the
war. Troy could not be taken without Philoctetes and
Neoptolemus. But while the matter of Troy as it jelled
into an "authorized version" fully verified the prophecy
with respect to Neoptolemus, it never did so for Philoctetes. Neoptolemus, succeeding his father Achilles,
finishes off the war. The father, Achilles, had killed the
son, Hector. Later the son, Neoptolemus, kills the father,
Priam. The poets convince us that Troy could not fall
without the help of Neoptolemus. But can we say as much
for the second recipient of Helenus' prophecy? If
Philoctetes too was indispensable, what else did his arrows do besides eliminate one of the less redoubtable
Trojans, the effete Paris? And does Pausanias help when

---

5. Which Odysseus had won for himself after the death of Achilles in a
celebrated contest with Ajax—the subject of another extant Sophoclean
tragedy.

he mentions another success, namely the slaying of a perfectly obscure Trojan named Admetus?

Pausanias *Description of Greece* 10. 27.1

These thin yields notwithstanding, the largest claims keep being made. Sophocles, for instance, lets Neoptolemus assure Philoctetes, at the solemn conclusion of the play, that "with me, and with your bow, you will demolish Troy," and more solemnly yet, Heracles himself confirms not only the killing of Paris, but separately, the conquest of Troy.[6] It may be objected that Sophocles is merely taking advantage of a poet's special privilege. But the union of large promise with small fulfillment occurs in nonpoetic texts as well. It appears, for example, in the history of Pompeius Trogus, epitomized by Justinus, where we hear of "those arrows of Hercules which *decided* the fate of Troy" (italics mine).

Sophocles *Philoctetes* 1335, 1428

Justinus 20.1

Pindar goes farther than any other known writer in explicitly ascribing the fall of Troy to Philoctetes. Addressing a compliment to the king of Syracuse, who has been waging a war though sick, "following the fashion of Philoctetes," Pindar writes in his First Pythian:

> They say that godlike heroes came to
>   bring Poias' son, the mighty archer
> from Lemnos, where he lay in pain of his festering
>   wound;
> and he sacked Priam's city and made an end of the
>   Danaans' labors;
> he came with flesh infirm, but a man of doom.

Pindar *I Pythian* 51–55

But the flattery of King Hieron intended here—Pindar even chooses to forget the well-attested cure of Philoctetes in order to keep up the analogy with the king—reduces the testimonial value of this passage. It fails to shake our faith that the ultimate weapon would be the Wooden Horse devised by Odysseus, inside of which, by the way, Philoctetes was to take a modest place as but one among many.

How are we to interpret this strange aposiopesis in the legend of Philoctetes? Had a version of the fall of Troy existed once in which Philoctetes had actually played the

---

6. "Thou shalt sack Troy" in R. C. Jebb's translation.

promised role? We shall be hearing by and by that his arrows were poisoned. Is there an ur-*Iliad,* later expurgated, in which, besides other atrocities, poisoned arrows were admitted, and those of Philoctetes felled Priam and brought Troy to its knees? Or was the Philoctetes matter intrusive from the beginning? If we start with a local heroic lay concerning a mighty archer, an innovative rhapsode can easily be pictured thrusting his story into the fashionable matter of Troy, and not losing any sleep over the fact that the conclusion was preempted by other personages and other engines of death. If his tale concerned a prediction made to Philoctetes that such or such a city (but not Troy) was destined to fall under his arrows, it would not be difficult to mortice this prophecy to the one by Helenus regarding Neoptolemus, and make the seer call for two saviors rather than one. Two saviors is an oddity, to be sure, for saviors prefer to work alone, but in this particular tale neither was so famous beforehand as to preclude a theoretical teaming up.

We know, furthermore, that the *Iliad* does not make much of the bow and arrows. They are favored by the Trojans more than the Greeks; but also—and this is more relevant here—in the Greek tradition they appear to belong to the previous generation, the generation in which Heracles rather than Achilles had flourished.[7] Once again we are led to surmise that an older legend was housed, and none too comfortably, in a later one. The cycle of Troy was too powerfully dedicated to the glorification of sword and spear to allow the war to be settled by a flight of arrows, poisoned or clean.

This solution to the problem of an aborted Philoctetes legend is of course highly speculative. Furthermore, it is a speculation which, as far as we can tell, the Greeks themselves did not indulge in. Now and then a text seems to

---

7. This is ably discussed by A. J. B. Wace and F. H. Stubbings, *A Companion to Homer,* chap. 19. A representative passage in the *Iliad* occurs when Paris has wounded Diomedes in the foot with an arrow. The sword-wielding Diomedes shouts at him:

This is the blank weapon of a useless man, no fighter.
But if one is struck by me only a little, that is far different,
The stroke is a sharp thing and suddenly lays him lifeless.
[11. 390–92, in Lattimore's translation]

imply a touch of puzzlement over the fact that a Malian or Magnesian hero of the Trojan War was a specialist of the bow, but the problem of giving the tale of Philoctetes a resounding conclusion is always finely evaded. Ovid, to give one instance, performed what can only be called a neat dodge:

> To the land of Queen Hypsipyle and the illustrious Thoas,[8] once infamous for its murdered men of olden time, victorious Ulysses now set sail to bring thence the Tirynthian[9] arrows. After he had brought these to the Greeks, and their master with them, the final blow was at last given to the long-drawn war.

Ovid *Meta-morphoses* 13. 399–403

A baffled lawyer could have done no better. If one so wishes, Philoctetes' arrows have conquered Troy; if one does not, they have done nothing of the sort.

6. Not much is said anywhere about the beginnings of Philoctetes. His father is Poeas, and his mother, according to Hyginus, is Demonassa. Apollodorus reports that Poeas was one of the Argonauts, and therefore a companion to Heracles, who was also taking part in Jason's expedition. But usually Philoctetes himself is named as the Argonaut, especially by those who emphasize his link with Heracles. Thus C. Valerius Flaccus in his *Argonautica:*

Apollodorus *Biblioteca* 1. 9.16

> Thou also, son of Poeas, twice destined to see Lemnos, art rowing to Phrixian Colchis,[10] famed now for thy father's spear, but one day shalt thou ply the arrows of Hercules.

Valerius *Argonautica* 1. 391–93

The younger Philostratus, in his *Imagines,* neatly ties the stories together:

---

8. That is, to Lemnos. Hypsipyle, daughter of Thoas, and apparently the first liberated woman of them all, had led the Lemnian women in murdering all male Lemnians with the exception of old Thoas.

9. That is, Heracleian; Heracles was the lord of Tyrins.

10. Colchis was at the eastern end of the Black Sea, in what is now the Russian Caucasus. Phrixus was a Boeotian prince who flew on a golden ram to Colchis. The fleece of this ram became the object of the Argonauts' expedition a generation later. Note that for Valerius, Philoctetes is a normal Greek hero equipped with spear and, presumably, sword. The bow and arrows will come to him as a special gift. The Heracleian connection is discussed in the next section.

Philostratus Jr.   The Achaeans, when they sailed for Troy and put in at the
Imagines 17   islands, were earnestly seeking the altar of Chryse, which Jason
                   had formerly erected when he made his voyage to Colchis; and
                   Philoctetes, remembering the altar from his visit to it with Hera-
                   cles, pointed it out to the searchers, whereupon a water-serpent
                   drove its poison into one of his feet.

This is better rounded, and closer to Sophocles, than
what we have teased out of the epic poems. We are given a
clear sequence: Philoctetes and Heracles as fellow Argonauts under Jason's command, the altar to Chryse on
one of the islands, the much later second expedition led
by Agamemnon, the return visit to Chryse (evidently the
Greeks were being careful to give every shrine on the way
its due), and the snakebite while good Philoctetes was
clearing the shrubbery or dusting off the altar. The bite
still looks like an accident in this account, but there is
slightly more thematic purpose to the ill-fated propitia-
tion of the goddess than in a wrong step at a banquet.

According to Dio Chrysostom, Euripides made use of
the Chryse episode in his *Philoctetes*. Dio reports the
hero's words as follows in his paraphrase of the Euripidean drama:

Dio *Discourses*   I met with disaster, because I showed the Greeks Chryse's altar,
59   where they must first make sacrifice if they would overcome the
                   foe; else, I declared, our expedition was being made in vain.[11]

The advantage of this pilgrimage to the shrine of Chryse
was that it put the Greeks in debt to Philoctetes. Writers
who wanted to condemn them for deserting the wounded
hero could use this tale to magnify their ingratitude.

Dares the Phrygian makes Philoctetes even more ser-
viceable to the Greeks:

Dares *De*   Philoctetes, who had gone with the Argonauts to Troy,[12] acted
excidio Troiae   as pilot.
historiae 15

---

11. For the full text, see the "Observations on the *Philoctetes* plays of
Aeschylus, Euripides, and Sophocles" below.

12. Heracles took time off from the *Argo* at Troy for one of his rousing
adventures, and Dares must be supposing that Philoctetes accompanied him.

As pilot, that is, to the entire Greek flotilla under Agamemnon's command. This was a role undreamed of in the *Iliad*.

7. As for the connection, filial or fraternal, with Heracles, after Homer it became firmly established and remained unquestioned from then on. Thus Lucan, in a description of Thessaly:

> . . . and Trachis, with near-by [?] Meliboeia, both of which Philoctetes made glorious by winning Hercules's bow, as a prize for setting alight the dying hero's funeral pyre.

Lucan *Pharsalia* 6. 353–54

Or Diodorus Siculus:

> Heracles, having abandoned hope for himself, ascended the pyre and asked each one who came up to him to put his torch to the pyre. And when no one had the courage to obey him, Philoctetes alone was prevailed upon; and he, having received in return for his compliance the gift of the bow and arrows of Heracles, lighted the pyre.

Diodorus Siculus *Biblioteca historica* 4.38

One of the church fathers, Lactantius, invoked this tale to pour scorn on the pagan worship of Heracles:

> And men think him a god! Philoctetes, his heir, did not think so, indeed, for he placed a torch under him as he was about to be buried, and he saw his limbs and sinews seared and scattered. He buried his bones and ashes on the Oetean Mount, and for this service he received the arrows.

Lactantius *Divinae institutiones* 1.9

A late and idiosyncratic tale found only in Servius's commentary on the *Aeneid* adds that Heracles made Philoctetes take an oath that he would never reveal the burial site to anyone. The "arrows dipped in the gall of the Hydra" were his reward. Servius does not explain why Heracles wanted secrecy; and when he adds that the Greeks subsequently pressured Philoctetes to reveal the site because they wanted the bow and arrows, all is confusion, since Philoctetes already has them in his possession according to Servius himself. Philoctetes then tries to escape from his quandary by saying nothing, and striking

Servius *Servianorum in Vergilii carmina commentarium* 3. 402

the burial site with his foot. This fable, weakly echoing perhaps some remote cult of the dead, seems alien to the spirit of the Philoctetes tradition.

That Heracles' arrows were dipped in poison is, however, an ancient tradition, though Sophocles and others expunged it from their civilized versions. In Seneca's *Hercules Oetaeus* the Hydra is named, but we are in effect talked into forgetting the venom. For the rest, Seneca's tragedy is worth citing here if only because it is the only complete classical drama extant, other than Sophocles', in which Philoctetes appears as a character.

He makes his entrance in the final episode of this long play. Earlier, we have seen Hercules' captive mistress Iole, his jealous wife Deianira, the latter's gift of the robe imbrued in the blood of Nessus, Hercules' atrocious suffering after he puts on the robe, his mother's lament; and we have heard the report of Deianira's death. Calmed down at last, Hercules turns to his followers:

Seneca
*Hercules
Oetaeus*
1480–87

Now let me choose a death glorious, renowned, illustrious, full worthy of myself. This day will I make famous. Go, cut down all the woods, heap Oeta's grove together, that a mighty pyre may receive Hercules, and that before he dies. Thou, son of Poeas, dear youth, perform this sad office for me; set the whole sky aglow with the flames of Hercules.

The actual death of Hercules takes place off stage, of course, and is reported by Philoctetes. On stage, the Chorus hears a great moan as the Savior (for so Hercules is consistently represented) expires:

Ibid.,
1595–1612

But what is this? The universe resounds. Behold, he mourns, the father mourns Alcides; or is it the outcry of the gods or the voice of his frighted step-dame? At the sight of Hercules does Juno flee the stars? Under the mighty weight has Atlas staggered? Or is it that the awful ghosts have trembled and at sight of Hercules the hell-hound in affright has broken his chains and fled? No, we are wrong; behold with joyful face comes Poeas' son and on his shoulders he bears the shafts and the quiver known to all, the heir of Hercules.
[*Enter* PHILOCTETES]
Speak out, good youth, and tell the end of Hercules, I pray, and with what countenance Alcides bore his death.

PHILOCTETES. With such as none e'er bore his life.
CHORUS. So joyous did he mount his funeral pyre?
PHILOCTETES. He showed that now flames were as naught to him. What 'neath the heavens has Hercules left by defeat unscathed? Lo, all things have been subdued.

The Chorus now asks for a close description, and Philoctetes willingly recounts the felling of the trees, the building of the gigantic pyre, and Hercules' climb onto the funeral pile.

But he, like some huge, suffering lion, which, in Libyan forest lying, roars out his pain, hurried along,—who would suppose him hasting to the flames? His gaze was of one who seeks the stars, not fires of earth, when he set foot on Oeta and with his eyes surveyed the pyre complete. The great beams broke beneath him. Then for his shafts and bow he called, and said: "Take these, thou son of Poeas, take them as Alcides' gift and pledge of love. These did the Hydra feel; by these the Stymphalian birds lie low, and all other pests which at distance I overcame. O youth with valour blest, never in vain shalt thou send these 'gainst a foe; or if birds from the very clouds thou wouldst fetch away, birds will fall down, and out of the sky will thy shafts, sure of their prey, come floating; and ne'er will this bow disappoint thy hand. Well has it learned to poise the feathered shafts and unerringly send them flying; while the shafts themselves, loosed from the string, fail never to find their mark. Only do thou, I pray, apply the fire and set the last torch for me. Let this club," he said, "which no hand but mine has wielded, burn in the flames with me; this weapon alone shall follow Hercules. This also shouldst thou have," said he, "if thou couldst wield it. Let it add fuel to its master's pyre." Then did he call for the Nemean monster's shaggy skin to burn with him; 'neath the skin the pyre was hidden.

Ibid., 1642–66

Presently another lament arises. Alcmena, like a second Mary, weeps and smites her breasts. But Hercules (still in Philoctetes' report) shames the weepers, and calls on Jove to revive him among the stars.

When he had thus said, he called for fire. "Up now, Alcides' willing friend," said he, "catch up the Oetaean torch; let my step-dame see how I can bear the flames. Why did thy right hand tremble? Did thy hand shrink timid from such unholy

Ibid., 1715–30

deed? Then give me my quiver back, thou undaring, unskilled,
unwarlike—*that* the hand to bend my bow! Why do thy cheeks
grow pale? Come, seize on the torch with courage, with face
thou seest on prone Alcides. Poor soul, have some regard for
him who soon will burn.

But lo! now doth my father call me and he opens heaven. I
come, O sire." Then was his face no more the same. With
trembling hand I applied the blazing pine; the flames shrunk
back, the torch resisted and would not touch his limbs; but
Heracles followed up the shrinking flames.

No one knows when or by whom the legend of Philoctetes
was first coupled to the Heracleian saga. But it is not
difficult to guess *why* the connection was made. For one
thing—the evidence is in the passage by Valerius cited
above (section 6)—a gift by Heracles made reasonable the
oddity of a Greek hero of the Trojan War relying on a
bow instead of a spear. For another, Heracles had already
subdued Troy once, when Priam's father Laomedon was
ruling (this takes us back to the *Argo*). But the first sack of
Troy had been eclipsed by the glamor of the second.
Storytellers had managed to draft Philoctetes into this
prestigious, we might even say best-selling, war. However, the same favor could not be done directly to the far
more renowned Heracles, for everyone knew that he had
died before the opening of hostilities. Instead, he was
given a share of the glory through his weapon. It was
common practice among poets to give important arms a
distinguished history of previous owners. Nothing then
was easier than fathering Philoctetes' bow on Heracles.
The idea was doubly good. It gave Philoctetes still greater
standing, and it allowed Heracles to participate vicari-
ously in the new victory over Troy. This is implied, for
instance, by Valerius in another passage, when he says of
Laomedon,

Valerius *Argo-*   He had heard that twice must Troy fall
nautica 2.   victim to the shafts of Hercules.
570–71

And the Chorus of Seneca's *Troades* cries out, concerning
Troy,

Seneca *Troades*   Twice she endured the battering of her Dardanian walls by
134–37   Grecian steel and twice felt the arrows of Hercules.

8. No wonder, then, that writers wavered between two interpretations of the central point in the Philoctetes legend. Some said that Philoctetes in person must be brought back to the Grecian camp. These writers were keeping faith, consciously or unconsciously, with the basic tradition of a Philoctetes unconnected with Heracles—his own man, the mightiest archer in the land. Others placed most or all of the stress on the bow and arrows. The weapon *rather* than Philoctetes or the weapon *more urgently* than Philoctetes must be recovered from Lemnos. These writers consciously or unconsciously subordinated Philoctetes to Heracles. The belated and peculiar Servius went so far as to separate Philoctetes from the arrows altogether, confining him to Lemnos while the Greeks plied the bow of Heracles against Troy:

When the Greeks could not bear the stench of the incurable wound, they left him at last on Lemnos after taking his arrows away.

Servius *Servianorum in Vergilii carmina commentarium* 3. 402

But no other writer subjects Philoctetes to this humiliation. Most versions take for granted that Philoctetes *and* the bow—Philoctetes *with* the bow, and *handling* the bow—are indispensable. Thus Dio again, paraphrasing a speech by Odysseus in Euripides' play:

So now a task most hazardous and hard brings me to Lemnos here, that Philoctetes and the bow of Heracles I may bear off for my allies. For . . . Helenus . . . disclosed that without these the city could never be seized.

Dio *Discourses* 59

Or Apollodorus:

When the war had already lasted ten years, and the Greeks were despondent, Calchas prophesied to them that Troy could not be taken unless they had the bow and arrows of Hercules fighting on their side. On hearing that, Ulysses went with Diomedes to Philoctetes in Lemnos, and having by craft got possession of the bow and arrows he persuaded him to sail to Troy. So he went, and after being cured by Podalirius, he shot Alexander.

Apollodorus *Epitome* 5.8

Or Hyginus:

Later it was prophecied to the Achaians that Troy could not be conquered without the arrows of Heracles. Thereupon

Hyginus *Fabulae* 102

Agamemnon sent Odysseus and Diomedes as messengers to him. They managed to reconcile him to them and to obtain his help in the conquest of Troy, and they brought him away at once.

So goes the dominant tradition, which the dramatists undoubtedly helped entrench. Yet Sophocles appears to waver between the two traditions. While his oracle (confirmed by Heracles) calls for Philoctetes in person, and Neoptolemus acts throughout as if he were taking this requirement for granted, Odysseus seems—seems to some readers, though not to others—to desire only the bow, or at any rate to be content with the bow if he cannot get Philoctetes—either because he is too coarse to understand or too arrogant to heed the oracle. There is no indication that such an ambiguity existed in the versions produced by Sophocles' predecessors. Either Sophocles exploited the two-headed tradition to achieve a subtler characterization of Odysseus, or he was careless—not because of his great age, but because the urgent message he wanted to convey did not require him to choose. Both traditions were compatible with his thesis.[13]

9. Let us now follow the Greek fleet on its way to Troy. We shall not insist with Dares that Philoctetes is acting as its pilot, but he does guide his companions to the altar erected by Jason in honor of Chryse. The less than momentous question, where this altar was located, has exercised a number of scholars. Some sources name Lemnos itself—and this is in fact the most natural place for the tragic episode to have occurred. Others refer us to Tenedos; still others to an unlocalized "Neai" near Lemnos. But most call the place Chryse, after the goddess (or the goddess after the place). An eligible island is mentioned by Appian in his *Mithridatic Wars*. The historian narrates how, in the year 73 B.C., Lucullus, general of the Romans, was pursuing King Mithridates:

Appian *Mithridatica* 77   He overtook Varius and Alexander and Dionysius near Lemnos on a barren island (where the altar of Philoctetes is shown with

---

13. See the "Observations" for further discussion.

the brazen serpent, the bow, and the breastplate bound with fillets, a memorial of the sufferings of that hero), and sailed against them contemptuously at full speed.

Appian fails to give this barren island a name or specific location. Pausanias, instead, has heard of an authentic Chryse:

No long sail from Lemnos was once an island called Chryse, where, it is said, Philoctetes met with his accident from the water-snake. But the waves utterly overwhelmed it, and Chryse sank and disappeared in the depths. *Pausanias De-scription of Greece* 10. 33.4

A geographical survey would seem to be called for, in hopes of dredging up a small island near Lemnos bearing the remains of an altar to a native goddess.

10. What matters here is that whenever the tradition has Philoctetes bitten on a small or deserted island, he is immediately transferred to Lemnos. Why so? We have seen that a tradition existed according to which Philoctetes was left on Lemnos so that he could be cared for. This provides the answer to Professor H. D. F. Kitto's shrewd observation that while the Greek leaders "had indeed some reason for not allowing Philoctetes to proceed with them to Troy, they had no reason whatever for marooning him as they did on this uninhabited island [Lemnos] instead of sending him home as an honourable ally who had become incapacitated" *(Form and Meaning in Drama,* p. 104). If the island was not uninhabited at all, but full of doctors and nurses, there is no puzzle. In order to make of Philoctetes a deeply injured party, Sophocles and his predecessors twisted a perfectly rational tradition into the irrationality which Professor Kitto detected— twisted, of course, for a higher poetic purpose, trusting, as poets could do before the advent of professors, that no one would notice.

But Sophocles carried this irrationality to an extreme position. For Aeschylus and Euripides Lemnos had *some* inhabitants, the Greeks were not monsters, and Philoctetes, though understandably resentful, had not quite the right to be so adamant as he is in Sophocles, who depopulated Lemnos entirely. Sophocles dared this irra-

tionality in order to present Philoctetes as a perfect martyr and the Greeks guilty of a monstrous and downright
unintelligible crime. In taking this splendid poetic step,
Sophocles committed another irrationality which has
hitherto escaped even the most meticulous inspectors of
his work, and which can therefore be dismissed as a
minor curiosity. Why did the playwright not allow the
wicked Greeks to abandon Philoctetes on Chryse itself?
Why the useless sailing from one deserted island to
another? Probably because the public might wink at an
uninhabited Lemnos,[14] but not at a dissociation of
Philoctetes from *his* island.

We can see now that Aeschylus and Euripides created a
transitional stage in the Philoctetes legend. Both were
looking backward in giving Lemnos a population, but
they looked ahead in making their Philoctetes bitterly
resentful nevertheless, for in their versions the central
problem had become "how to overcome the resistance of
Philoctetes and thus bring him and the bow back to the
siege." Now a man may be resentful even if the place
where he has been marooned is not utterly unpeopled, so
neither playwright was guilty of any inconsistency.
Sophocles merely went to the limit. Interestingly, however, his audacity in sequestering Philoctetes from all
human intercourse did not gain general acceptance.
Even the bitterness theme introduced by Aeschylus
found its dissenters who kept faith with the older tradition of a deed of mercy *recognized* by Philoctetes as such.
As we take up other aspects of the Philoctetes legend, we
shall see examples of both traditions facing one another.

11. What made the water serpent bite Philoctetes?
Apollodorus of Athens, who places the incident on
Tenedos, retells the well-worn story:

Apollodorus   As they were offering a sacrifice to Apollo,[15] a watersnake ap-
Epitome 3. 27   proached from the altar and bit Philoctetes; and as the sore did

---

14. Or at any rate—if Jebb is right—an uninhabited northeastern region of
Lemnos. The Lemnos known to Sophocles' audience had in fact a rich human
history—and a bloody one, as evidenced by Queen Hypsipyle.

15. Chryse, of course, cannot be placed on Tenedos.

not heal and grew noisome, the army could not endure the stench, and Ulysses, by the orders of Agamemnon, put him ashore on the island of Lemnos, with the bow of Hercules which he had in his possession; and there, by shooting birds with the bow, he subsisted in the wilderness.

Here, as in several other texts, we are in the realm of pure accident. Most writers do not seem to have looked any farther, for the main issue lay in the question of what was done to Philoctetes as the *result* of the bite. Yet not everyone was satisfied with the notion of an accident. In Hyginus, for example, we find something more purposeful, namely revenge by Hera, the inveterate enemy of Heracles:

While Philoctetes, the son of Poias and Demonassa, was staying on the island of Lemnos, a serpent bit him in the foot. Hera had sent it, being angry with him, because he alone, before all others, had dared to build the pyre for Heracles, when the latter was released from his body and he entered into immortality.

Hyginus Fabulae 102

Another explanation was attempted by Servius, who, it will be remembered, had Philoctetes strike the resting place of Heracles with his foot. Heracles apparently failed to appreciate this trick and got even with his erstwhile friend, for

later, proceeding to the war, while [Philoctetes] was practicing with his arrows, he was wounded upon the foot with which he had struck the tomb.

Servius Servianorum in Vergilii Carmina Commentarium 3. 402

Incidentally, this event took place before Troy, and Servius ignores the snake altogether.[16]

Another slight improvement on pure accident was the explanation that Philoctetes had somehow disturbed Chryse when he sought out her altar. This may well have been the etiological account used by Aeschylus and Euripides, and we discover it in Sophocles, where Neoptolemus offers it perfunctorily to Philoctetes near the end of the play:

---

16. Fénelon adapted Servius's account in chapter 12—the Philoctetes chapter—of his didactic romance, *Télémaque* (1699).

Sophocles
Philoctetes
1326–28

This suffering is sent on you from heaven because you once went near to Chryse's serpent, the secret guardian of her roofless home.

Since he is making his final effort to sway Philoctetes, he may be using a touch of innocent cunning in suggesting that Philoctetes had committed a little sin. The implication would be: "Since you have yourself to blame, why not make amends by forgetting your anger against the Greeks?" But Sophocles did not put his heart into this argument. Philoctetes does not even seem to hear it. Had he taken note, he would probably have replied indignantly that far from trying to violate Chryse's sanctuary, he had sought the altar as an act of piety and a service to his companions.[17] Curiously enough, this tale of disturbing Chryse may have been deeply rooted, as we shall see, in the pre-Trojan *myth*. It takes us back to a world of brutal spirits who punish accidental infractions without the slightest consideration of pure or impure motive. No wonder it flits in and out of Sophocles' work without leaving a trace.[18]

By far the best explanation for the bite occurs again in Sophocles, though we do not know whether he received or invented it. Early in the play, Neoptolemus is addressing the Chorus:

Sophocles
Philoctetes
191–200

By heavenly ordinance, if such as I may judge, those first sufferings came on him from relentless Chryse; and the woes that now he bears, with none to tend him, surely he bears by the providence of some god, that so he should not bend against Troy the resistless shafts divine, till the time be fulfilled when, as men say, Troy is fated by those shafts to fall. [R. C. Jebb's translation]

---

17. This is in fact conveyed by Euripides, as quoted by Dio (see section 5 above).

18. A similar layer of "precivilized" amoral tales preceded the moralized Don Juan legend first dramatized by Tirso de Molina in the seventeenth century. See my *Theater of Don Juan,* (Lincoln: University of Nebraska Press, 1964). At the same time, it is not excluded that Aeschylus, and perhaps Euripides, gave Philoctetes a small dose of guilt, and that the Sophoclean passage is a vestige with a minor, fleeting function, a "charged moment." See, in this connection, Mario Untersteiner's hypotheses concerning Aeschylus's version *(Gli "Eraclidi" e il "Filotette" di Eschilo).* One point is beyond controversy: Sophocles' Philoctetes is innocent; he has done *nothing* to deserve his fate.

Neoptolemus expresses himself modestly: "if such as I may judge," "surely," "some god," "as men say"; hence it is not surprising that this explanation is never mentioned again. Neoptolemus is hesitant, the Chorus ignores it (ll. 676–729), and Sophocles does not seem to be interested. If we tally the two explanations, however—the one offered at the beginning of the play and the other delivered at the end—we can construct a logical sequence. The gods decide to remove Philoctetes from combat for nine or ten years (this can be our given). Therefore they plant in Philoctetes the idea of leading his fellow officers to Chryse's altar. They see to it that he takes a wrong step at the shrine, offends the goddess, and suffers the snakebite. The Greeks leave him on Lemnos to get rid of him, and nine years later the oracle informs them that his presence at the siege is indispensable.

This composite does nothing to endear the gods to a humane reader. Surely there are more amiable ways of removing a man from battle—for instance, consigning him to the care of Calypso—than crippling and isolating him for ten years. But the real trouble with our construction is precisely that it is no more than that. The attentive scholar can extract it from the text, but it does not function *in* the text. I believe, in fact, that I am the first to have performed this exercise. And although Sophocles did provide the materials for a coherent story, quite possibly without having himself noticed it, that interesting if cruel tale of divine manipulation never got itself told.

12. The reprehensible role played by the Greeks in general, or Odysseus in particular, in leaving their stricken companion behind, had probably been an invention of Aeschylus's, which allowed him to dramatize a thesis dear to him, that of a divine order, or the state, triumphant over personal grievance. Philoctetes has only a limited right to bitterness. He did disturb the goddess. And he was not left on Lemnos untended. It is only right that the good of society should prevail.

This thesis seems to have been further developed by Euripides, and then, as we shall see, boldly reversed by Sophocles. Later writers prudently turned either to a pre-Aeschylean scheme of kind-hearted Greeks, or an Aeschylean one of more or less guilty Greeks who should

Hyginus *Fab-
ulae* 102 nevertheless be forgiven. Hyginus, for example, echoes
Euripides in granting Philoctetes the company of a
shepherd, Aktor. Thus the stricken hero has at any rate a
little less cause for despair than he does in Sophocles. One
of the Homeric scholiasts goes farther:

Scholia Graeca
in Homeri
Iliadem 2.722 The story runs that Philoctetes, cleansing the altar of Chryse
(called Athena) on Lemnos, was bitten by the serpent and,
succumbing to a painful wound, he was abandoned there by the
Greeks, for they knew that the priests of Hephaistos tend to
people who have been bitten by snakes.

The same approach is followed by Dictys of Crete. The
scholiast had Philoctetes bitten on the island of Lemnos
itself, as suggested by Homer. Dictys places the event in
the Greek camp before Troy, as Servius will do later.
Since Dictys is distinctly a pro-Ulyssian, he makes the
Ithacan hero kill the serpent at once.[19]

Dictys *Ephem-
eris belli Troiani*
2. 14 Soon afterwards we sent Philoctetes, with a few other men, to be
cured of his poison on Lemnos, for the inhabitants of the island,
which was sacred to Vulcan, claimed that their priests were wont
to cure cases like this.

Significantly, there is no stench: Philoctetes cannot com-
plain that the Greeks are getting rid of a nuisance. But the
good will of the Greeks does not stop there. While the war
was raging,

Ibid., 2. 33 we also sent Philoctetes' share of the booty across to Lemnos,
where he was.

Naturally, his return to the siege is uneventful, and un-
Sophoclean in the extreme:

Ibid., 2. 47. The next event was the return of Philoctetes from Lemnos,
along with those who had gone to take him his share of the
booty. He was still rather sick and walked with difficulty.

But he made no trouble.

---

19. In a vase painting at the Louvre dated before 400 B. C., the killing of the
snake is clearly depicted (pls. 2, 3). It is Agamemnon, however, who kills the
snake. Dictys, writing several centuries later, may have modified a particular
tradition in favor of his hero Odysseus.

13. Ovid, on the contrary, took full advantage of the tradition of an embittered Philoctetes. He shows us Ajax and Odysseus in the famous contention over Achilles' weapons, which Sophocles had so effectively used in his play. Ajax is speaking. The madness he refers to is that of Odysseus, who, according to one legend, had tried to shirk war duty:

And oh, that his madness either had been real, or had never been detected, and that this criminal had never come with us against the Phrygians! Then, son of Poeas, Lemnos would not possess you, set off there to our sin and shame, you who, they say, hidden in forest lairs, move the very rocks with your groans and call down curses on Laërtes' son [Odysseus] which he has richly merited, and which, if there are any gods, you do not call down in vain. And now he, who took oath with us for this same war, alas! one of our chieftains, who fell heir to Alcides' shafts, now, broken with disease and hunger, is clothed and fed by the birds, and in pursuit of birds uses those arrows which fate intended for Troy!

Ovid *Meta-morphoses* 13. 43–54

Odysseus, however, refuses to acknowledge that his was a criminal act. To begin with, it should not be imputed to him alone; and furthermore, it was meant as a kindness:

Nor should I be blamed because Vulcanian Lemnos holds the son of Poeas. Defend your own deed, for you consented to it. But I will not deny that I advised that he withdraw from the hardships of the war and the journey thither, and seek to soothe his terrible anguish by a time of rest. He took the advice—and lives! And not alone was this advice given in good faith, but it was fortunate as well; though it is enough that it was given in good faith. Now, since our seers say that he is necessary for the fall of Pergama [Troy] do not entrust the task to me! Telamon's son [Ajax] will better go, and by his eloquence he will calm the hero, mad with pain and rage, or else by some shrewd trick will bring him to us. Nay, Simoïs will flow backward, Ida stand without foliage, and Greece send aid to Troy before the craft of stupid Ajax would avail the Greeks in case I should cease to work for your advantage. Though you have a deadly hatred, O harsh Philoctetes, for the allied Greeks and the king and me myself; though you heap endless curses on my head and long in your misery to have me in your power, to drink my blood, and pray that, as I was given a chance at you, so you may have a chance at me; still would I go to you and strive to bring you back

Ibid., 3. 313–38

with me. And I should get possession of your arrows (should Fortune favour me), just as I got possession of the Dardanian seer, whom I made captive; just as I discovered the oracles of the gods and the fate of Troy; just as I stole away from the midst of the enemy the enshrined image of Phrygian Minerva.

Yet Odysseus concurs with Ajax that Philoctetes is indeed resentful. Thus Ovid gets the benefit of both traditions: the Greeks meant well, *yet* Philoctetes is angry.

The *Heroicus* of Flavius Philostratus also provides a pro-Greek account:

Flavius Philos-tratus *Heroicus* 5

True, Philoctetes was left behind on Lemnos, but not without medical care, nor neglected by the Greek army; for numerous Meliboians, whose chief he was, remained at his side, and the Achaians shed tears at being deprived of this warrior "worth many men" [*Iliad* 11.514]; and the Lemnian earth, upon which Hephaistos had fallen, cured him right away. . . . During the time the Achaians were at Ilium, Philoctetes, together with Euneos, Jason's son, conquered the little islands [near Lemnos] and drove off the Carians who lived there. As a reward for this support he received a part of Lemnos, which he named Akesa [akesis = cure] because he had been healed there. From Lemnos Diomedes and Neoptolemus led him of his own free will to Troy.

Perhaps this quite late account should be linked with Appian's reference to an island near Lemnos where an altar to Philoctetes was exhibited.

14. Quintus of Smyrna paints one of the most colorful pictures of the suffering Philoctetes, reconciles everyone as quickly as possible, and then sends him on to Troy, restored like another Job after his long and inexplicable afflictions.

Quintus *Posthomerica* 9

When Odysseus and Diomedes reached the land of Lemnos and the stone cavern where Philoctetes, the son of glorious Poeas lay, wonder came over them, as they looked upon the hero lying on the hard ground and groaning with hideous pains. Round about him, by his couch, were strewn the feathers of many birds. Others had been sewn together and put around his body as a protection against bitter cold. Whenever melancholy hunger seized him, he shot an irresistible arrow, wherever his mind directed it. In part he ate the prey, and in part put them over his grisly wound to keep off the black anguish.[20] His dry locks of hair streamed around his head, like those of a fierce wild beast that the snare of a painful trap has caught by the foot as it went swiftly through the night. Under pressure of necessity, it cuts off the tip of its foot with its destructive teeth and so arrives at its cave, its heart suffering at once from hunger and cruel pains; so evil suffering overpowered Philoctetes in his wide cavern. His whole body was wasted away; he was nothing but skin and bones. His cheeks were filthily squalid, and he was hideously dirty. Pain beyond curing overwhelmed him, and the eyes of the terribly suffering hero were sunk deep under his brows. He never stopped groaning, because severe pains kept gnawing at the base of his black wound. It had putrefied on the surface and penetrated to the bone. Just as when on a cliff that juts into the dashing sea the water of the vast ocean overwhelms a rock crag by cutting it away at the base, strong though it is, and as it is lashed by the wind and the blustering storms holes are hollowed out in it, eaten away by the sea; so the wound in his foot kept growing larger from the putrefying poison which a fierce water snake had injected in him with its cruel fangs. (Men say its bite is loathsome and incurable whenever the power of the sun dries it out as it crawls around on dry land.) So the wound was wearing out the supremely great hero, overpowered as he was by obstinate pain. The floor of the vast cave was spattered with the purulent discharge that dripped steadily from the wound onto the ground—a great marvel even for men of later generations. Beside his bed stood the long quiver, full of arrows. Some he used for hunting, some against enemies, and these he smeared with the deadly poison of the noxious water snake. In front of the quiver, there was placed nearby the great bow fitted with curving horns, the work of Heracles' tireless hands.

When he caught sight of Odysseus and Diomedes coming to his wide cave, he resolved at once to send against them both his cruel arrows, remembering his terrible anger because they had previously abandoned him and his loud groans and left him alone on deserted shores of the sea. He would have immediately executed the desire of his bold spirit if Athena had not dispersed his melancholy anger as he looked upon the familiar men. They came close to him, both of them looking like men in deep distress. The two of them sat beside him in the hollow cave,

---

20. The text is doubtful. There may well be a line lost which contained a reference to leaves used for his wound. Cf. Sophocles *Philoctetes* 649–50. [Tr.]

one on each side, and questioned him about his ruinous wound and severe pains, and he explained his miseries to them. They kept giving him words of encouragement and told him that his horrible wound would be healed after all his cruel trouble and pain, if he came to the Greek army. The army itself, moreover, they said, was in great distress at the ships, the Atreussons [sons of Atreus: Agamemnon and Menelaus (ed.)] themselves as well as the others. No one of the Greeks in the army was responsible for his troubles, they said, merely the cruel Fates. "No man can avoid them as he moves over the earth. They always move unseen by the side of toiling men all their days, sometimes in their pitiless spirit harming the race of mortals, at other times again exalting them, because they are the ones who contrive for mortals quite all that is sad and pleasant, just as they themselves desire." As Philoctetes listened to Odysseus and godlike Diomedes, his spirit quickly and easily gave up its obstinate anger, although he had been terribly angry before, at all that he had suffered.

Swiftly and joyfully they carried him and his weapons to the ship and the roaring beach. They thoroughly wiped his body and the cruel wound with a porous sponge and washed the wound well in quantities of water. He received a little relief, and they busied themselves at once in preparing a good meal, which he was glad to have. They ate along with him, on board the ship. Ambrosial night came on, and they fell asleep quickly, remaining until dawn on the shore of the island of Lemnos. With dawn, they busied themselves with the cables and raised from the sea the curving anchors. Athena sent a wind blowing astern of the slim-prowed ship. They spread their sails at once with both the sheets, steering their sturdy ship straight. Under the breeze, she ran swiftly over the level sea. The black wave broke with a roar around her, and the gray froth boiled everywhere about her. Shoals of dolphins darted around her, making their way swiftly along the pathways of the gray sea.

Soon the heroes reached the Hellespont, that abounds in fish, where the other ships were. The Greeks were delighted when they saw the men who had been much longed for in the army, and they were naturally pleased to disembark from the ship. Philoctetes, Poeas' bold son, kept his thin hands on the other two, and they led him to the glorious earth, limping badly and supported by their powerful arms. Just as in the forests an oak tree or a fat pine tree cut halfway through by a strong woodcutter still stands for a little while—as much, that is, as the woodcutter left when he cut away at the resinous trunk, so that the pitch, set on fire, might provide a torch in the mountains—and the tree, heavily burdened, is bent down by the wind and weakness onto flourishing young trees, and they hold up its weight; so Philoctetes, weighed down by intolerable pain, leaned upon the bold heroes who brought him into the crowd of Greek soldiers.[21]

As they looked upon him, every man felt pity for this archer suffering from a loathsome wound. But quicker than swift thought, Podalirius, equal to the heavenly gods, made him hale and sound, carefully sprinkling many drugs over his wound and making proper invocation of his father's name.[22] The Greeks raised a quick shout, all of them together glorifying Asclepius' son. They zealously washed Philoctetes clean and anointed him with olive oil. His pernicious despondency and pain disappeared, through the will of the immortals, and the Greeks were glad at heart as they looked upon him. He had relief from his misery, color succeeded to his pallor, great strength to his wretched weakness, and all his frame filled out. Just as when a grainfield grows strong with ears of grain, although it had previously been wasting away, and the rain of a hard winter had fallen heavily upon it and swamped it, and then, made strong by the winds, it smiles, flourishing on a carefully worked farm; so the whole body of Philoctetes, previously so afflicted, at once took on a flourishing appearance. He had left in the rounded hull of the ship all the cares that had been overwhelming his spirit.

The Atreussons looked with wonder on the man who had, as it were, returned from the dead. They thought this was the work of the immortals. This was, indeed, the truth, just as they thought. Noble Athena Tritogeneia [thrice-born (ed.)] shed over him size and grace. He took on at once exactly the appearance he had had before among the Greeks, before he was laid low by misfortune. Then all the princes together brought the son of Poeas to the quarters of rich Agamemnon and glorified him with the honor of a banquet. When they had had their fill of drink and fine food, then Agamemnon of the good ashen spear spoke to him:

"My friend, do not now put terrible anger into your heart because we abandoned you years ago on the island of Lemnos,

---

21. An obscure passage with many difficulties of detail. As Köchly says, *locus vexatissimus*. The text may be defective, and there may be lacunae. [Tr.]

22. Homer had named both sons of Asclepius—Podalirius and Machaon—as the physicians who treated Philoctetes. Later authors chose one or the other. The treatment is illustrated on the back of a bronze Etruscan mirror which partially survives at the Museo Civico of Bologna (pl. 1). Two serpents can be detected in this work. Perhaps one of them is meant to be the evil one of Chryse, and the other the gentle one associated with Asclepius.

when our minds were deluded by the will of the gods. We did not do this apart from the blessed ones, but the immortals themselves, I fancy, wanted to inflict many evils upon us in your absence, because you are an expert in destroying with your arrows enemies who fight against you. [The paths of human life] over all the earth and over the great sea are hidden from our eyes by the will of the Fates. The paths have many branches, are numerous and crooked, turn in all directions. Men are carried along them by the Fate of a supernatural power, like leaves swept along by the blasts of the wind. The good man often lights upon an evil path, the man who is not good, on a good one. No man upon earth is able to avoid them, any more than he can have his free choice. The sensible man must endure his misery with a stubborn mind, even if the winds carry him along a hard way. Since, then, this act of ours was foolish and wrong, we will in return make recompense with great gifts, if ever we take the fine citadel of Troy. For the moment, take seven women, twenty fast prize-winning horses, and twelve tripods. Your heart will find pleasure in these all your days. Moreover, in my quarters you will always have a king's honor at the feast."

So he spoke, and gave the hero splendid gifts. The son of stout-hearted Poeas said to him:

"My friend, I am no longer angry at you, nor at any other Greek, if, perhaps, there was also someone else involved in the wrong done me. I know how pliable the minds of good men are. It is not right to be always hard and headstrong, but sometimes to be formidable and sometimes gentle. But let us now go to our beds, because if a man is eager to fight, it is better for him to sleep than to linger at banquets."

With these words, he hurried away to his comrades' quarters. They quickly and with great joy in their hearts got a bed ready for their war-loving king, and he lay down gladly until the dawn.[23]

Thereafter Philoctetes does yeomanly work for the Greeks, dealing Paris the fatal wound, but failing to kill Aeneas (says Quintus), and even—another new point for us—objecting to the use of the wooden horse. He and Neoptolemus both prefer open war. But a thunderclap from Zeus brings them to their senses. Without further talk they take their places inside the horse, and then, as usual, we lose sight of our hero.

---

23. From *The War At Troy: What Homer Didn't Tell*, by Quintus of Smyrna, translated and with an introduction and notes by Frederick M. Combellack.

15. For a close view of Philoctetes killing Paris, Dictys is useful, and seems to reflect the ancient tradition of the *Little Iliad:*

Philoctetes advanced against Alexander and challenged him to fight, if he dared, a duel with the bow. Alexander agreed, and thus Ulysses and Deiphobus marked off a place for the contest. Alexander was the first to shoot and missed. Thereupon Philoctetes hit Alexander in the left hand, and then—he was howling with pain—struck his right eye, and then—he was trying to flee—pierced both his feet, and finally finished him off. Philoctetes' arrows had once been Hercules', and the Hydra's lethal blood had stained their points. *Dictys Ephemeris belli Troiani 4. 19–20*

The barbarians, seeing that their leader was dead, rushed in and tried to snatch his body away. Philoctetes killed many of them, but they kept pressing on, and eventually got the body into the city. Ajax the son of Telamon pursued them as far as the gate, and there the slaughter was huge. Many were unable to enter; the crowd was frantic, with everyone shoving, everyone striving to get in first. Those who had entered went to the walls and hurled down rocks of every description, rolled down earth collected from everywhere, onto the shield of Ajax, hoping to drive him off. But our illustrious leader, shaking his shield whenever it grew too heavy, relented not in the least. And Philoctetes, shooting from a distance, killed many of those on the wall and drove the others away.

In other parts of the field the rest of our soldiers met with equal success. That day would have seen the walls of Troy destroyed, the city sacked, if the swift arrival of night had not restrained us. Thus we returned to the ships, rejoicing, our spirits tremendously buoyed because of the deeds Philoctetes had done. To him we gave our highest praise and showed our deepest gratitude.

At daybreak, Philoctetes, accompanied by the rest of our leaders, returned to the field. And the Trojans, even with the help of their walls, could scarcely protect themselves, so great was their terror.

If we stop our breaths now expecting to hear at last that Philoctetes has delivered the coup de grâce to Troy, we will be disappointed as usual. When the last sentence I have quoted comes to its period, Philoctetes sinks from the text without a trace.

We have now arrived beyond the events narrated by Sophocles in his extant masterpiece, but it will be recalled that he also wrote a *Philoctetes at Troy,* a few surviving fragments of which suggest that it covered the cure of Philoctetes and the killing of Paris. We do not know what thesis, if any, this play proposed.

16. It is comforting to hear from Quintus that Agamemnon presented Philoctetes with seven women (one for each of his ships?) to compensate him for nine years of abstinence. But the truth is that romantic or sexual adventures do not sit well with the austere Philoctetes matter. Apollodorus feebly casts him as one of Helen's wooers before she was given to Menelaus. A Sophoclean scholiast, disturbed perhaps by the master's perfunctory explanations, absurdly informs us that the nymph Chryse, unable to win Philoctetes' love, took revenge by causing her serpent to bite him.[24] And an epigram by Martial calls him a homosexual. These are all painfully false notes. But they give us a clue, I think, to the relative obscurity in which the tale of Philoctetes has remained since the passing of ancient civilization. The missing note of romance left his story too harsh and bleak. It wanted lusciousness. When Jean-François de La Harpe—a discerning critic of ancient literature—published his somewhat free translation of Sophocles' play in 1781, he expressed in his preface misgivings about staging it: "Is it credible that an audience would enjoy today so simple and bare a Greek drama—three characters on a desert island—a work not only without love interest, but without a woman in it?"[25] And he recalled with some asperity the *Philoctète* of Jean-Baptiste de Chateaubrun (which had received seven performances in 1755), where the suffering hero is given a daughter, supported by the inevitable female companion. Neoptolemus falls in love with this Miranda at first sight, to the understandable chagrin of Odysseus who, in two and a half millennia, had not been called upon to cope with such a queer turn of events. For all we know, Philoctetes' sexual problems may

Apollodorus Biblioteca 3. 10.8

Scholia in Sophoclis tragoedias vetera 194

Martial Epigrams 2. 84

---

24. Professor Robert Torrance has directed me to a brief passage in Carl Jung's *Symbols of Transformation* in which Chryse becomes the Unconscious, and the serpent's bite the revenge of that primordial "mother" for being neglected by the ego. Comment seems superfluous.

25. Albin Lesky, *Die Tragische Dichtung der Hellenen*, reminds us that *Philoctetes* is the only surviving all-male Greek play.

have beguiled the *comic* playwrights of antiquity—Epicharmos, Strattis, and Epiphanes—who had written Philoctetes plays. But only in the century of mawkish fathers would anyone have thought up a daughter for the stricken hero. Daughter or mistress—what Chateaubrun failed to understand was that so long as a love interest was indispensable, Philoctetes must be left alone. Only when serious literature emancipated itself from its enforced alliance with romance—and this happened as the nineteenth century drew to its end—could the tale of Philoctetes be narrated again without compromise.

17. G. E. Lessing argued in the *Laokoon* (1766) that literature is free to exhibit pain in all its horror, with shrieks and groans, and that Sophocles had in fact portrayed Philoctetes without stoical niceties. This was allowable because Sophocles had been careful to preserve the moral greatness of his hero in the midst of his uninhibited outcries: "He moans, he shrieks, he falls into the most horrible convulsions," but "his eyes were not so dried up with pain that they had no tear to bestow upon the fate of his former friends; neither was his spirit so subdued by it that to obtain a release from it he could forgive his enemies and willingly lend himself to all their selfish ends" (p. 30).

In our own century, Edmund Wilson has adapted and perverted Lessing's insight in an essay entitled "The Wound and the Bow"—affirming that *Philoctetes* demonstrates "the conception of superior strength as inseparable from disability"—a characteristic twentieth-century grimace of an idea. "Genius and disease . . . may be inextricably bound up together" (pp. 257, 259). Thus the classical concept that great virtue or genius may survive or overcome disability or disease becomes the recherché notion, first spread by Thomas Mann (for reasons well known to himself) that a wound is the very *condition* for superiority, for it sharpens the sensibilities and the intelligence. Such a notion was unthinkable in a civilization that imagined Heracles, Theseus, Achilles, and Hector.

In actuality, Sophocles' tragedy (or rather paratragedy) eludes both Lessing and Wilson. Nothing is said and little is implied about a greatness of spirit that shines out in spite of pain. Sophocles' thoughts are on other things. And of course he does not dream of making

Philoctetes' affliction a source or a condition of his greatness. But that he dwells on, that he explores, indeed that
he exploits the suffering of Philoctetes with the same almost complacent relish we sense in his treatment of Ajax
and Oedipus and Electra and Heracles is undeniable. He
obviously liked to make his audiences cry. But for
Philoctetes he had good precedents. Again and again, the
rank misery of the abandoned, sick, helpless, ragged
Philoctetes had given the cue to poets, sculptors, and
painters alike, and was to fascinate them for centuries
after Sophocles—even when they allowed the wounded
hero a little help or company. *There* lay the peculiar appeal of Philoctetes. *This* is what made him memorable to
antiquity. Not the weapon that would bring Troy down
but somehow never did, not the wrath which many writers underplayed or denied, and not the undefeated
greatness shining through as in another Prometheus; but
his relentless pain, his solitude (partial or absolute), his
weather-wrinkled face, his disheveled hair, the herbs he
must eat, the birds he must shoot, the tatters he must
wear—these, with or without further meaning, enthral-
led and begot extreme "pity and fear."

We cannot even call Philoctetes a legitimate ancestor
to Robinson Crusoe, for the vigorous stance of making
the best of it—this very British pride in technical
adaptability—this triumph of Baconian empiricism—
interests the writers of antiquity much less than the un-
mitigated woes which the man endures. We know that for
the Greeks no affliction was more terrible than exile—the
fate of being cut off from communion with one's own. In
Philoctetes they saw the figure of the exile at its most
pathetic, even when his removal was pictured in a kindly
light. Homer's Odysseus, helplessly crawling on the
Phaeacians' beach, excited commiseration. But that was
for a night and a morning. Philoctetes had been beached,
so to speak, for nine years, and he had a festering wound,
and he was half-starved. There was no personage quite
like him among the numberless heroes of Greek saga.

In several texts quoted so far we have read eloquent
expressions of Philoctetes' desolation—notably in Ovid
and Quintus of Smyrna. Brief though it is, the passage
concerning Philoctetes in the *Iliad* also hints strongly at

the central interest. And all the clues lead us to believe that Aeschylus and Euripides both made the most of this motif well before Sophocles.

Other testimonials abound. In Aristophanes' *Acharnians,* when some ragged clothes are mentioned, the actor representing Euripides asks,

Aristophanes
Acharnians 423

> Can it be those of beggarly Philoctetes?

Plutarch, referring to a *Philoctetes* painted by Aristophon, speaks of the hero pining away on stage.[26] Then again, he quotes an unnamed person taunting Philoctetes:

Plutarch *The
Right Way of
Hearing Poetry*
3

> What bride, what virgin in her youth, you wretch, would take you? You're a pretty one to wed!

Plutarch
*Whether an Old
Man Should
Engage in Pub-
lic Affairs* 9

(This may be Odysseus' reaction to the attempt by Paris, probably in Euripides' version, to entice Philoctetes to the Trojan side.) Cicero contributes two eloquent passages from the *Philoctetes* of Accius:

> Look at Philoctetes, whose moans we must pardon, for he had seen the mighty Hercules on Oeta shrieking aloud in the extremity of his pains. No comfort, therefore, did the arrows he had received from Hercules give this hero when

Cicero *Tus-
culanae disputa-
tiones* 2. 6. 19

---

26. The four most famous visual representations of Philoctetes in antiquity all showed the hero suffering rather than acting. They are (1) A lost picture of limping Philoctetes by Aristophon in the mid-fifth century. (2) A lost statue by Pythagoras of Rhegium of the same period, again showing the lamed Philoctetes. This statue stood in Syracuse. Pliny the Elder mentions it in his *Natural History* (34. 8) without naming Philoctetes. L. A. Milani suggested that a surviving wall painting in Pompei dated after A. D. 63 is a late derivative from this statue (fig. 2). (3) A lost painting by Parrhasios (late fifth century) in which, perhaps for the first time, Philoctetes was portrayed in a sitting position. This painting probably inspired the painter of the *aryballos* (fig. 1), dated mid-fourth century. (4) A surviving gem by Boethos, a notable artist of the Hellenistic period (third to second century B. C.) in which Philoctetes, seated once again, is seen fanning his injured foot in order to chase the flies from it (fig. 3). A number of copies and imitations have likewise survived. For the basic illustrated survey of Philoctetes representations in antiquity, see L. A. Milani, *Il mito di Filottete nella letteratura classica e nell'arte figurata* and *Nuovi monumenti di Filottete,* supplemented by W. M. Calder III, "A Reconstruction of Euripides' *Philoctetes.*"

From vipers' bite the veins of all his flesh
Tainted with venom, cruel torture stirs.

And thus he cries out in the longing for aid and desire of death:

Ah! who to the salt sea-waves can consign
Me from the summit of the cliff on high?
Now, now pierces the pain and the killing
Might of the wound and the ulcer's fire.

Later, Cicero turns again to Accius on Philoctetes:

Ibid. 2. 13. 33   in dwelling dank,
Where from the dumb walls re-echo piteous sounds
of lamentation, plaints and groans and cries.

Other fragments from Accius in the same vein have come
down to us:

Nonius *De*
compendiosa
doctrina ad fili-   Look long at this my resting-place, in which
um 469. 34   Stretched on the stone I have endured nine winters.

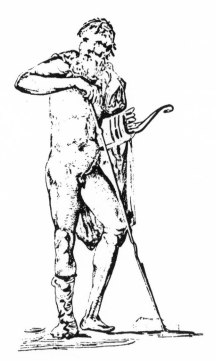

FIGURE 2. The limping Philoctetes. Drawing after a Pompeian
wall painting. After A.D. 63. *From L. A. Milani,* Nuovi
monumenti di Filottete, *1882*

And:

But, I beseech you, allow not this my uncared-for hideousness   Ibid., 179. 32
to make me a thing of scorn.

The same voice issues from a number of vase paintings
depicting Philoctetes, the best one of which is reproduced
as figure 1, and from several lost works of art described in
the *Greek Anthology:*

Only after Parrhasios truly saw Philoctetes, the long-suffering   *Anthologia*
hero from Trachis [?], did he paint him. For in his afflicted eye   *Graeca* 16. 3
lurks a dry tear, and deep in his breast churns his consuming
pain. Admirable painter, your skill is masterful, but would you
not have done better to free the suffering man of his misery?[27]

This artist, this second Odysseus, who reminds me of my dread-   Ibid., 112.
ful misery and sickness, hates me more than the Danaans do.
Not content with sore, blood, rags, wound and cave, he poured
my pain and woe into brass as well.[28]

Yes, this is Philoctetes. I see it. Everyone recognizes him from   Ibid., 113.
afar because of his groans and.suffering. He is wildly dishevel-
led; behold, his dirty hair falls about his temples in unkempt
strands. His skin is raw and cracked to look upon, and if one
touched it, no doubt it would feel parched. From his dry eye
hangs a frozen tear as the sign of a torment that knows no
sleep.[29]

---

27. This epigram is ascribed to Glaukos of Athens, about whom nothing is
known. The date of the painting by Parrhasios is also unknown, but even
though this master was much younger than Sophocles, it is tempting to guess at
a connection of some sort. The temptation becomes even stronger when we
remember that Plutarch in his *Moralia* (18a) mentions two other paintings by
Parrhasios of events alluded to in Sophocles' play: *Odysseus Pretending to Be Mad,*
and *The Struggle for the Arms of Achilles.* It is certain, at any rate, that Sophocles
knew Polygnotos, a man of his own generation (see T. B. L. Webster, *Athenian
Culture and Society,* p. 262), while a remarkable anecdote told by Ion of Chios
enables us to listen to Sophocles chatting about poetic images which do not
translate literally into painting. For the rest, one can only concur with Lesky
when he remarks that "the small dimensions of Attic life must have placed
Sophocles in contact with a series of important men" (*Die Tragische Dichtung der
Hellenen,* p. 172). Among them, no doubt, most of the leading artists of his day.
    28. The artist in question is Pythagoras of Rhegium.
    29. This epigram is by Iulianos, a Byzantine civil servant who lived in Egypt
in the sixth century A.D.

FIGURE 3. Boethos. The Philoctetes gem. A drawing after the
gem. Mid-second century B.C. H. 30 cm. *From L. A. Milani,
Nuovi monumenti di Filottete, 1882*

I repeat: the pure suffering of the innocent hero, the
suffering as such, the suffering upon a ground of
innocence—this is what kept Philoctetes alive in the
memory of Greece and Rome. Such elemental pathos
required no philosophical coloring to impress itself on
artists, mythographers, and their audiences. Sophocles
extracted from it a shattering ethicopolitical conclusion;
but—unless we have lost in Accius a worthy sucessor—no
one followed him on this difficult track. If the extant texts
are representative, it is fair to say that he was not even
understood by his own posterity in Greece and Rome. For
that matter, our own civilization has only recently dared
to handle again, in all frankness, the problems Sophocles
posed in his *Philoctetes*.

18. Even though Philoctetes never gets to play the
decisive role promised by the oracle, the tradition assures
us that no one could beat him as an archer.

Odyssey 8. 219   Philoctetes was the only man who could shoot better than I
when we Achaians were before Troy,

says Homer's Odysseus. Dictys shows us Philoctetes winning a curious archery contest over Odysseus and Meriones at the games following the death of Hector. A dove is hanging from a string (vertical, of course) which is tied to a longer one stretched horizontally between two masts. Both Odysseus and Meriones hit the dove, but the arrow of Philoctetes cuts the string holding it, and the bird falls to the ground. This is perhaps the context in which we should read the passage in Sophocles where Odysseus boasts to Philoctetes that he or Teucer will be able to handle the bow should Philoctetes refuse to join them. On the one hand Odysseus is aware of Philoctetes' preeminence; on the other his challenge is not that of a bluffer or boaster.

Dictys Ephemeris belli Troiani 3.8

19. Like most of the surviving heroes of the Trojan War, Philoctetes ultimately disappears into a mist. In the *Odyssey,* Nestor associates Neoptolemus and Philoctetes in the happy ending, as is only poetic justice, but there is nothing of substance to report:

They say the Myrmidons returned safely under Achilles' son Neoptolemus; so also did the valiant son of Poias, Philoctetes.

Odyssey 3. 190

Home is Meliboia, not Malis; for according to a tradition preserved by Strabo, the Magnesian town was the place from which Philoctetes was eventually driven away as the result of a "political quarrel." Thereafter he is unanimously settled in what is now Calabria as one of the Greek colonists of southern Italy. Here is Strabo in full:

Petelia, then, is regarded as the metropolis of the Chones, and has been rather populous down to the present day. It was founded by Philoctetes after he, as the result of a political quarrel, had fled from Meliboia.

Strabo Geographica 6. 1.3

Or, as Virgil has it:

Here is the well-known little town of the Meliboian leader Philoctetes, Petelia, resting on the wall he built.

Aeneid 3. 401–2

A pseudo-Aristotelian text is more explicit:

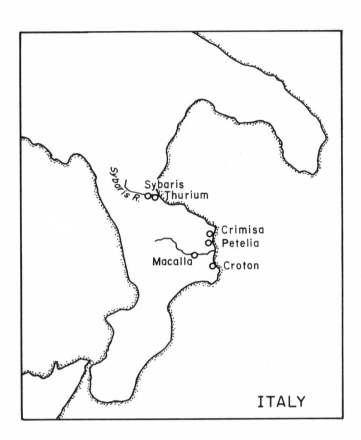

Aristotle *On Marvelous Things Heard* 107

It is said that Philoctetes is honored among the Sybarites. For when he was brought back from Troy, he lived in a place called Macalla in the region of Croton, which they say is a hundred and twenty stades [fifteen miles] away, and they relate that he dedicated Heracles' bow and arrows at the temple of Apollo the sea god. There they say that the Crotoniates during their supremacy dedicated them at the Apollonium in their own district. It is also said that, when he died, he was buried there by the river Sybaris, after helping the Rhodians who landed at the spot with Tlepolemus, and joined battle with the barbarians, who dwelt in that part of the country.

Pompeius Trogus in Justinus 20.1

Pompeius Trogus has Philoctetes buried at Thurium, where, he says, one can visit a temple to Apollo featuring the famous arrows. Finally, the Byzantine scholar Tzetzes, citing a lost passage in Apollodorus, places Philoctetes and the temple at Crimissa. This is as far as we need to pursue the matter, since all the places mentioned by these writers are near one another on the instep of the Italian boot.[30]

Tzetzes *Scholia in Lycophron* 902

20. A final question. Can we speak of a *myth* of Philoctetes which would take us behind the scenes of the legend or legends we have examined up to now? In particular, we may well ask whether, in the absence of any really sensible explanation of the snakebite, we are not entitled to read into the confrontation between Philoctetes and Chryse a significance of its own, unrelated to the Trojan War. For everything about the Philoctetes matter suggests that his "true" story antedates his appearance in the Homeric sagas, and that he was belatedly inserted into them.

The *Little Iliad,* if we can trust Photius, flatly identified Chryse with Athena. L. A. Milani, writing a century ago, regarded her instead as an Artemis figure. If we follow the lead of scholars like Uberto Pestalozza and his student Mario Untersteiner, the precise identification does not matter; for Chryse is then a minor *Potnia,* or "Lady," that is to say one of many representations of the Mediterranean Great Mother, or Earth Goddess, who reigned before the Achaeans descended upon Greece with their Zeus and other male gods. Everywhere they went, the male and martial Olympians encountered the Mother worshipped by peasant populations, and lodged her by hook or crook in their own divine mansions. Sophocles' Chorus invokes this very Mother early in the play (ll. 391–402).

In this perspective, the encounter between Philoctetes and Chryse takes on meaning and loses the enigmatic character it exhibits in all the legends that have come down to us. Chryse, protected by the serpent, faces a

---

30. Archaeological evidence shows—so far—no Greek settlements in southern Italy before the mid-eighth century B.C. We can suppose that historians and poets were ennobling Greek settlements by ascribing their foundation to ancient heroes.

minor bow-carrying Apollo.[31] Early this century, Otto Gruppe identified Philoctetes, whose name means "greedy of gain," with a Thessalian Apollo *Kerdoos,* that is, "seeking gain." We can therefore interpret the confrontation between Philoctetes and Chryse as a momentary setback, on Lemnos, of the conquering Olympians. Perhaps the Trojan saga into which poets later threw Philoctetes half conceals but also half reveals a cure, a full restoration of power, and a conquest of Lemnos, of which a faint echo possibly remains in the account by Flavius Philostratus the Lemnian (see section 6 above) to the effect that Philoctetes conquered several islands around Lemnos and was finally given Lemnos itself. A more solid testimonial would be that of Appian (see section 9 above) concerning the altar to Philoctetes on one of the islands. The fact that in one tradition the guardian snake is killed by a member of Philoctetes' party may be suggestive.

Or does the violation of Chryse's shrine flatly signify a victory *over* the goddess, which the younger god has to expiate (via the avenging snakebite, the wound he receives during the struggle) through nine years of bondage and pain?

Such, at any rate, is one direction which speculation can take. Other scholars have tried different routes. As soon as we press into the hinterland of Homeric saga, we reach an obscure intersection, where bards—the makers of saga—take over mythical tales whose significance is being forgotten, and adapt them to newer interests—struggles among city-states rather than epic battles for supremacy among gods.

With this, however, we wander sheer out of the arena of this volume, which begins with Homer, and confines itself to legend and literature. Neither Homer, nor the tragedians, nor the modern interpreters of the Philoctetes matter radiate intimations of ancient theomachies or other mythical rumors from the infancy of mankind. If Philoctetes, and numerous other characters of saga, had indeed begun their careers as minor local divinities, we can only admire the thoroughness with which their

---

31. Here the bow is Apollo's appanage and has nothing to do with Heracles.

origins were suppressed and their humanity perfected. Even those, like Achilles, who are still allowed to be children of a god or goddess—or at least a nymph—retain no supernatural powers of their own, but are compelled to live and die like their fully human peers. With a figure like Philoctetes, the process of decay has completed itself. He is absolutely separate from the gods. Fortunately, at this pristine stage of human history, he is still a hero "trailing clouds of glory." He has doffed divinity, but he still *counts*. Tragedy can sit on his broad shoulders.

Register of Sources

The Loeb Classical Library editions, all published by Harvard University Press (Cambridge, Mass.), are abbreviated LCL. For the other sources, whenever no translation is listed, I owe the English versions to the kindness of my colleague George W. Pigman III, whose help I here acknowledge with gratitude.

ACCIUS. Roman dramatist, born in 170 B.C. Fragments of his *Philoctetes on Lemnos* are collected by E. H. Warmington in the LCL *Remains of Old Latin,* vol. 2 (1936).

AESCHYLUS (525–456 B.C.). The Fragments can be found in the second volume of the LCL *Aeschylus,* translated by H. W. Smyth (1926).

Anthologia Graeca (Greek Anthology). Under this title are understood two separate but overlapping manuscripts of Greek poems and epigrams, printed nowadays as one great collection. Book 16 is based on the so-called *Anthologia Planudea,* one of these two manuscripts. I have used Hermann Beckby's second edition of the text, vol. 4 (Munich: Heimeran, 1965).

APOLLODORUS OF ATHENS. Scholar who lived around 140 B.C. His *Biblioteca (Library),* followed by an *Epitome* of fragments surviving from lost sections of the *Biblioteca,* constitutes a valuable compilation of myths. Authorship in doubt. Translated by J. G. Frazer for the LCL (1921).

APPIAN. Graeco-Roman historian born in Alexandria (ca. 95–ca. 165). The *Mithridatica (Mithridatic Wars)* is translated by Horace White in vol. 2 of the LCL edition of *Roman History* (1912).

ARISTOPHANES. The greatest of the Attic writers of comedy was born around 448 B.C. and died after 388 B.C. His *Acharnians* was produced in 425 B.C.

47

ARISTOTLE (384–322 B.C.). The *On Marvelous Things Heard* is not by the philosopher himself but consists of jottings emanating from his Peripatetic School. The LCL translation is by W. S. Hett in Aristotle, *Minor Works,* vol. 1, (1936).

MARCUS TULLIUS CICERO (106–43 B.C.). The *Tusculanae disputationes (Tusculan Disputations),* one of his major philosophical works, is translated by J. E. King for the LCL (1927).

Cypria (Poem of Cyprus). The reason for the name of this lost post-Homeric epic is not known. A summary by Proclus, which appeared in the ninth century A.D. *Biblioteca* of Photius, is translated in Albert Severyns: *Recherches sur la Chrestomathie de Proclos,* vol. 4, *La "Vira Homeri" et les sommaires du cycle,* (Paris: Droz, 1963), pp. 77–85.

DARES PHRYGIUS (Dares the Phrygian). His *De excidio Troiae historiae (History of the Fall of Troy)* is probably a first century A.D. text, but it survives only in a sixth century version. See DICTYS.

DICTYS CRETENSIS (Dictys the Cretan). First century A.D. author of an *Ephemeris belli Troiani (Journal of the Trojan War)* which survives in a fourth century version. The translations of Dares and Dictys are by R. M. Frazer, *The Trojan War: The Chronicles of Dictys of Crete and Dares the Phrygian* (Bloomington: Indiana University Press, 1966).

DIO CHRYSOSTOM (ca. 40–120). The *Discourses* of this Graeco-Roman rhetorician is translated by J. W. Cohoon for the LCL (1932–51). The fifty-second and fifty-ninth Discourses are in the fourth volume.

DIODORUS SICULUS. Diodorus the Sicilian died after 21 B.C. His historical compilation known as the *Biblioteca historica (Library of History)* is translated for the LCL by C. H. Oldfather in vol. 2 (1935).

EURIPIDES (485?–406 B.C.). I have used Wilhelm Nestle's *Euripides* (Stuttgart: W. Kuhlhammer, 1901) for the Fragments.

HOMER (before 700 B.C.). The translation from the *Iliad* is that of Richmond Lattimore (Chicago: University of Chicago Press, 1951). The *Odyssey* quotations are from Samuel Butler's prose version, 2d ed. (London: Jonathan Cape, 1922).

Scholia Graeca in HOMERI Iliadem (Greek Scholia to Homer's Iliad), ed. Wilhelm Dindorf (Oxford, 1875).

GAIUS JULIUS HYGINUS. The *Fabulae (Fables)* are probably a school text written before A.D. 270, the date of an extant Greek text. Actual authorship doubtful. I have used Ludwig Mader's German translation in *Griechische Sagen* (Zurich: Artemis, 1963).

MARCUS JUNIANUS JUSTINUS. See C. POMPEIUS TROGUS.

LACTANTIUS (ca. 260–340). Christian apologist, whose *Divinae institutiones (Divine Institutes)* were published sometime after 303. The translation is by Mary F. McDonald (Washington D.C.: Catholic University of America Press, 1964).

Little Iliad. See *Cypria* for the preservation and transmission of this post-Homeric epic, attributed to Lesches. I have taken the text from *Homeri carmina et cycli epici reliquiae* (Paris, 1845).

MARCUS ANNAEUS LUCANUS (39–65). Ten books of Lucan's epic poem *Pharsalia* survive. The translation is by Robert Graves (London: Cassell, 1961).

LYCOPHRON. An Alexandrian poet, born around 330 B.C., whose *Alexandra,* or *Cassandra,* is an occult report of the latter's prophecies. Translated for the LCL by A. W. Maier (1921).

MARCUS VALERIUS MARTIALIS. The great epigram writer Martial died around the year A.D. 104. Numerous translations of his *Epigrammata* (usually in selections) exist in English.

PUBLIUS OVIDIUS NASO (43 B.C.–A.D. 18). I have used vol. 2 of Ovid's *Metamorphoses* in the LCL translation by F. J. Miller (1916).

NONIUS MARCELLUS. Latin grammarian who lived around the end of the third century A.D. His *De compendiosa doctrina ad filium (Brief Instruction to His Son)* was edited by Lucianus Mueller (Leipzig, 1888).

PAUSANIAS (fl. A.D. 174). Geographer and traveler who wrote a voluminous *Description of Greece.* The six-volume LCL translation is by W. H. S. Jones (1931–35).

PHILOSTRATUS. Four writers belonging to the same family answer to this name, and ascriptions are uncertain. The dialogue entitled *Heroicus (Of Heroes)* may be from Flavius Philostratus the Lemnian (fl. A.D. 217). Two others wrote descriptions of paintings called *Imagines.* The second set, perhaps by the so-called Younger Philostratus, was written about 300. A collected edition of all works under the name of Philostratus was made by C. F. Kayser (Leipzig, 1870–71). There is no English translation of the *Heroicus.* Both sets of *Imagines* are in the LCL, however, where they are translated by Arthur Fairbanks (1931).

PHOTIUS (ca. 820–ca. 891). See *Cypria.*

PINDAR (518?–ca. 438 B.C.). The first of Pindar's *Pythian Odes* is dated 470 B.C. I have used the translation by Richmond Lattimore in *The Odes of Pindar,* 2d ed. (Chicago: University of Chicago Press, 1976).

PLUTARCH (46?–ca. 120). The author of the renowned *Parallel Lives* also wrote a mass of essays and dialogues collected under the title of *Moralia (Morals).* They are published in the LCL in fifteen volumes (1927–76). I have used two of these essays: *The Right Way of Hearing Poetry* in vol. 1, translated by Frank C. Babbitt, and *Whether an Old*

Man Should Engage in Public Affairs in vol. 10, translated by H. North-Fowler.

PROCLUS. His lost *Chrestomateia (Anthology)* has been assigned variously to the second or fifth century A.D. See *Cypria*.

QUINTUS SMYRNAEUS. The "pale Homer of the fourth century" (A.D.), as Quintus of Smyrna has been called, wrote a *Posthomerica (Sequel to Homer)*, which F. M. Combellack has translated under the title *The War at Troy: What Homer Didn't Tell* (Norman: University of Oklahoma Press, 1968).

LUCIUS ANNAEUS SENECA (ca. 3 B.C.–A.D. 65). His *Troades (The Trojan Women)* and *Hercules Oetaeus (Hercules on Mount Oeta)* are translated by F. J. Miller for the LCL in the first and second volumes, respectively, of *Seneca's Tragedies* (1917).

MAURUS HONORATUS SERVIUS. The commentator on Virgil lived around the year 400. The relevant comment appears in vol. 3 of the *Servianorum in Vergilii carmina commentarium* (Oxford: Oxford University Press, 1965).

Scholia in SOPHOCLIS tragoedias vetera (Old Scholia to the Tragedies of Sophocles. Ed. Petrus N. Papageorgius (Leipzig, 1888).

STRABO (ca. 63 B.C.–after A.D. 21). His *Geographica (Geography)* appears in LCL, translated by H. L. Jones (1917–32).

C. POMPEIUS TROGUS. A forty-four-book history by this writer, who lived in the time of Caesar Augustus, is preserved in a condensed form through the *Epitome* by Marcus Junianus Justinus, who lived in the second or third century A.D. I have used the French translation by Désiré Nisard in his *Cornelius Nepos, Quinte-Curce, Justin.* . . . (Paris, 1864).

TZETZES. Two Byzantine brother-scholars who annotated LYCO-PHRON. I have taken my quotation from an editorial note to Apollodorus's *Epitome* 6. 15b.

GAIUS VALERIUS FLACCUS (died ca. A.D. 90). Minor Roman poet. J. H. Mozley has translated his *Argonautica* for the LCL (1934).

PUBLIUS VERGILIUS MARO (70–19 B.C.). I have used the special edition of the third book of Virgil's *Aeneid* by R. D. Williams (Oxford: Oxford University Press, 1962).

Sophocles

PHILOCTETES
(409 B.C.)

Translated by Robert Torrance

Robert Torrance's translation of Sophocles' *Philoctetes* was produced by the Adams House Drama Society of Harvard University in 1961, and again, in 1964, by the Group of Ancient Drama at the East River Park Amphitheater in New York City. Both productions were directed by Anthony Keller with music by Raphael Crystal and design by David Follansbee. The text was published by Houghton Mifflin in 1966 together with *The Women of Trachis*. Professor Torrance has revised his translation especially for this volume. It is now inscribed *To the memory of Cedric Whitman.*

CHARACTERS

ODÝSSEUS, son of Laertes and king of Ithaca
NEOPTÓLEMUS, son of Achilles
PHILOCTÉTES, son of Poeas
SPY, a sailor of Odysseus later disguised as a merchant
ANOTHER SAILOR
HERACLES
CHORUS, sailors of Neoptolemus

[*Scene: the island of Lemnos, in front of* PHILOCTETES' CAVE.]

[*Enter* ODYSSEUS *and* NEOPTOLEMUS *followed by the sailor*
who will return later as Odysseus' SPY.]

ODYSSEUS. This is the shore of the sea-encircled isle
of Lemnos, uninhabited and forlorn.
Here long ago, great Neoptolemus,
son of Achilles, noblest of the Greeks,
under strict orders from my two commanders   5
I left the Malian archer Philoctetes.
His swollen foot groaned with a festering ulcer,
and we could not so much as sacrifice
in peace of mind, when all our camp was filled
with savage, sacrilegious screams of pain,   10
moaning and wailing. But, why speak of that?
Now is no time for lengthy words, for he
may learn that I am here, and I may ruin
the scheme by which I hope to snare the man.
    Listen: in what remains you must assist me.   15
Go forth and seek a twin-mouthed rock: a cave
such that in winter each of the entrance-ways
faces the sun, but in the summertime
a gentle breeze sends sleep through both the chambers.
Down to the left a little you will find,   20
I think, a stream—unless its source has failed.
Approach it silently, and signal me
whether he still lives there, or someplace else.
Then you must listen to the plan which I

55

will tell you, and we'll carry out together.   25
NEOPTOLEMUS. Look, prince Odysseus—what you ask is easy;
    I think I see the cave you just described.
ODYSSEUS. Far up, or further down? I cannot see it.
NEOPTOLEMUS. Up high—and I can hear no sound of footsteps.
ODYSSEUS. Make sure that no one lies asleep inside.   30
NEOPTOLEMUS. I see an empty chamber—no one near.
ODYSSEUS. And are there no provisions there for living?
NEOPTOLEMUS. A pile of leaves pressed down for a man to sleep on.
ODYSSEUS. Is all the rest of the cave deserted then?
NEOPTOLEMUS. All but a cup carved from a piece of wood   35
    by a clumsy workman's efforts—and some kindling.
ODYSSEUS. This treasure-house which you describe is his.
NEOPTOLEMUS. And over here—ugh!—filthy rags are lying,
    set out to dry, and full of hideous pus.
ODYSSEUS. Clearly this dwelling-place belongs to him;   40
    he must be somewhere near. A man whose leg
    was maimed so long ago will not walk far.
    Either he's gone to look for food, or else
    to find a soothing medicine for his wound.
    Send this man here to spy, and to prevent him   45
    from coming suddenly; for he would rather
    take me than all the other Greeks combined.
NEOPTOLEMUS. Done—be assured the path will be well guarded.

                        [SPY *withdraws.*]

    Now, if you will, speak further of your plan.
ODYSSEUS. Son of Achilles, now is the time to show   50
    your true nobility, not with strength alone,
    but, if you hear some unexpected plan,
    yet serve me—for you came as my assistant.
NEOPTOLEMUS. What are you asking?
ODYSSEUS.   This: you must beguile
    the mind of Philoctetes with your words.   55
    When he inquires about your name and country,
    tell him the truth: you are Achilles' son.
    Then say you're sailing home, leaving the fleet,
    leaving the army of those hated Greeks
    who summoned you from home with earnest prayers—   60
    since only thus could Troy at last be captured—
    yet, when you came, cheated you of the arms

of great Achilles, which you rightly claimed,
and gave them to Odysseus. Slander me
in terms as harsh and bitter as you wish: 65
you won't hurt me at all. But if you fail
in this, you bring disaster on the Greeks.
For if his bow cannot be taken, you
will never capture Priam's ancient land.
   Now, let me tell you why this undertaking   70
is safe for you, but perilous for me.
You were not one of those who first set sail
to Troy, constrained by great and solemn oaths,
yet none of this can I disclaim. And so
if he once sees me, with that bow in hand,   75
I die—and you, as my accomplice, with me.
No, we must plan this deed more cleverly:
steal his resistless weapon like a thief!
I know, my son, you were not meant by nature
to speak, or to contrive, such evil acts;   80
but what we gain by victory is sweet,
so do it—later on we will seem just.
Now, but for one day's brief and shameless time
give yourself to me—and forever after
you shall be called most reverent of men.   85
NEOPTOLEMUS. Son of Laertes, when I hear a plan
which pains me, I recoil from acting on it.
I was not born to act on false contrivance,
nor, so they tell me, was my father. I
will freely lend myself to take the man   90
by force, not guile: he has one foot; he cannot
by force defeat such men as we. . . . And yet
I came to help, and would not willingly
be called a traitor. Prince, I would prefer
to fail with honor than to win by evil.   95
ODYSSEUS. Son of a valiant sire, I once was young;
my tongue, like yours, was slow; my hand was active.
But now, by long experience, I see
the tongue, not deeds, is ruler in all things.
NEOPTOLEMUS. What are you asking but that I should lie?   100
ODYSSEUS. I say, snare Philoctetes by deception.
NEOPTOLEMUS. But why deceive him rather than persuade him?
ODYSSEUS. He will not listen—nor be caught by force.
NEOPTOLEMUS. What dreadful strength could make a man so bold?

ODYSSEUS. Arrows which bring inevitable death.   105
NEOPTOLEMUS. Then do we not so much as dare approach him?
ODYSSEUS. Only if by deception—as I said.
NEOPTOLEMUS. Do you not think that telling lies is shameful?
ODYSSEUS. No—not, at least, if lies lead on to safety.
NEOPTOLEMUS. How can a man face speaking words like these?   110
ODYSSEUS. None should recoil when what he does brings profit.
NEOPTOLEMUS. How will I profit if he comes to Troy?
ODYSSEUS. Troy will be captured only by his bow.
NEOPTOLEMUS. Then will *I* not sack Troy, as it was promised?
ODYSSEUS. Not without it, nor it apart from you.   115
NEOPTOLEMUS. It must be taken then, if that is true.
ODYSSEUS. When you accomplish this, two gifts are yours.
NEOPTOLEMUS. What? Tell me, and I will no longer scruple.
ODYSSEUS. To be proclaimed at once both wise and good.
NEOPTOLEMUS. I'll do it then—and lay all shame aside.   120
ODYSSEUS. Do you remember all that I have told you?
NEOPTOLEMUS. Be sure of it—for now I have consented.
ODYSSEUS. Then stay here by the cave and wait for him.
    I will depart—he must not see me here—
    and take our spy back to the ship again.   125
    Later, if you should seem procrastinating
    or spending too much time, then I will send
    this very man to you again, disguised
    as a ship's captain: his secrecy will help you.
    Listen, my son, to him, and when he speaks   130
    artfully, benefit from what he says.
    Now I must go: this task is in your hands.
    May guileful Hermes guide us on our way,
    and Nike, and Athena—my protectress!

        [ODYSSEUS *and the* SPY *leave. The* CHORUS *enter.*]

                                                    [*Parados*]
                                                    [*Strophe A*]
CHORUS. O master, how must I, a stranger in a strange land,   135
    speak or dissemble before this wary man?
    Tell me: for that man
    surpasses other men
    in wisdom and in skill who rules
    with the sanction of God.   140
    To you, my son, has come now

all of that ancient power: tell me,
how may I assist you?

NEOPTOLEMUS. As for now you may wish to view the land
　he inhabits here by the farthest shore: 145
　survey it boldly, but when the dreadful
　traveller stumbles home again,
　come when I beckon you, and try
　to serve as the moment requires.

　　　　　　　　　　　　　　　　　　　　　　[*Antistrophe A*]
CHORUS. For long, O prince, my chief concern has been   150
　watching for your best interest over all.
　Tell me now: what chamber
　does this man inhabit,
　and what land is his? for I
　must learn, lest suddenly   155
　he fall upon me here.
　Where is his dwelling? where is he,
　at home or far away?

NEOPTOLEMUS. Here you behold the rocky entrance-way
　of his twin-mouthed lair.   160
CHORUS. But where has this miserable man gone now?
NEOPTOLEMUS. I would surmise that he is dragging
　his foot nearby in search of food.
　They say it is thus he gains a living,
　hunting wild beasts with wingèd arrows,   165
　leading a hateful, hateful life. And no one
　comes near to him
　to heal his heavy hardships.

CHORUS. How I pity this lonely man!   [*Strophe B*]
　No one living will care for him,   170
　no companion is by his side,
　wretched, always alone,
　afflicted with a savage wound,
　and lost when need arises.
　How can he live?   175
　　　　　　How can he bear such insufferable pain?
　O inscrutable plan of God!
　O most miserable race of men,
　never is destiny mild.

He was born of an ancient race,   [*Antistrophe B*] 180
yielding never to any man;
now, bereft of the gifts of life,
he lives apart from all others
along with spotted and shaggy beasts,
piteous, hungry, in pain,   185
bearing incurable ills—
                    and afar in the mountains
she of the babbling voice,
Echo, responds to his cries of pain,
wailing sadly around him.   190

NEOPTOLEMUS. None of these things surprise me at all:
they come from heaven, and, if I may judge,
the first of his troubles was sent on him
long since by Chryse with savage intention;
and now, though he suffers with none to help him,   195
surely some god is watching his course
to hold him back from aiming at Troy
his god-given arrows, until the time
shall come when, the oracles say, she is destined
to fall and be vanquished by them.   200

[PHILOCTETES *screams offstage.*]

CHORUS. Be silent, my son!   [*Strophe C*]
NEOPTOLEMUS.   What is it?
CHORUS. A cry has arisen
    as if from a man worn down by pain—
    from there—or over there—it came. . . .
    Surely I hear the voice of someone   205
                    helplessly creeping along;
    I cannot ignore
    that grievously wearying voice from afar—
                    it comes too distinctly.

    Then change, my son . . .   [*Antistrophe C*]
NEOPTOLEMUS.   Change what?   210
CHORUS. . . . your plan of action;
    for he must be close, cannot be far,
    and not to the sound of the flute
    does he come, like a pasturing shepherd,
                    but, stumbling helplessly near,   215

he wails from afar,
beholding the harbor all barren of ships—[1]
          his moaning is dreadful!

[*Enter* PHILOCTETES.]

PHILOCTETES. O strangers!
Who are you, and what country are you from,   220
who sail to this ill-harbored, homeless land?
What city do you come from? How may I
address you? The appearance of your clothing
is Greek—and oh, how sweet it seems to me!—
but let me hear your voices; and do not   225
recoil in terror at my wild appearance,
but pity me, a wretched man, alone,
deserted on this island, friendless, wronged:
speak to me! . . . if, indeed, you come as friends.
Oh, answer! It would not be right if you   230
refused to hear my words and speak to me.
NEOPTOLEMUS. Stranger, be certain, first of all, that we,
as you most wish to learn, are Greeks indeed.
PHILOCTETES. Oh, sweet, sweet voice! How strange it seems, to be
greeted by such a man after so long!   235
What purpose made you come, my child, and led you
so far? What impulse was it? what fair wind?
Answer me all—and tell who you are.
NEOPTOLEMUS. My country is the sea-encircled isle
of Skyros; I am sailing home; my name,   240
Neoptolemus, son of Achilles. That is all.
PHILOCTETES. O son of a dear father! O sweet island!
Foster-child of the agèd Lycomedes,[2]
why did you sail to this land—and from where?
NEOPTOLEMUS. In truth, I am sailing on my way from Troy.   245
PHILOCTETES. What are you saying? You were not one of those
who came with us when we set out for Troy.
NEOPTOLEMUS. Then did you, too, share in this enterprise?

---

1. A disputed line. It has also been read: "seeing the ship at its inhospitable anchorage." The tone of Philoctetes' opening address will differ markedly depending on which reading is adopted. (All notes are by the editor.)
    2. King of Scyros. Achilles had allowed himself to be concealed on the island in order to avoid the Trojan War. There he fathered Neoptolemus by Deidamia, daughter of Lycomedes.

PHILOCTETES. My child, can you be ignorant who I am?
NEOPTOLEMUS. How should I know a man I never saw?   250
PHILOCTETES. Have you not heard my name, or learned the story
    of all the suffering that has been my ruin?
NEOPTOLEMUS. Be certain I know nothing that you ask me.
PHILOCTETES. Oh, how I suffer—how the gods must hate me!
    No tale of how I live has reached my home   255
    or found its way to any part of Greece;
    but those ungodly men who left me here
    conceal their deed, and laugh, while my disease
    continues, flourishes, grows even greater.
        O child, son of Achilles, I am he   260
    whom you perhaps have heard of, he who wields
    the bow of Heracles: I am the son
    of Poeas, Philoctetes. Long ago
    the king of Ithaca and his commanders
    deserted me unjustly on this island,   265
    to rot with savage plagues inflicted by
    the noxious poison of a deadly viper.
    With only this, my son, they left me here
    alone, and sailed away. At first they brought me
    from Chryse to this island in their ships;   270
    then, overjoyed to see me fast asleep
    here in this rocky cave, they sailed away
    and left me nothing but a few soiled rags
    such as a beggar wears, and a small pittance
    of food. May such a fate soon crush them too!   275
        But you, my child—perhaps you can imagine
    the awakening I had when they were gone.
    Oh how I wept and cursed my evil fortune
    when I beheld the ships which I had sailed in
    all vanished. Not a man remained behind: 280
    no one to help me live, and none to soothe
    my wearying disease. I searched all over
    and soon discovered only grief was there,
    but that in plentiful supply, my son.
        Time in its unremitting course went on,   285
    and I, within this narrow cave alone,
    provided for myself; my bow supplied
    my stomach's needs by striking down the doves
    that flew above me; and when my swift arrow
    sped from the string and struck one, I would crawl   290

in pain and drag my throbbing foot behind me
toward it; and when I needed drinking-water
or firewood, even when the frosts of winter
were hard upon me, I crept forth in pain,
and somehow managed. Yet, I had no fire: 295
I ground two stones together till, at last,
a spark appeared from nowhere—and preserved me.
And now a home to live in and a fire
suffice—except to free me from this illness.
  Let me, my child, describe this island to you.   300
No sailor, of his own free will, comes near it;
there is no harbor here, no place to land
and sell his goods with profit, or be welcomed:
no one with any sense would anchor here!
But if one did, against his will (for often   305
in the long life of man these things occur),
he, when he came, my son, would speak to me
with pity, and would give me, from compassion,
some portion of his food or of his clothing;
yet none, when I would mention it, was willing   310
to take me home, and I have wasted here
for ten long years in hunger and in pain,
feeding the ravenous maw of my disease.
  The sons of Atreus and the strong Odysseus
have done this to me, child: and may the gods   315
in heaven grant me vengeance for my wrongs!
CHORUS. I think that I must pity you as greatly
  as they who came before me, son of Poeas.
NEOPTOLEMUS. And I bear witness to your words: I know
  how true they are. I too have felt the hand   320
  of Atreus' evil sons and strong Odysseus.
PHILOCTETES. What? do you also bear a grudge against
  these cursed sons of Atreus? Do you hate them?
NEOPTOLEMUS. Would that this hand could satisfy my hatred!
  Then would Mycenae and Sparta come to know[3]   325
  that Skyros too has fathered valiant men.
PHILOCTETES. Good, child! But what foul crime have you endured
  to come with such a mighty wrath against them?
NEOPTOLEMUS. Ah, son of Poeas, it is hard, but I

---

3. Agamemnon ruled over Mycenae, Menelaus over Sparta.

will tell you how I suffered at their hands.   330
After Achilles met his destined end . . .
PHILOCTETES. Oh wait! say nothing more until you tell me,
has he, the glorious son of Peleus, died?
PHILOCTETES. He has—not killed by any man, but struck
(so they say) by the arrow of Apollo.   335
PHILOCTETES. Well, both the slayer and the slain were noble.
My child, I cannot say if I should first
ask of your suffering or mourn for him.
PHILOCTETES. Unhappy man! your own misfortunes are
enough—you need not mourn for any other.   340
PHILOCTETES. Yes, you are right. Go on, then, with your story
of how these violent men have done you wrong.
NEOPTOLEMUS. Mighty Odysseus and old Phoenix came
to fetch me in a painted ship, and said—
either sincerely or with false intent—   345
that, since my father died, it was decreed
that Troy be taken by no hand but mine.
Stranger, when they had spoken thus, believe me
it was not long before I sailed. I yearned
above all else to see my father's body   350
before his burial—I had never seen him—
but also there was magic in their pledge
that I alone should take the towers of Troy.
    After we sailed two days, a friendly breeze
advanced us on our way, and soon we reached   355
the port of cruel Sigeum. When I landed
all of the army welcomed me, and swore
that they beheld their dead Achilles living.
But he was dead: and after I had wept
for him and my misfortune, I approached   360
the sons of Atreus, thinking them my friends,
and asked them for the arms and all the rest
my father owned; but they in turn replied
presumptuously: "Achilles' son, choose freely
among your father's other goods, but now   365
Laertes' son is master of those arms."
I sprang to my feet immediately, in tears,
and, in a towering passion at my wrong,
I cried: "Wretch, have you dared to give my arms
to another man without first asking me?"   370
Odysseus was standing near, and said:

"Yes child, these men have allocated justly:
I saved your father in his time of need."
But I immediately assailed him then
with every bitter insult I could think of,   375
enraged that he should steal my arms from me.
He was a man not quickly angered, but,
stung by the words he heard me speak, he answered:
"You were not here with us, but shirked your duty.
Now, since you dare to boast so, you will never   380
sail back to Skyros with these arms again."
I listened to his taunts and insults: now
I am sailing home, deprived of what is mine
by that most evil of evil men, Odysseus.
Yet, I would blame his leaders even more: 385
a city's welfare, like an army's, lies
with those who rule, and many who do wrong
are led astray by what their leaders tell them.
    That is my story—and may the man who hates
these sons of Atreus be my friend and God's.   390

                                                            [*Strophe*]
CHORUS. All-fertile guardian of the mountains, Earth,
                                        mother of God,
    thou who rulest the golden stream Pactolus:
    there once I called upon thee, sacred mother,   395
    when this man felt the wrath of Atreus' sons,
    when they were giving the arms of his father,
    unequalled in splendor,   400
    to the son of Laertes, O blessèd one,
    thou who ridest
                    bull-slaughtering lions.

PHILOCTETES. You and your comrades, stranger, as it seems,
    have sailed to me with signs of suffering
    so similar to mine, that I am sure   405
    they come from Atreus' sons and from Odysseus.
    I know full well that he would lend his tongue
    to any evil word or wicked deed
    by which he might accomplish some injustice.
    Nothing surprises me in that—except   410
    that Ajax could endure to see it done.
NEOPTOLEMUS. He was not living, stranger: I would never

have been despoiled if he had been alive.
PHILOCTETES. What? are you telling me he too is dead?
NEOPTOLEMUS. Be certain he will see the light no more.   415
PHILOCTETES. Oh wretched that I am! but Tydeus' son[4]
and the bastard child that Sisyphus sold Laertes,[5]
they will live on—for they deserve to die.
NEOPTOLEMUS. They do, most surely: but they are still living
and prospering in the army of the Greeks.   420
PHILOCTETES. But is my old and faithful friend alive,
Nestor of Pylos? He, at least, could sometimes
restrain their evil deeds with his wise counsels.
NEOPTOLEMUS. Yes, but he lives in sorrows, for his son
Antilochus is dead, who once stood by him.   425
PHILOCTETES. Oh, you have mentioned the two men whose death
I wanted least to hear you tell me of!
What must we look for when such men as these
have died, and yet Odysseus lives, though he
deserves to be a corpse instead of them!   430
NEOPTOLEMUS. He is a shrewd contestant, Philoctetes;
but even shrewd plans often trip themselves.
PHILOCTETES. Tell me, I pray you, where Patroclus was—
he whom your father loved beyond all others.
NEOPTOLEMUS. He was dead too—and I, in short, will tell you   435
that war, of its own choice, will take no man
who is evil, but will always take the good.
PHILOCTETES. I will bear witness there! and on these grounds
will ask about a paltry, worthless man
I knew, whose tongue was clever: how is he?   440
NEOPTOLEMUS. Who else besides Odysseus can you mean?
PHILOCTETES. Not him—there was a man, Thersites, there,
who always spoke so long that all the others
refused to listen: is he still alive?
NEOPTOLEMUS. I never saw him, but I heard he lives.[6]   445

---

4. The son of Tydeus is Diomedes, closely associated with Odysseus throughout the Trojan War. Perhaps Sophocles is remembering that in the Euripidean version it was Diomedes rather than Neoptolemus who helped steal Philoctetes' bow.

5. One tradition has it that Odysseus's true father was Sisyphus, not Laertes, and that Laertes paid Sisyphus a sum of money to carry off the latter's pregnant wife, Anticlea.

6. The foul-mouthed Thersites had actually been killed by Achilles. It is clear that Sophocles has kept him alive for his poetic purpose.

PHILOCTETES. He would—for nothing bad has ever died!
  The gods themselves take special care of that,
  and somehow seem delighted to allow
  the evil and villainous to live; but always
  banish whatever things are right and good.   450
  How can I praise the deeds these gods have done
  when I discover they themselves are evil?
NEOPTOLEMUS. Son of Oetean Poeas, as for me,
  I in the future will beware of Troy
  and watch the sons of Atreus from afar;   455
  and where the worse is stronger than the better,
  and what is good dies out, and villains rule—
  never will I make friends with such as they.
  No, it will satisfy me after this
  to find my happiness in rocky Skyros.   460
    Now to my ship: farewell, a long farewell,
  great son of Poeas! May the gods release you
  from this disease, as you yourself desire.
  We must be going so that, when the gods
  grant us to sail, we may set forth at once.   465
PHILOCTETES. Child, are you leaving me?
NEOPTOLEMUS.   The time commands:
  we must keep closer watch upon our ships.
PHILOCTETES. Child, in your father's and your mother's name,
  by everything you value most, I beg you,
  do not abandon me to live alone   470
  with all these many hardships you yourself
  have seen, and others you have only heard of.
  Give me a passing thought: I know this burden
  is great, and will perhaps offend you, yet
  bear with it; for the truly noble man   475
  will hate a shameful act, and prize a good one.
  If you forsake me, only shame is yours,
  but if you take me safely home to Oeta,
  my son, a rich reward of fame awaits you.
  Come: I will trouble you for just one day;   480
  make the endeavor—place me where you will,
  down in the hold, or in the prow, the stern,
  wherever I will be least in the way.
  Consent—by the god of suppliants, child, I pray,
  listen: I fall upon my knees, though I   485
  am weak and lame and wretched: do not leave me
  forlorn, and far from human footsteps, here.

Save me, and take me to your home, or else
farther, to prince Chalcodon's land, Euboea:
then we will not have far to go to Oeta,   490
the Trachinian hills and the fair-flowing river
Spercheius, and you may take me to my father—
though I have been afraid for many a year
that he is gone: for I have often sent
prayers with my visitors, and summoned him   495
to come for me and take me home again.
But either he is dead, or else, more likely,
my messengers neglected what I asked them,
and, in their haste, sailed on their homeward way.
But now I have found in you both messenger   500
and escort: have compassion, and preserve me!
The life of man is full of dread and danger;
its happiness is fleeting; and the man
who dwells apart from grief must watch that danger,
and when he lives at ease must be most careful   505
lest suddenly his life slip by in ruin.

                                                      [*Antistrophe*]
CHORUS. Have pity, prince, for he has told of pains
                                          many and hard,
  such, I pray, as my friends will never suffer.
  Prince, if you hate the cruel sons of Atreus,   510
  turn their evil deeds to his advantage:
  come, let us take him and carry him now   515
  in our swift-flying ship
  to his home, to the land where he yearns to go,
  fleeing far from
                  the wrath of the gods.

NEOPTOLEMUS. Beware lest you be ready now, but later,
  when you have come in contact with his illness   520
  and tire of it, you change to other plans.
CHORUS. No, never fear, for you will never have
  just cause to utter that reproach against me.
NEOPTOLEMUS. I would account it shameful to be slower
  than you to serve this stranger in his need.   525
  Come, let us sail and leave at once, for surely
  our ship will not refuse to carry him.
  And may the gods convey us from this land
  safely, wherever we may wish to sail.

PHILOCTETES. Oh sweetest day of days, oh kindest man!   530
  Sailors, my friends, I wish that I could show you
  truly how dear you have become to me!
  Son, let us go—but first we must salute
  this home which is no home, for you must learn
  how I sustained myself with patient heart.   535
  I think no other man than I could even
  look for a moment on this sight and bear it;
  but destiny has taught me to endure.
CHORUS. Wait, let us listen, for two men are coming—
  one from our ship, the other man a stranger.   540
  Listen to what they say before you enter.

[*Enter* SPY, *with another sailor.*]

SPY. Son of Achilles, I asked this sailor here,
  who, with two other men, was standing guard
  over your ship, to tell me where you were.
  I met you when I least expected to,   545
  for only chance has brought me to this island.
  I was sailing as a merchant back from Troy
  with a small crew to my grape-clustered home
  Peparethus. When I learned that all these sailors
  were members of your crew, why, I decided   550
  not to sail on my way in silence, but
  to speak with you—and take my due reward.
  You see, you don't know anything at all
  about the new plans which the Greeks are making
  concerning you—not only plans, but deeds,   555
  and deeds in progress, not just thought about.
NEOPTOLEMUS. Stranger, if I have any seed of virtue
  I will remember your concern for me.
  Now, tell me what you mean, for I must learn
  about whatever plan the Greeks have made.   560
SPY. The aged Phoenix and the sons of Theseus
  have launched an expedition to pursue you.
ÑEOPTOLEMUS. To take me back by force or by persuasion?
SPY. I only know what I have heard from others.
NEOPTOLEMUS. Are Phoenix and his fellow-sailors really   565
  so anxious to appease the sons of Atreus?
SPY. Be certain they are doing so—and now.
NEOPTOLEMUS. Why did Odysseus not set forth with them
  and tell me this himself? Was he afraid?

SPY. He and the son of Tydeus were sailing   570
   after another man when I left port.
NEOPTOLEMUS. Who is it that Odysseus is seeking?
SPY. There was a certain man—but tell me first
   who *he* is; and speak softly when you say it.
NEOPTOLEMUS. This is the famous Philoctetes, stranger.   575
SPY. Ask me no more, but sail from here as quickly
   as possibly you can, and leave this island.
PHILOCTETES. What is he saying, child? what shadowy bargain
   is this man making with you about me?
NEOPTOLEMUS. I am not certain yet; but he must speak   580
   openly, to my sailors, and to you.
SPY. Son of Achilles, do not charge me here
   with saying what I should not: I am poor,
   and these men are the means of my subsistence.
NEOPTOLEMUS. I hate the sons of Atreus; this man   585
   is my best friend, because he hates them too.
   You, if you come in friendship for me, must
   not hide from us whatever you have heard.
SPY. Watch yourself, son.
NEOPTOLEMUS.   I know what I am doing.
SPY. You are responsible.
NEOPTOLEMUS.   I am: speak on.   590
SPY. I will. The men I told you of before,
   the son of Tydeus and the strong Odysseus,
   are sailing under oath to bring this man
   back—by persuasive words, or by brute force.
   It was Odysseus who informed the Greeks   595
   about this plan: he was more confident
   than his companion that he would succeed.
NEOPTOLEMUS. Why did the sons of Atreus turn their thoughts
   again, when so much time had passed, to him
   whom they deserted here so long ago?   600
   What passion came upon them? what constraint
   or vengeance from the gods, who punish evil?
SPY. I will explain these matters, for it seems
   you have not heard about them. Helenus,
   a noble prophet and the son of Priam,   605
   was captured one night by this guileful man
   Odysseus, who is known for shameful acts
   and insults: he was taken then in chains
   and shown to the Achaeans as a prize.

He prophesied to them of many things, 610
and said the towers of Troy would never fall
unless they could persuade this man to come
back from the island he inhabits now.
And when Laertes' son had heard the seer
thus prophesy, immediately he promised 615
the Greeks would see the man brought back to them.
He hoped he would come willingly, but said,
willing or not, that he would come; and then
offered his head if he should fail to bring him.
Now you have heard me, son: I would advise 620
haste for yourself and any man you care for.
PHILOCTETES. Oh oh, has he, that universal plague,
sworn that he will persuade me to return?
I shall as soon come back from hell to see
the light, when I have died, as be persuaded! 625
SPY. I cannot vouch for that; but I am going
back to my ship—and may the gods be with you!

[SPY *and sailor leave.*]

PHILOCTETES. Is it not strange indeed, my child, that this
son of Laertes hoped by soothing words
to bring me back among the Greeks again? 630
No, I would rather listen to the hateful
serpent that crippled me than hear this man!
He would say anything to serve his end;
but now, at least, I know that he is coming.
Then, child, let us be going; let us place 635
wide tracts of sea between us and Odysseus.
Come, let us hasten; timely speed will bring
sleep and repose for us when toil is over.
NEOPTOLEMUS. As soon as favoring breezes fill our sails,
then we will go; but now they are adverse. 640
PHILOCTETES. Those who flee evil always have fair sailing.
NEOPTOLEMUS. These winds are adverse to our enemies, too.
PHILOCTETES. No wind will ever blow against those pirates
when they have any chance to steal or plunder!
NEOPTOLEMUS. Well, let us sail then: but first go inside 645
and fetch whatever things you have most need of.
PHILOCTETES. I do need some things, though I have but few.
NEOPTOLEMUS. What can you need that my ship does not have?

PHILOCTETES. A certain medicine I own, with which
  I soothe my wound until the pain dies down.   650
NEOPTOLEMUS. Take it then: what else do you wish to bring?
PHILOCTETES. The arrows I have overlooked and left
  behind me: no one else must find them here.
NEOPTOLEMUS. Is that the famous bow you have there? Tell me.
PHILOCTETES. This which my hands are holding, and no other.   655
NEOPTOLEMUS. Will you allow me to behold it closer,
  and take it, and revere it as a god?
PHILOCTETES. Child, I will grant this favor to you, and
  whatever else is in my power to help you.
NEOPTOLEMUS. I long to hold it—but my desire is such   660
  that, if it were not right, I would not wish it.
PHILOCTETES. Child, do not doubt your wish is right and holy.
  You and you only have allowed my heart
  to hope once more to see my native land,
  my agèd father and friends: you have restored me   665
  and saved me from the snares of evil men!
  Take heart, for I will let you hold it, and,
  when you return it, you may boast that you
  alone of men were good enough to touch it.
  I won this bow myself through my good deeds.   670
NEOPTOLEMUS. I am glad I found you and acquired a friend.
  He who repays one good deed with another
  is such a friend as riches cannot buy.
  Now go inside.
PHILOCTETES.   I will, and you must follow:
  I need someone to help me in my illness.   675

              [PHILOCTETES *and* NEOPTOLEMUS *withdraw into the cave.*]

                                                            [*Stasimon*]
                                                          [*Strophe A*]
CHORUS. Such suffering my eyes have never seen: they say
    Ixion once went near to the sacred bed
    of Zeus, and was cast by the god to the depths on
                                        a wheel of fire;   680
    but I have never beheld or heard of another
    whose fate was harder than this man's.
    He did no wrong to any man alive,
    but lived at peace with all: yet now   685
    he wastes away unjustly.
    I cannot understand how he

ever was able to live all alone
　　　　　and hear the waves around him,
enduring a life so full of tears.　　　　　　690

　　　　　　　　　　　　　[Antistrophe A]
He had no neighbor but himself, he could not walk,
and none was near to share in his suffering
or listen when he would lament of his cruel,
　　　　　　　　　　　devouring pain,
or soothe the burning-hot blood that would ooze from
　　the wound　　　　　　695
in his poisonous foot, or gather
soft herbs from the fruitful earth, whenever
the agony would fall upon him.　　　　　　700
He crept from place to place
and crawled with slowly painful steps
(just like a child who has lost his nurse)
　　　　　　　wherever he might hope to find
the means to live when the pain died down.　　705

　　　　　　　　　　　　　[Strophe B]
He found no food on all of the sacred earth,
nor anything which laboring men enjoy,
except when he could limit his hunger　　　　710
with arrows shot from his swift-striking bow.
　　　　　　　　How black his life was,
he who never for ten long years
　　　　　　　rejoiced in the taste of wine,　715
but searched to find a place where he
　　　　　　might but drink of stagnant water.

　　　　　　　　　　　　　[Antistrophe B]
Yet soon at last he will become great and happy,
for he has met the son of a noble race,　　　720
who, now that many months have departed,[7]

---

　　7. R. C. Jebb's reading here is "in the fullness of many months," and David Grene's translation follows closely with "after the fullness of many months." Critics have usually explained that the sailors are lying because they have just caught sight of Philoctetes, but Eilhard Schlesinger ("Die Intrige in Aufbau um Sophokles Philoktet") has made the interesting suggestion that they are telling the literal truth. Neoptolemus will indeed restore Philoctetes to his native land—right after the two have captured Troy.

will carry him in his ship to his country,
                                   land of sea-nymphs,   725
near Spercheius's banks where once
                            the bronze-armored Heracles
Approached the gods all splendid with fire
            atop Oeta's craggy mountain.

[NEOPTOLEMUS *comes out from the cave, followed by*
      PHILOCTETES.]

NEOPTOLEMUS. Come now—why are you suddenly so silent?   730
  Why do you stand dumfounded without cause?
PHILOCTETES. Ah ah ah ah!
NEOPTOLEMUS. What is it?
PHILOCTETES.   Nothing much, my son: go on.
NEOPTOLEMUS. Are you in pain from your habitual illness?
PHILOCTETES. No—I am certain it is better now.   735
  O gods!
NEOPTOLEMUS. Why do you call the gods with such loud moans?
PHILOCTETES. To come to me and soothe me and preserve me—
  ah ah ah ah!
NEOPTOLEMUS. What are you suffering from? Come, speak: do not 740
  be silent—you are clearly in great pain.
PHILOCTETES. Child, it is killing me: I can no longer
  hide my distress from you—oh oh!—it comes,
  it comes! wretch that I am! the pain, the pain!
  Child, it is killing me: child, it devours me!   745
  Ah oh ah oh ah oh ah oh ah oh!
  Child, if you have a sword at hand, I pray you,
  in God's name, take it, strike this foot of mine,
  now, cut it off, now—never mind my life—
  come child!   750
NEOPTOLEMUS. But what has happened now to cause this outburst
  of sudden screaming and groaning that I hear?
PHILOCTETES. You know, my son.
NEOPTOLEMUS.   What is it?
PHILOCTETES.   Child, you know.
NEOPTOLEMUS. I do not know.
PHILOCTETES.   How can you not know? Oh!
NEOPTOLEMUS. Frightful must be the burden of your illness!   755
PHILOCTETES. Frightful beyond the power of speech: have pity!
NEOPTOLEMUS. What can I do?

PHILOCTETES. Do not forsake me in fear:
this comes upon me at times, when it has finished
wandering elsewhere.
NEOPTOLEMUS. Oh unhappy man,
truly unhappy with these many pains! 760
Shall I take hold of you and give my hand?
PHILOCTETES. No, no—but take this bow of mine, and hold it
just as you asked before, until the pangs
from the disease which pains me now die down. 765
Preserve it for me; guard it well—for sleep
will take me when this agony has passed,
and only then will free me: you must let me
slumber in peace. But if in the meantime
these men should come, I pray you, by the gods, 770
do not by any means, willing or not,
give them the bow, or you will kill yourself
and me, who am your suppliant, together.
NEOPTOLEMUS. Trust my discretion, for no hands will touch it
but yours and mine: so give it in good faith. 775
PHILOCTETES. Take it, my son, and pray it may not bring
such pain and suffering to you as it
brought me, and him who wielded it before me.
NEOPTOLEMUS. Grant this, O gods, to both of us, and grant
fair sailing to us and a prosperous voyage 780
wherever God and our intentions take us.
PHILOCTETES. My child, I fear your prayers are said in vain:
the bloody gore drops oozing from the depths
of my wound, and yet the worst is still to come.
The pain, the pain! 785
O my foot, how great will be the pain you cause me!
It is creeping,
it is coming nearer, wretched that I am!
You know it now; but do not flee from me!
Ah ah ah ah! 790
O king of Ithaca, would this anguish might
pierce through your breast: ah ah ah ah ah ah!
Oh oh oh oh! Agamemnon, Menelaus,
you captains of the Greeks, would that you might
suffer instead of me this lifelong pain!
Oh oh! 795
Death, Death, why, when I always call upon you,
day in, day out, can you not ever come?

O child, my noble friend, come, take me now
and burn me in the famed volcanic fire   800
of Lemnos' mountain: I myself once dared
to do this for the son of Zeus to gain
that bow which you are now preserving for me.
Say something, child.
Speak; break your silence—child, what are you thinking?   805
NEOPTOLEMUS. I have long now been grieving for your hardships.
PHILOCTETES. But, O my child, take heart: it comes to me
grievously, but it quickly goes away.
I only pray, do not leave me alone.
NEOPTOLEMUS. Take heart: we will remain.
PHILOCTETES.   Will you?
NEOPTOLEMUS.   Be certain.   810
PHILOCTETES. I will not place you under oath, my son.
NEOPTOLEMUS. It is not right that I should go without you.
PHILOCTETES. Give me your hand as pledge.
NEOPTOLEMUS.   Here: I will stay.
PHILOCTETES. Now take me there.
NEOPTOLEMUS.   Where do you mean?
PHILOCTETES.   Up there.
NEOPTOLEMUS. Why do you rave and look up at the sky?   815
PHILOCTETES. Let me go, let me go!
NEOPTOLEMUS.   Where?
PHILOCTETES.   Let me go!
NEOPTOLEMUS. I will not.
PHILOCTETES.   You will kill me if you touch me!
NEOPTOLEMUS. I will let you go if you are in your senses.
PHILOCTETES. Earth, take me here to die now in your arms:
I can no longer stand erect for pain.   820
NEOPTOLEMUS. I think that sleep will come upon this man
soon now: his head already is bent back;
the sweat is pouring over his whole body;
a thin black stream of blood has broken from
his wounded foot. Friends, let us leave him here   825
in peace, and hope that sleep may come upon him.

                                                                        [*Commos*]
                                                                        [*Strophe*]
CHORUS. Sleep who art stranger to sorrow and suffering,
come to him gently, gently,
and grant him, lord, thy blessing now;

let him behold this light 830
which now spreads over his lustrous eyes:
come, Healer, I pray.
    Child, you must make your decision now
what to do and how to think,
seeing how these matters stand. 835
Why should we be slow to act?
The moment is judge over every deed,
and often allows unexpected achievements.

NEOPTOLEMUS. I know he cannot hear me but I see that we must fail
    if we should take the bow alone without the man and sail: 840
    the crown is his and he it was the god meant for our prize—
    it is a shameful thing to boast of futile deeds and lies.

[*Antistrophe*]

CHORUS. Child, be assured that the gods will attend to that.
    When you reply to me next,
    speak softly, softly, O my child, 845
    the tone of the words you utter:
    the sleep of men who are ill is light
    and quick to perceive.
        Now be especially careful to
    take no possible chance here: 850
    do it, do it secretly.
    You know what I am speaking of.
    But if you follow some other plan,
    a man of discretion can see only danger.

Child, the wind is with us now: [*Epode*] 855
the man cannot see us: he lies
defenseless, in darkness,
fearlessly sleeping,
without the use of his hands or feet
like a man who lies in the kingdom of death. 860
Be sure the plan you choose
is best: in my opinion, child,
the wisest counsel is that
which involves the minimum danger.

NEOPTOLEMUS. Silence, I say, and keep your wits about you: 865
    he is lifting up his head with open eyes.

PHILOCTETES. O light of heaven, how little I expected,
on waking, to behold these strangers here!
Never, my child, could I have hoped that you
would wait upon my suffering with such pity,   870
and stay beside me and help me in my need.
The sons of Atreus—those noble captains!—
were not so patient as you to bear with me.
But you are good by birth, my child, and come
from noble parents; you have lightly done   875
all this, and borne with my screams and foul smell.
And now, since some oblivion and release
from my disease has come to me, my child,
raise me yourself, and lift me up, my child,
so that when pain releases me we may   880
set forth in our ship and not delay to sail.
NEOPTOLEMUS. How glad I am to see you living still,
and breathing without pain, beyond my hopes!
I almost might have thought, as I was watching
your agony, that you were dying. Come,   885
raise yourself up now, or, if you prefer,
I will command these men to carry you;
for you and I are of the same intention.
PHILOCTETES. Thank you, my child: now help me rise again,
and leave these men alone. They should not suffer   890
this smell before they need to. On the ship
they will have pain enough from living with me.
NEOPTOLEMUS. So let it be—now take my hand and rise.
PHILOCTETES. Fear not—my ingrained habit will restore me.
NEOPTOLEMUS. Ah me, what course of action must I take?   895
PHILOCTETES. What is the matter, child? Why do you waver?
NEOPTOLEMUS. I find myself unable to reply.
PHILOCTETES. Unable? Child, do not say such a thing.
NEOPTOLEMUS. Yet even so is the turmoil I am in.
PHILOCTETES. Has my disease become offensive to you,   900
and will you not now take me in your ship?
NEOPTOLEMUS. Everything is offensive when a man
departs from his own nature and does wrong.
PHILOCTETES. Surely your words and actions will be like   905
your father's if you help a worthy man.
NEOPTOLEMUS. I will seem base, and that thought tortures me.
PHILOCTETES. Not if you help me—yet I fear your words.
NEOPTOLEMUS. O God, what shall I do? Must I be guilty
again of hiding truth and spreading lies?

PHILOCTETES. Unless my judgment fails it seems that he   910
　is falsely leaving me, to sail away.
NEOPTOLEMUS. I am not leaving you, but I may bring you
　to greater pain—and that thought tortures me.
PHILOCTETES. My child, I cannot understand your words.
NEOPTOLEMUS. I will hide nothing: you must sail to Troy,   915
　to the Greek army of the sons of Atreus.
PHILOCTETES. What are you saying?
NEOPTOLEMUS.   Wait, until you learn . . .
PHILOCTETES. Learn what? What do you mean to do with me?
NEOPTOLEMUS. To save you from this suffering, and then
　to go along with you and capture Troy.   920
PHILOCTETES. Can you really mean this?
NEOPTOLEMUS.   Yes: a strong compulsion
　necessitates it: do not be enraged.
PHILOCTETES. Oh, you have killed me and betrayed me! Stranger,
　what have you done to me? Give back my bow.
NEOPTOLEMUS. That is not possible. My duty and   925
　expedience both make me obey my rulers.
PHILOCTETES. You monstrous plague, you hateful instrument
　of craft and cunning, think what you have done,
　how you have tricked me! Are you not ashamed
　even to look at me, who trusted you?   930
　You took my bow, and with it took my life:
　give it back I pray, give it back I beg, my child;
　by all your father's gods, do not destroy me! . . .
　Oh wretched that I am, he will not speak,
　but looks away and keeps it for himself.   935
　　Harbors and promontories—fellow-creatures
　who roam the mountainside—steep-rising cliffs—
　I have no one but you whom I may speak to
　(for you have heard me often) and lament
　the wrongs Achilles' son has done to me.   940
　He swore to take me home, yet sails for Troy;
　he gave me his right hand, yet now he holds
　the sacred bow of Zeus' son Heracles
　and plans to show it off before the Greeks.
　He uses force, as if I could oppose him: 945
　I who am but a corpse, a smoky shadow,
　a vision! He would not have captured me
　before—or even now, except by guile.
　Yet he has tricked me now: what must I do?
　Oh give it back and be yourself again!   950

What do you say? Nothing? Then I am lost!
My twin-mouthed cave, I come to you again,
naked now, and deprived of my subsistence.
I shall soon waste away within this chamber,
killing no wingèd birds or mountain beasts 955
now with my arrows; I will perish here
in pain, providing food for those who fed me:
they whom I hunted once will track me down.
I must pay for the blood that I have shed
because of one who seemed to know no evil. 960
Curses—yet not until I learn if you
will change your mind: if not, may you be damned!
CHORUS. What shall we do? Prince, you must tell us now
whether to sail or yield to this man's words.
NEOPTOLEMUS. A strange compassion for him comes upon me, 965
which I first felt, not now, but long before.
PHILOCTETES. Have pity, child, in God's name: do not give
men cause to blame you for deceiving me.
NEOPTOLEMUS. What shall I do? I wish that I had never
left Skyros to be burdened by these troubles! 970
PHILOCTETES. You are not evil—yet it seems that you
have learned from men who are: leave that to them,
but sail away, and give me back my weapon.
NEOPTOLEMUS. What shall we do?

[ODYSSEUS, *who has entered unnoticed, steps forward.*]

ODYSSEUS.   Rash man, what are you doing?
Step back, I tell you: give the bow to me. 975
PHILOCTETES. Who is it? Do I hear Odysseus speak?
ODYSSEUS. Odysseus, yes! Now you may see me clearly.
PHILOCTETES. Oh, I am ruined, lost! then it was you
who snared me and deprived me of my weapon!
ODYSSEUS. I and no other—I confess it freely. 980
PHILOCTETES. Child, give me back my bow.
ODYSSEUS.   No, he will never
do that, not even if he wishes: you
must come with us, or *they* will force you to it.
PHILOCTETES. Boldest and evilest of wicked men,
will they use force on me?
ODYSSEUS.   Yes, if you struggle. 985
PHILOCTETES. Lemnos, my island, whose almighty flame

the god of fire engendered, can you bear
to see this man force me away from you?
ODYSSEUS. Zeus, let me tell you, Zeus rules in this land; 990
Zeus has done this—and I am but his servant.
PHILOCTETES. Villain, what pretext will you think of next?
By crediting the gods you make them liars!
ODYSSEUS. No, they are true. And now we must set forth.
PHILOCTETES. I will not.
ODYSSEUS. But you will: you cannot help it.
PHILOCTETES. Wretch that I am! was I my father's son 995
to be a slave and never live in freedom?
ODYSSEUS. Not so, but equal to our noblest men,
with whom you will take Troy and bring it low.
PHILOCTETES. No, never! I would suffer any evil
to keep this rocky land beneath my feet. 1000
ODYSSEUS. What can you do about it?
PHILOCTETES. Throw myself
down on those rocks and dash my brains upon them!
ODYSSEUS. Two of you, seize him: this must not take place.

[*Two* CHORUS *members seize* PHILOCTETES *and
bind his hands.*]

PHILOCTETES. My hands, oh how you suffer now without
your bowstring, bound together by this man! 1005
But you, whose thoughts are foul and servile, you
stole on me, hunted me, and took this boy
whom I had never seen to be your shield—
my equal, but too good for you!—who only
tried to perform what you had ordered, though 1010
clearly he is remorseful now for what
he did in error and for what I suffered.
But your base soul, peeping from hidden corners,
trained him against his nature and his will
to be a shrewd contriver of evil deeds; 1015
and now, O wretch, you bind me and intend
to take me from this shore where once you left me,
a friendless, lonely, homeless, living corpse.
Oh!
May you be cursed, as I have often prayed!
Yet no . . . the gods grant nothing sweet to me, 1020
and you will live in happiness while I

drag on my wretched life with further pains,
laughed at by you and by your twin commanders,
the sons of Atreus, whom you serve so well.
And yet when we first sailed for Troy, *you* were   1025
deceived and forced,[8] while I, who suffer now,
came willingly, with seven ships, until
you cast me off—or they, if you prefer!
Why will you take me? what can you intend?
I am a worthless nothing, long since dead!   1030
Why do I seem, god-hated man, no longer
crippled and putrid to you? How will you
sacrifice if I sail with you? for that
was your excuse for leaving me before.
May you be damned!—you *will* be damned for all   1035
the wrongs I suffered, if the gods are just.
I know they are, for you would not have sailed
on such a trip after a man like me
unless some god had spurred you on your way.
O fatherland of mine, O gods who watch me,   1040
avenge, avenge, however late, my wrongs
on all these men, if you have pity for me.
I live most piteously, but if I saw
them perish, I would think my illness cured.
CHORUS. This stranger's words are strong, and strongly spoken, 1045
Odysseus: he will not submit to hardships.
ODYSSEUS. If I had time I could reply to him
at leisure; now I will say one thing only:
where any man is needed, I am there.
If you will speak of just and noble men,   1050
you will find none more reverent than I.
By nature I want victory everywhere—
except from you, to whom I freely yield.
Release him; do not touch him any longer;

[CHORUS *members release* PHILOCTETES.]

---

8. Like Achilles, Odysseus tried to shun service in the war at first. He
feigned madness, and the Greek leaders found him in Ithaca sowing salt into
the furrows as he went plowing the earth. But when Palamedes flung his baby
son Telemachus before the team, Odysseus reined in the animals and so was
proved sane and fit for duty.

let him remain. We have no need of you   1055
now that we have your bow, for Teucer lives
among us still, a master of his craft,
and I myself, I think, can handle it
no worse than you, and aim it just as well.
What need for you? Take pleasure in your island,   1060
for we must go. Perhaps this prize will bring
to me the honor which you might have had.
PHILOCTETES. What shall I do in my unhappiness?
Will you display my weapon to the Greeks?
ODYSSEUS. Talk to me now no longer—I am going.   1065
PHILOCTETES. Seed of Achilles, will you not address me
now, but depart from me without a word?
ODYSSEUS. Come with me—do not look at him—you are
too noble, and you may yet spoil our fortunes.
PHILOCTETES. Strangers, will you too leave me here alone,   1070
and not have pity on my solitude?
CHORUS. This boy is our commander, and whatever
he says to you, we must agree with him.
NEOPTOLEMUS. *He* will say that my nature is too full
of pity; but, if this man wishes, stay   1075
until the others have prepared the ship
and we have made our offering to the gods.
Meanwhile perhaps his attitude toward us
will soften. Now the two of us must go:
as soon as we send word, be prompt to follow.   1080

[NEOPTOLEMUS *follows* ODYSSEUS *out.*]

                                                  [*Commos*]
PHILOCTETES. O my hollow cavern of stone,   [*Strophe A*]
now hot, now icy cold, was I
never again to leave you then,
unhappy that I am, but die
with no one near but you?   1085
Ah ah ah ah!
O my chamber, so full of grief
brought upon you by me alone,
how can I now survive here
day by day, and where will I find   1090
hope to provide me with food in my pain?
The tremulous doves will

fly on their way through the piercing air
above my head, unhindered.
CHORUS. You have caused this, you alone,   1095
harsh-fated man, and no one
is forcing this fortune
upon you but you.
You had your chance to choose
a better fate, but chose instead   1100
one which is harder for you.

PHILOCTETES. Oh unhappy man that I am,   [*Antistrophe A*]
dishonored in my suffering:
I will never, never behold
another man to share my grief,   1105
but soon will perish here—
oh oh oh oh!—
bringing food to my home no more
such as once, with my wingèd shafts
held in my mighty hands, I   1110
caught; but now the deceitful words
born of a treacherous mind have snared me.
Oh how I wish that he,
he who has brought all this evil on me,
could feel my never-ending pain.   1115
CHORUS. Only fate has done this to you.
As for me I have not lent
my hand to any guile:
so speak your dreadful
ill-fated curse on others.
My only wish is that you will   1120
not now reject my friendship.

PHILOCTETES. Ah ah ah! he is sitting now   [*Strophe B*]
down by the shore of the white-waved sea
laughing at me and brandishing   1125
the only prop of my wretched life,
which no one before had ever taken.
O my bow, my only friend,
torn away from loving hands,
surely if you have a heart   1130
you are looking with pity on me,
the comrade of Heracles.

Never again will I hold you hereafter:
you will be wielded now by the hands
of another, a man of deceitful guile,   1135
and watch his shameful tricks, and see
that hateful man, my wicked foe,
bringing his evil plans to fulfillment
with thousandfold shames for me, my God!
CHORUS. Man should always attempt to speak with justice;   1140
    but his tongue should not ever say
    galling words which derive from envy.
    The man you speak of was ordered
    by many other men, and he
    has done a great service for all his friends.   1145

                                            [*Antistrophe B*]
PHILOCTETES. O birds of the air, O bright-eyed tribes
    of wandering beasts who inhabit
    this rocky, mountainous pasture-land:
    no longer need you flee from your lairs,
    for I will never hold in my hands   1150
    the arrows which used to protect me.
    Oh how miserable am I now!
    Roam wherever you wish: the land
    no longer is dangerous for you;
    now it is only just that you   1155
    should take my blood in return for yours
    and sate yourselves on my yellowed flesh.
    Soon I shall leave this life of mine.
    How can I find myself a living?
    How can a man with none of the gifts   1160
    the nourishing earth supplies to others
    feed himself on the winds of the air?
CHORUS. In God's name, if you respect a friendly stranger,
    come to me as I come to you.
    Pray consider, consider well   1165
    how you may flee from this plague.
    It eats without remorse, and no one
    ever could learn to endure such pain.

PHILOCTETES. Again, again you have brought
    to my mind my ancient pain,   1170
    O kindest of men to visit me:

why will you kill me, what have you done?
CHORUS. What can you mean?
PHILOCTETES.   You wished to take me
    back to that hated land of Troy.   1175
CHORUS. I think it is best.
PHILOCTETES.   Then leave me alone!
CHORUS. What you have spoken is welcome to me
                        and joyfully will I perform it!
    Let us go, let us go,   1180
    each to his place on our ship.
PHILOCTETES. By Zeus who is god of curses, I pray you, stay!
CHORUS.   Be calm!
PHILOCTETES. Strangers, remain for God's sake!
CHORUS.   Why do you scream? 1185
PHILOCTETES. Ah ah ah ah!
    O God, I am dying, wretchedly dying!
    My foot, my foot, how will I ever
    take care of you in the time to come?
    Strangers, come back to me now again!   1190
CHORUS. But what can we do for you now
    more than what you have told us before?
PHILOCTETES. You must not blame me, for I
    am distraught with tempestuous pain,
    and my screams are beyond my control   1195
CHORUS. Come with us then, poor man, as we bid you.
PHILOCTETES. Never, oh never: be certain of that!
    not though the god of the fiery lightning
    came to envelop me in his flame!
    May Troy soon perish with all of those   1200
    who cast me off because of my foot!
    But strangers, grant me, I beg you, one prayer.
CHORUS. What are you asking?
PHILOCTETES.   Give me a sword,
    or an axe or whatever weapon you have.   1205
CHORUS. What will you do? what terrible thing?
PHILOCTETES. I will cut up my flesh and my limbs with my hands,
    for all of my thoughts are of blood!
CHORUS. What?
PHILOCTETES. I will go to seek my father.   1210
CHORUS. Where?
PHILOCTETES.   In the land of the dead,
    for he is no longer alive!

O my country, home of my fathers,
would that I might behold you: how foolish I was
to leave your sacred river and go   1215
to assist those hated Greeks.
And now I am nothing, nothing at all.

[PHILOCTETES *withdraws into his cave.*]

CHORUS. I would have left you long ago and gone
   down to my ship, if I had not beheld
   Odysseus approaching us; and with him   1220
   Achilles' son is also coming toward us.[9]

[NEOPTOLEMUS *enters rapidly, followed immediately*
by ODYSSEUS.]

ODYSSEUS. Will you not tell me why you are returning
   along this pathway with such earnest speed?
NEOPTOLEMUS. To undo the error which I made before.
ODYSSEUS. Your words are strange: what "error" do you mean? 1225
NEOPTOLEMUS. Obeying you and yielding to my sailors.
ODYSSEUS. What have you done that was not proper for you?
NEOPTOLEMUS. I have snared a man by shamefulness and guile.
ODYSSEUS. But whom? Oh, what new plan are you now making?
NEOPTOLEMUS. No new plan: I will give the son of Poeas . . .   1230
ODYSSEUS. What do you mean? I am suddenly afraid.
NEOPTOLEMUS. . . . his bow, which I took from him, back again.
ODYSSEUS. O God! what are you saying? Give it back?
NEOPTOLEMUS. I took it shamefully, and not with justice.
ODYSSEUS. In God's name, are you saying this to mock me?   1235
NEOPTOLEMUS. Only if telling truth is mockery.
ODYSSEUS. Son of Achilles, tell me what you mean.
NEOPTOLEMUS. How many times must I repeat my words?
ODYSSEUS. I wish I had never heard them even once!

---

9. Oliver Taplin ("Significant Action in Sophocles' *Philoctetes*") has argued
that these choral lines are a post-Sophoclean interpolation. The manuscripts
give no stage directions—all such directions are the work of editors and
translators—but it is clear that Philoctetes has indeed withdrawn before these
lines are spoken, for upon his reappearance (l. 1263) he is surprised at the
presence of Odysseus and Neoptolemus. Thus in the passage as it stands the
Chorus is speaking of rather than to Philoctetes.

NEOPTOLEMUS. Now you may rest assured you have heard all.   1240
ODYSSEUS. There is, I say, there is a way to stop you!
NEOPTOLEMUS. What are you saying? Who can stop me now?
ODYSSEUS. The army of the Greeks—and I among them.
NEOPTOLEMUS. Shrewd though you are, your words are far
    from shrewd.   1245
ODYSSEUS. Surely your speech and deeds are not so shrewd!
NEOPTOLEMUS. If they are right they do not need your shrewdness.
ODYSSEUS. How is it right to give back what you took
    on my advice?
NEOPTOLEMUS.   I made a shameful error,
    and I must now endeavor to retrieve it.
ODYSSEUS. Do you not fear the army of the Greeks?   1250
NEOPTOLEMUS. With justice on my side I have no fears;
    and I will not submit to do your bidding.
ODYSSEUS. Then must I fight with you instead of Troy?
NEOPTOLEMUS. If you so wish.
ODYSSEUS.   Look: do you see my hand
    upon my sword-hilt?
NEOPTOLEMUS.   Yes. And do you wish   1255
    to see my hand on mine—without delay?
ODYSSEUS. Well, I will let you be. But I am going
    to tell the army: they will punish you.

[ODYSSEUS *withdraws.*]

NEOPTOLEMUS. Now you are showing wisdom; and if you
    continue thus, you may stay clear of trouble.   1260
        Philoctetes, Poeas' son, I call upon you
    to leave your rocky chamber and come forth.

[PHILOCTETES *emerges from the cave.*]

PHILOCTETES. What is this sound of shouting near my cave?
    Why do you call? what can you want from me?
    There must be something wrong: have you come to me   1265
    bringing new hardships to add to my others?
NEOPTOLEMUS. Take heart and listen to the words I speak.
PHILOCTETES. I am afraid. I suffered bitterly
    from your fair words before, because I listened.
NEOPTOLEMUS. Is it not possible to change one's mind?   1270
PHILOCTETES. Your words seemed just as true when you were stealing

my bow from me, and yet they were deceptive.
NEOPTOLEMUS. They are not now: I wish to learn from you
  whether you will remain here and endure,
  or sail with us.
PHILOCTETES. Wait, say nothing more! 1275
  Every word that you speak will be in vain.
NEOPTOLEMUS. Are you resolved?
PHILOCTETES.   Much more than I can say.
NEOPTOLEMUS. I wish you had been persuaded by my words;
  but if I speak to no avail, then I
  will cease.
PHILOCTETES. All that you say will be in vain, 1280
  for you will never make my mind your friend.
  You robbed me of my life and took my bow,
  yet now you come to me to bring advice,
  most hateful son of a most noble father!
  Damn all of you—the sons of Atreus first, 1285
  and then Laertes' son: then you!
NEOPTOLEMUS.   Do not
  curse me, but take your bow back from my hand.
PHILOCTETES. What do you mean? is this another trick?
NEOPTOLEMUS. No, by the sacred majesty of God!
PHILOCTETES. How sweet your words are if your words are true! 1290
NEOPTOLEMUS. My deed will show how true they are: reach out
  your hand and take your weapon once again.

[ODYSSEUS *steps forward.*]

ODYSSEUS. But I forbid it, calling God to witness,
  in the name of Atreus' sons and all the army!
PHILOCTETES. My child, whose voice is that? did I not hear 1295
  Odysseus?
ODYSSEUS. Yes, you did: and now you see him,
  him who will take you back to Troy by force
  whether Achilles' son approves or not.
PHILOCTETES. Not without paying, if my aim is true!

[ODYSSEUS *turns and leaves.*]

NEOPTOLEMUS. Wait! for the sake of God put down your
  arrow. 1300

PHILOCTETES. For God's sake take your hand off mine, dear
    child.
NEOPTOLEMUS. No, I will not.
PHILOCTETES.   Oh, why have you not let me
    kill my hated enemy with my bow?
NEOPTOLEMUS. That would be right for neither you nor me.
PHILOCTETES. Well, this much is certain: the false-hearted   1305
    commanders of the army of the Greeks
    are cowards in fight, however bold in words!
NEOPTOLEMUS. So be it. Now you have your bow, and have
    no reason to be angry, or to blame me.
PHILOCTETES. Yes, you are right, my child; and you have
    shown   1310
    what nature you were born with. Sisyphus
    was not your father, but Achilles, most
    renowned of men when living, as when dead.
NEOPTOLEMUS. I am truly glad to hear you praise my father
    and me; now listen to the benefit   1315
    I hope to win from you. Men must endure
    the fortunes which are given them by God;
    but when they willingly persist in pain,
    like you, it is not right for anyone
    to pardon them or have compassion on them.   1320
    You are too harsh, and will not hear advice;
    and if one counsels you with good intentions
    you hate him and consider him your foe.
    Yet I will speak, and call God as my witness:
    so hear my words and write them in your heart.   1325
    This suffering is sent on you from heaven
    because you once went near to Chryse's serpent,
    the secret guardian of her roofless home.
    Be certain you will never find relief
    from your hard illness while the sun continues   1330
    to rise and set again, until you come
    of your own will to Troy, where you will find
    the children of Asclepius among us,
    and they will soothe your illness; then, with me,
    and with your bow, you will demolish Troy.   1335
    Now I will tell you how I know all this.
    We have a Trojan prisoner among us,
    Helenus, best of prophets, who declares
    that these things shall occur, and furthermore

he says it is ordained that Troy shall fall 1340
this very summer: he will give his life
willingly if his prophecy proves false.
Now that you are aware of this, yield freely.
It is a fair reward to be acclaimed
the noblest of the Greeks, and find your way 1345
to healing hands, and then, when you have captured
sorrowful Troy, to win immortal glory.
PHILOCTETES. My hateful life, why do you keep me here
instead of letting me go down to Hades?
What shall I do? how can I disobey 1350
his words, when he has counseled me in friendship?
Shall I submit? But then, in my misfortune,
how could I face the light? whom could I speak to?
My eyes, who have beheld my many wrongs,
how could you ever bear to see me with 1355
the sons of Atreus, who have ruined me,
or with that villainous son of Laertes?
Resentment for the past is not what hurts me,
but thinking on the pains that I must suffer
hereafter: for when men have given birth 1360
to evil thoughts once, they will soon learn others.
Your actions, too, surprise me: you should never
have thought of going back to Troy or taking
my bow: for these men have insulted you
and robbed your father's arms.[10] Can you intend 1365
to go and fight for them, and force me also?
No, child, not that! You must fulfill your promise
to take me home; and you must stay in Skyros
and let those evil men die and be damned.
Thus you will win a double gratitude, 1370
mine and my father's; and though you have served
bad men, your nature will not seem like theirs.
NEOPTOLEMUS. You speak with reason; yet I hope that you
will put your trust in God and in my words,
and sail from here with me, who am your friend. 1375
PHILOCTETES. What, sail to Troy and to the hated son
of Atreus with this cursèd foot of mine?
NEOPTOLEMUS. To those who will relieve your pus-filled limb
from suffering, and cure you of your illness.

---

10. It has not occurred to Philoctetes that this story was also a lie.

PHILOCTETES. These are strange words indeed: what are you
   saying?   1380
NEOPTOLEMUS. What will be best for you as well as me.
PHILOCTETES. When you speak thus, do you not fear the gods?
NEOPTOLEMUS. Why should I be afraid to help my friend?
PHILOCTETES. But will you help me or the sons of Atreus?
NEOPTOLEMUS. You—for I am your friend, and speak in
   friendship.   1385
PHILOCTETES. Yet you would give me to my enemies!
NEOPTOLEMUS. My friend, be less defiant in misfortune.
PHILOCTETES. Surely you will destroy me with your words.
NEOPTOLEMUS. Not *I* . . . but you will not know what I mean.
PHILOCTETES. I know the sons of Atreus left me here.   1390
NEOPTOLEMUS. They did; and yet they may restore you also.
PHILOCTETES. Not if I must consent to go to Troy.
NEOPTOLEMUS. What must I do then, if my words cannot
   persuade you to do anything I ask?
   The easiest course for me is to be silent   1395
   and let you live without help, as before.
PHILOCTETES. Yes, let me suffer what I have to suffer.
   But you, my child, must now fulfill the promise
   made when you touched my hand, and send me home.
   Do not delay, or speak again of Troy,   1400
   for I have had my fill of lamentation.
NEOPTOLEMUS. If you wish, then let us go.
PHILOCTETES.   O nobly spoken word!
NEOPTOLEMUS. Plant your footsteps firmly now.
PHILOCTETES.   With all the strength I have.
NEOPTOLEMUS. How can I escape the anger of the Greeks?
PHILOCTETES.   Fear not.
NEOPTOLEMUS. What if they destroy my country?
PHILOCTETES.   I shall be at hand.   1405
NEOPTOLEMUS. How can you assist me?
PHILOCTETES.   With the bow of Heracles.
NEOPTOLEMUS. How?
PHILOCTETES.   I will prevent them.
NEOPTOLEMUS.   Bless this land, then, and depart.

[HERACLES *appears above.*]

HERACLES. Not yet, until you have heard the words
   which I will speak to you, son of Poeas.   1410

Be certain that you are hearing the voice
and beholding the presence of Heracles.
For your sake I have departed from
my heavenly home,
to tell you the counsels of Zeus on high,   1415
and prevent you from making this journey.
Now hear my words, and obey them.

First I will say that in my varied fortunes
I have passed through many sufferings and toils,
and won, as you may see, eternal glory;   1420
and now it is ordained for you as well
to build from suffering a noble life.
First you will travel with this man to Troy
and there will find release from your disease;
and then, foremost among the ranks in courage,   1425
you will slay Paris with that bow of mine,
Paris, who was the cause of all these hardships,
and conquer Troy, and choose the prize of valor
from all the army's spoils, and take them to
your father Poeas by the plains of Oeta.   1430
But when you bring these spoils home from the army,
take some, in gratitude for my bow, to
my funeral pyre. You too, son of Achilles,
must listen: for without *him* you cannot
take Troy, nor he apart from you. Like lions   1435
you roam together, and together guard
each other's lives. And I will send to Troy
Asclepius to cure you of your illness;
for it is fated Troy shall be once more
captured by my bow. When you spoil the land,   1440
remember this: to reverence the gods;
for of all things that is the most important
to father Zeus. Such reverence will not die
with men, but go with them in life and death.
PHILOCTETES. O voice which I long have yearned to hear,   1445
revealed to me now,
I will not disobey your words.
NEOPTOLEMUS. And I will also grant assent.
HERACLES. Do not delay your action long;
occasion is calling,   1450
and the wind at your stern is urging you on.

[HERACLES *withdraws.*]

PHILOCTETES. Now as I leave I will call on my island.
Farewell to the chamber that shared in my vigil,
and the nymphs of the meadows, nymphs of the streams,
and the masculine roar of the sea-swept coast.   1455
Often my head has been damp with the blowing
of southerly winds, though deep in my cave;
and often the distant mountain of Hermes
has heard my voice and answered to me
with echoing groans in my tempest of sorrow.   1460
But O my streams and my Lycian spring,[11]
I am leaving you now, I am leaving at last,
though I had thought I would never depart.
O land of sea-circled Lemnos, farewell!
Do not begrudge me a fair voyage now   1465
to whatever place great Destiny calls,
and my friends' advice, and the almighty god
who has brought these things to fulfillment.
CHORUS. Come let us go now all together,
and pray to the nymphs of the sea   1470
to grant us a prosperous voyage.

---

11. A spring sacred to Apollo Lyceius—a traditional title whose meaning is
in dispute.

Observations on the
Philoctetes Plays of
Aeschylus, Euripides,
and Sophocles

The bulk of our information concerning the Philoctetes plays of Aeschylus (about 475) and Euripides (431) comes to us from two Discourses by Dio Chrysostom, an orator and philosopher who lived in the first century of our era. Dio wrote an essay "On Aeschylus and Sophocles and Euripides; or, The Bow of Philoctetes," and another which appears to be a direct imitation or paraphrase of the prologos (that is, the opening scene) of Euripides' play. A few allusions and direct quotations in other authors, and some papyrus fragments give us further hints for the two predecessors' versions. Many questions remain—especially about Aeschylus's play—but a certain degree of reconstruction is feasible, enabling us to place Sophocles against the background of his precursors.

Thus it is generally agreed that it was Aeschylus's idea to send Odysseus rather than Diomedes as the emissary of the Greeks to Lemnos. The traditional despatching of Odysseus to Scyros to present Neoptolemus with the armor of his defunct father Achilles was of course more plausible. Odysseus had won this armor for himself, but now, in response to the oracle, it was to be taken to Neoptolemus as an entice-ment to join the Greeks at Troy. Why did Aeschylus decide to tamper with this tradition?[1] A reasonable guess is that, many years before the *Oresteia,* he had detected somewhat similar possibilities in the Philoctetes legends: a man deeply wronged, then going too far in his vengeful bitterness, but finally submitting to a higher reconciling power—a divine power concerned with the good of the state. Great as the distance is between Orestes and Philoctetes, Albin Lesky's words regarding the trilogy seem entirely appropriate here: "Man's path through guilt and sorrow is his path toward insight into God's law. The proverb, 'Suffering is learning' . . . here becomes the key expression of a profound religious cosmology."[2]

But to be convincingly guided from his strictly personal sense of wrong to a larger, communal reconciling vision, Philoctetes had to be met by a challenger of enormous prestige and intelligence or cunning. As long as no difficulty had been anticipated, the tradition had quietly sent Diomedes to Lemnos, and Odysseus to Scyros. Aeschylus made the simple and satisfying substitution. Odysseus had the intelligence and cunning required, and he was a king. The final step was to sharpen the sense of injury—and thus raise the obstacle to be overcome still higher—by making Odysseus personally responsible for abandoning Philoctetes on Lemnos in the first place.

Here in summary is what one can reconstruct of Aeschylus from Dio and the fragments:

1. Odysseus is the lone emissary to Lemnos.[3]
2. He finds a chorus of Lemnians on the scene: Philoctetes is not alone.
3. Philoctetes does not recognize him.
4. The unrecognized Odysseus tells Philoctetes stories of rack and ruin among the Greeks, including the lie that Agamemnon is dead and that Odysseus has been caught in some disgraceful act (possibly involving the armor of Achilles).

---

1. Needless to say, a source for Aeschylus is not excluded.
2. Albin Lesky, *Die Tragische Dichtung der Hellenen.* Aeschylus's Philoctetes may have been a less innocent figure than he appears in Sophocles. Mario Untersteiner *(Gli "Eraclidi" e il "Filottete" di Eschilo)* suggests an offense against Hera through his services to Heracles—an offense punished by Chryse, who is a Hera figure. Any application of guilt to Philoctetes would contribute to the sense that he exceeds due measure in his stubborn hatred against the Greeks.
3. Thus it is possible that Aeschylus required only two actors for his play, unless a divine epiphany at the end, in the presence of both Odysseus and Philoctetes, involved a third.

5. Philoctetes succumbs to an access of pain, and leans the bow and quiver against a shady pine.
6. Odysseus seizes the weapon.

Nothing more can be positively asserted, but since Dio speaks of "the deception which Odysseus practiced upon Philoctetes and the arguments by which he won him over," we know that the art of oratory, so highly regarded by the ancients—and so dramatically demoted in the Sophoclean version—played a decisive role in finally changing Philoctetes' mind. Another passage in Dio shows, however, that the utter helplessness of Philoctetes when deprived of his weapon contributed mightily to his newfound reasonableness:

These tragedies were the work of topmost artists, I may say, Aeschylus and Sophocles and Euripides, all dealing with the same theme, which was the theft—or should I say the seizure?—of the bow of Philoctetes. However that may be, Philoctetes was portrayed as being deprived of his weapons by Odysseus and as being carried off to Troy along with them, for the most part willingly, though in some measure also yielding to the persuasion of necessity, since he had been deprived of the weapons which furnished him with not only a living on his island, but courage in his sore affliction, and at the same time fame. [*Discourses* 52. 2]

Did Sophocles rebel in his heart against the spectacle of a man talked into good sense and patriotism after being robbed of his only means of subsistence? I believe that some such indignation—applicable to Euripides' version as well—triggered Sophocles' eloquent rebuttal in his own conception of the tale.

Unfortunately for us, Dio's criticism is of the shallowest sort. He worries like a pedestrian schoolmaster about the plausibility of Philoctetes' not recognizing Odysseus, the likelihood of Philoctetes retailing his tale of woe to the Lemnians (who must after all have heard it before), and the credibility of the stories of disaster Odysseus tells Philoctetes. Naturally, the Sophoclean stroke—so bold, so plangent, and of such high philosophical importance—of a totally isolated Philoctetes could elicit no response from this good-natured plodder. Like all good plodders, he wanted realism:

Again, it was quite impossible to conceive that not a single Lemnian had come near Philoctetes or given him any attention at all, for in my opinion he could not even have survived those ten years without receiving some aid; no, it is reasonable to suppose that he did get some aid, though but rarely and of no great importance, and, furthermore, that no one chose to take him into his house and give him medical attention because of the disgusting nature of his ailment. At any rate Euripides himself does bring upon the scene one Lemnian, Actor, who approaches Philoctetes as being already known to him and as having often met him. [*Discourses* 52. 8]

Since Aeschylus had already provided Philoctetes with a chorus of Lemnians, Euripides' contribution of Aktor does not constitute a thematic advance. It does appear, however, that his Odysseus was a more brutal figure than Aeschylus had made him, and that he was accompanied by Diomedes. In a far more significant innovation, Euripides brought in a band of Trojans, headed by none other than Paris, to lure Philoctetes to Troy on their side. Here was a sprightly idea, to say the least, and one that must have led Euripides to one of his rousing debates, namely between Paris and the still disguised Odysseus.

Dio's imitation of the prologos deserves to be given in full.

The Fifty-ninth Discourse: Philoctetes

ODYSSEUS. I fear 'twill prove that my allies were rash when they conceived of me the thought that I, in sooth, am best and wisest of the Greeks. And yet what kind of wisdom and prudence may this be which makes a man to toil beyond the others to gain the salvation and the victory of the group, seeing that, were he deemed to be but one among the throng, 'twere his to share these blessings with the best? Ah well, no doubt 'tis difficult to find a thing so proud, so jealous of honour, as man is born to be. For 'tis the prominent, those who dare to undertake more labours than the rest, I dare say, whom we all do view with wonder and regard as truly men.

This thirst for glory is what leads even me to bear unnumbered woes and live a life of toil beyond all other men, accepting ever fresh peril, fearing to mar the glory won by earlier achievements. So now a task most hazardous and hard brings me to Lemnos here, that Philoctetes and the bow of Heracles I may bear off for my allies. For the one most gifted in prophecy of all the Phrygians [Trojans], Helenus, Priam's son, when by good fortune taken captive, disclosed that without these the city never could be seized.

Now to the princes I did not agree to undertake the venture, knowing well the malice of that man [Philoctetes][4], since 'twas I myself caused him to be marooned, that day when by ill fortune he was stung by a fierce and deadly viper. Thus I could not hope to find persuasion such that he should ever feel a kindly feeling toward me; nay, I thought he'd slay me out of hand. But afterwards, Athena urging me in dreams, as is her wont, boldly to go and fetch the man—for she herself would change my form and voice, that I might meet him safe from detection—so did I pluck up courage, and am here.

---

4. The gist of this contorted clause is simply, "I did not commit myself to the Greek princes." [Ed.]

But word has come that envoys from the Phrygians too have secretly been sent, if haply they may win Philoctetes by means of bribes, and through his hatred of us Greeks as well, and so take back to Troy him and his bow. With such a prize before him, why should not any man grow keen? For, should one fail in this endeavour, all previous achievements, it seems, have been but labour lost.

[*Aside*] Hah! the man draws nigh. 'Tis he himself, the son of Poeas, as is plain from his affliction, toiling along with labour and in pain. Oh what a grievous, awful spectacle! Aye, his person is frightful, thanks to his disease, his garb unwonted too—skins of wild beasts cover his nakedness. Come, Mistress Athena, be thou mine aid, nor show thyself to have promised me safety all in vain!

PHILOCTETES. What is thy purpose, whoe'er thou art, by what audacity inspired hast thou come to this my poor retreat—to pillage, or to spy upon my evil fortune?

ODYSSEUS. Believe me, no man of violence dost thou see.

PHILOCTETES. Yet surely not of thy former wont has thou come here.[5]

ODYSSEUS. Aye, not former wont; yet may it prove that coming even now is opportune.

PHILOCTETES. Methinks thou dost betray much lack of reason in thy coming here.

ODYSSEUS. Then rest assured, not lacking reason have I come, and to thee at least no stranger shall I prove.

PHILOCTETES. How so? This first of all 'tis fair that I should know.

ODYSSEUS. Well, I'm an Argive, one of those who sailed for Troy.

PHILOCTETES. How can that be? Repeat thy words, that I may more clearly know.

ODYSSEUS. Then dost thou hear it yet a second time: of those Achaeans who advanced on Troy I claim to be.

PHILOCTETES. Faith, thou didst well in claiming to be friend of mine, seeing thou art revealed among my bitterest foes, the Argives! So for their injustice shalt thou this very instant pay the penalty.

ODYSSEUS. Nay, by the gods, forbear to loose thy shaft!

PHILOCTETES. It cannot be, if haply thou art Greek in truth, that thou shouldst fail to die this very day.

ODYSSEUS. Nay, I have suffered at their hands such things that I should rightly be a friend to thee, to them a foe.

PHILOCTETES. And what is this thou hast suffered so terrible?

ODYSSEUS. Odysseus drove me an exile from the camp.

PHILOCTETES. What hadst thou done to meet with such a doom?

ODYSSEUS. Methinks thou knowest Palamedes son of Nauplius.

PHILOCTETES. In truth no common man was he who sailed with us, nor little worth to men and generals.

---

5. That is, "Surely it has not been your habit to come here." [Ed.]

ODYSSEUS. Aye, such the man the common spoiler of the Greeks destroyed.
PHILOCTETES. O'ercoming him in open fight, or with some guile?
ODYSSEUS. Charging betrayal of the camp to Priam's sons.
PHILOCTETES. But was it so in fact, or has he met with calumny?
ODYSSEUS. Could aught at all that scoundrel did be just?
PHILOCTETES. Oh thou who hast refrained from naught most cruel, thou utter
   villain in both word and deed, Odysseus, once more how fine the man thou
   hast destroyed, of no less value to the allied host than thou, methinks,
   inventing and devising the best and sagest plans! Just so in fact didst thou
   make me a castaway, when for the salvation and the victory of us all I met with
   this disaster, because I showed them Chrysê's altar, where they must first
   make sacrifice if they would overcome the foe; else, I declared, our expedition was being made in vain. Yet what hast thou to do with Palamedes' lot?
ODYSSEUS. Know well, the cursed feud was visited on all his friends, and all have
   perished, save such as could take to flight. Thus I too during the night just
   sped, sailing across alone, found refuge here. So I myself am placed in much
   the same necessity as thyself. If, then, thou hast some scheme, by adding thy
   eagerness to mine touching my voyage home, thou wilt have done a kindly
   deed toward me and wilt besides send home to thy own friends him who will
   bear the story of thy present ills.
PHILOCTETES. Nay, wretched creature, thou art come for aid to such another as
   thou art, helpless himself and lacking friends besides, an outcast on this
   shore, in niggard fashion and with toil providing with this bow both food and
   clothing, as thou dost see. For what raiment I had before time hath consumed. But if thou wilt share with me here this life of mine until some second
   chance of safety falls thy way, I'd grudge it not. Distressing, truly, what thou
   wilt see indoors, my friend—wrappings polluted with an ulcer's filth and
   other tokens of my malady—and I myself am far from being pleasant
   company when the pain comes on me. And yet the worst of my disease time
   hath assuaged, though at the start it was in no wise bearable.

At this point Dio's Discourse ends. What happens afterwards? The
reconstruction made a century ago by L. A. Milani on the basis of the
extant fragments has not been bettered.[6] I shall make broad use of his
conception.

---

6. Milani, *Il mito di Filottete nella letteratura e nell'arte figurata*, pp. 34–41. It
seems, however, to have been slighted or forgotten. Jebb fails to acknowledge it
as a source for his reconstruction in the introduction to his Sophocles text of
1890. Gilbert Murray *(Euripides)* and J. S. Kieffer ("Philoctetes and Arete")
make no reference to it in the course of their own unsatisfactory attempts.
Neither is he mentioned in a survey by Herman van Looy ("Les Fragments
d'Euripide") and in W. M. Calder's recent "A Reconstruction of Euripides,
Philoctetes." But Milani's contributions to Philoctetes scholarship are wide-
ranging, and after a century they retain almost all their original

The end of Dio's paraphrase has shown us that in Euripides' play the trick offer of conveying Philoctetes back to Malis—crucial in Sophocles—did not exist. Quite the reverse happens; the supposed refugee asks Philoctetes for help, and is offered asylum. All three tragedians, however, made use of a false story concerning Greek oppression, designed to make Philoctetes lower his defenses.

Odysseus naturally accepts Philoctetes' modest hospitality. Now the Chorus speaks, and Dio's earlier Discourse indicates that the Lemnians apologize for not having been more helpful to the suffering hero in the past. They listen to the story of his suffering and his resentment.

Odysseus having stepped into the cave with his host, suddenly the Trojans appear, led by Paris. The Chorus points toward or summons Philoctetes. A highly charged encounter follows, with Paris attempting to "bribe" and argue Philoctetes into joining up with the Trojans. But Odysseus has overheard this transaction.[7] He advances and, without revealing himself (Athena has veiled his identity from Philoctetes), confounds the Trojans. Here Milani cites a famous fragment: "It is shameful to be silent on behalf of the entire army of the Greeks and to allow barbarians to speak." Since the speaker has allegedly suffered terrible injuries himself at the hands of his fellow Greeks, his indignant denunciation of treason is particularly effective, and moves Philoctetes to reject the Trojans' offers.

The disappointed Trojans depart, whereupon the Chorus sings in praise of Philoctetes. Now the Lemnian Aktor makes his appearance. Perhaps, says Milani, he knows that the time has come around again for an attack of pain, and he offers his customary help. Presently spasms overcome the hero. A line quoted by Aristotle in the *Poetics* about "the gangrene feasting on this foot" may be uttered here. The Chorus, seeing Philoctetes visibly failing, perhaps speaks the "He has breathed out his life," which has also been preserved.

Milani supposes that Odysseus has been lending a hand in comforting Philoctetes; but at a favorable moment he gives a signal to Diomedes, who seizes the bow and disappears. Milani's assertion that Diomedes plays a strictly secondary role as Odysseus' strong-man is

importance. He can also be recommended for his examination of German studies of Philoctetes published in and before his time. In sum: a mistakenly forgotten authority.

7. Milani *(Il mito di Filottete)* prints two drawings taken from Etruscan urns, one of which is reproduced here (fig. 4). Each shows the Trojans on the right hand soliciting Philoctetes (their ship is clearly portrayed in the illustration not printed here), while Odysseus and Diomedes anxiously listen behind Philoctetes' back.

FIGURE 4. Drawing after an Etruscan urn. Philoctetes in the
center, Diomedes and the bonneted Odysseus on the left,
Paris in a Phrygian cap and another Trojan on the right. *From
L. A. Milani, Il mito di Filottete, 1879*

soundly supported, first by an examination of Dio's two texts, and second by a scholium to the first line of Sophocles' play: "Euripides attri-
butes everything to Odysseus, but Sophocles introduces Neoptolemus."[8] As for the bow, we have seen that Aeschylus had already
made Philoctetes leave it leaning against a tree.

There is no question that Odysseus gets the weapon through theft.[9]
It was Sophocles who invented the pathetic and ethically significant act
by which Philoctetes *gives* the bow to his enemy.

---

8. Diomedes may well have been a mute character.
9. This is beautifully shown in the so-called Hoby beaker in Copenhagen, a
silver cup of the Augustan Age probably inspired by a fifth-century B.C.
painting (pls. 4, 5). Odysseus is furtively slipping the bow to a tense Diomedes
behind him while Philoctetes suffers his fit. Another segment of the cup
portrays a Lemnian preparing a splendidly enormous bird for dinner, while
other attendants are bathing Philoctetes' foot. W. M. Calder ("A
Reconstruction of Euripides' *Philoctetes*") conjectures that the Lemnian holding
the bird is Aktor. He also suggests, not implausibly, that Aktor has appeared
together with the Chorus earlier in the play and has announced the landing of
the Trojans. Readers can choose between his and Milani's notion regarding this
detail.

After a second choral song, a scene which Sophocles will imitate has Philoctetes confronting Odysseus, who now reveals his true identity. Philoctetes explodes with anger and hatred. Odysseus discloses the prophecy and the purpose of his mission. Here belongs another pre-served fragment, namely a sarcastic remark by Philoctetes about people who interpret prophecies to suit their own ends. Odysseus stoutly defends himself (as later in Ovid), ascribes the relegation of Philoctetes to the will of the gods, points out that the Greeks have been suffering the consequences too, and argues that a man should not persist forever in his rancor. This last sentiment also appears in a fragment.

All this eloquence finally breaks down the martyr's resentment. A reconciliation occurs, ratified by Athena or another divine personage. In the concluding lines of the Chorus we hear another preserved passage: "Alas, may I never be anything but dear to the gods, as they bring everything to pass, even if they do it slowly."

This must have been an attractive play. But it was also an uncontro-versial one. If Milani's reconstruction is approximately correct, Sopho-cles' brilliance becomes as impressive as Shakespeare's when we set him against *his* predecessors. It is clearly not by chance or error that, when all the anonymous sifting which took so many centuries ended, the surviving version was the last of the three.

For Aeschylus and Euripides, the question posed by the play had been, "Will Philoctetes yield to Odysseus?" But Sophocles dropped this question, and decided from the beginning that Philoctetes would *not* yield to Odysseus or any other mortal. He turned Philoctetes into a fixed and ultimately unproblematic character, and wrote instead a Neoptolemus play dealing with a movement from lie to truth in the mind and action of his new hero.

Two passages in Aristotle's *Nicomachean Ethics* make it appear that the ancients too were struck by the importance of this motif. In the first, Aristotle speaks of a good sort of incontinence, "of which Sophocles' Neoptolemus in his *Philoctetes* will be an instance; for he is to be praised for not standing by what Odysseus persuaded him to do, because he is pained at telling a lie" (1146a). A little later, Aristotle remarks of Neoptolemus that "it was for the sake of pleasure that he did not stand fast—but a noble pleasure; for telling the truth was noble to him, but he had been persuaded by Odysseus to tell the lie" (115lb). These com-ments in no way prove that Aristotle, or the Greeks in general, re-garded Neoptolemus as the protagonist of the play, yet they are suggestive and reassuring.

Not that our interest in Philoctetes recedes. In a sense, Lesky is right when he asserts that *Philoctetes* is a play with three central characters

(Die Tragische Dichtung der Hellenen, p. 246). But centralities can be of different kinds. If two men are quarreling about the best way to move a notable monument, our philosophical concern will attach itself to the rightness and wrongness of their strategies, but the notable monument, to which the argument is directed, and whose splendor is evident to our own eyes, dominates the contention "ceremonially." It "outranks" the contenders. And yet the contention is what needs to be explored and resolved. In Sophocles' play, Philoctetes dominates by sheer presence: his importance to the cause, his greatness, his grief. But it is Neoptolemus who creates and enacts the problem to be solved: shall the crookedness which Aeschylus and Euripides so glibly accepted be countenanced? This new question places Neoptolemus at the philosophical and dramatic center of the action.

The lay reader may be surprised to hear that this centrality of Neoptolemus is in question. The title notwithstanding, Sophocles seems to have gone to great pains to prevent any doubt. And in part he succeeded, as a few quotations from modern critics will show. For example, Heinrich Weinstock defines the problem of the play as "the seduction of youth or Neoptolemus at the crossroads." H. D. F. Kitto writes: "Our interest in the *Philoctetes* is not directly in the sufferings of the outcast and his tragic case . . . it is in watching Neoptolemus moving between two fixed points." And again: "If the spiritual journey which befalls Neoptolemus is not very close indeed to the real theme of the play, Sophocles has miscalculated badly, for we cannot imagine that any responsive audience would have been disposed to give its most serious attention to something else." Manara Valgimigli is more direct: "Neoptolemus is the center of Sophocles' inspiration, the nucleus of his creation, the figure from which the entire drama develops with perfect unity of tone. His title is taken from the mythological tradition, where the chief issue is the point of arrival and conclusion, that is to say the return of Philoctetes to Troy; but the fact remains that this is Neoptolemus' play much more than Philoctetes'." This viewpoint does not preclude the definition offered by Beniamino Stumbo, who speaks of two principles struggling for supremacy, "one legal and political, embodied in Odysseus, the other ethical and universal, in Neoptolemus," a view echoed by Agostino Masaracchia: "The struggle between Odysseus and Philoctetes for the soul of Neoptolemus constitutes the theme of the tragedy."[10]

On the other hand, many critics continue to look for light in the

---

10. Heinrich Weinstock, *Sophokles,* p. 102; H. D. F. Kitto, *Greek Tragedy,* 2d ed., p. 319; Kitto, *Greek Tragedy,* 3d ed., p. 297; Manara Valgimigli, *Poeti e filosofi di Grecia,* p. 215; Beniamino Stumbo, "Il Filottete di Sofocle," p. 98; Agostino

penumbras of the action. The most naïve comment is perhaps that of C. H. Whitman, who exclaims, "Weinstock . . . actually asserts that the chief person of the play is Neoptolemus. This despite the title" *(Sophocles: A Study of Heroic Humanism,* p. 274). One may as well argue that the chief character of the *Trachinian Women* is the chorus. Obviously—as the Italian critic saw—Sophocles was not about to oust the famous Philoctetes from his title in favor of a stripling newcomer to the story. Besides—and here we might try another metaphor—it is perfectly sound practice to name the story of a mountain climber after the mountain he has to climb.

For Whitman, the whole point of the drama is that Philoctetes must come away of his own free will. This human freedom thesis is common to a substantial number of critics. Others emphasize the gradual fulfillment of the will of the gods. For Hartmut Erbse, Neoptolemus, like Odysseus, exists only so that Philoctetes can exhibit his own nature through him.[11] C. M. Bowra reads in the play "a struggle between the will of the gods and the will of men" in which all the human characters are deluded. Karin Alt agrees and defines the thesis as "human inadequacy." Ignacio Errandonea regards the action as centered on the change of mind of Philoctetes from hatred to compliance. For B. M. W.

Masaracchia, "La scena dell'*emporos* nel Filottete di Sofocle," pp. 86–87.

Kitto's formula—to which I subscribe—was strikingly anticipated by Émile Faguet: "In Sophocles' work, Odysseus and Philoctetes are rigid. They are inflexible—one of them sheathed in his intransigent patriotism and his principle, 'The only law is the salvation of my land'; the other, completely so, in his implacable resentment and the sense of his right and right itself violated in his person. Only Neoptolemus goes from one point to the other" ("Sophocle: *Philoctète,* par André Gide," p. 36). And: "Neoptolemus: that is the hero of *Philoctetes*" (p. 31).

A vast study of *Philoctetes* by Jens U. Schmidt *(Sophokles Philoktet: Eine Strukturanalyse)* documents every controversy surrounding the play. Unfortunately Schmidt does not include the views of Weinstock, one of the most perceptive writers on *Philoctetes,* and several useful critics outside the Germanic and Anglo-Saxon family circle. His work is indispensable, but not definitive. J. C. Kamerbeek's *The Philoctetes,* the sixth in a series of commentaries under the collective title of *The Plays of Sophocles,* appeared as the present volume was in press, and while it was possible to enter it in the bibliography, I was most regrettably unable to stop the presses long enough to obtain a copy.

11. Hartmut Erbse, "Neoptolemos und Philoktet bei Sophokles." Erbse's interpretation will serve as a fair sample of misfocusing. For him, the final point of *Philoctetes* is that "whoever compromises too readily with the machinations of the everyday world forfeits the trust of upright men, while the man who shrinks from contact with the community offends against the order of that world" (p. 201).

Knox, the central problem of the play is finding the morally right method to sway Philoctetes. A trigger-happy article by W. M. Calder protests against "Neoptolemus-idolatry" and argues that Neoptolemus is as complete a villain as Odysseus. T. B. L. Webster simply asserts, "It is Philoctetes' play, a study in suffering." This position is reaffirmed by G. H. Gellie, who sees at the center of the play "the passionate single-mindedness of a man whom long suffering has not broken and who cannot be made to break at the prospect of more." And again by Joe Park Poe: "The emphasis of this play is upon the torments suffered by Philoctetes." However, as Lesky has observed, critics who place Philoctetes at the center of the action usually proceed at once to discuss not Philoctetes but Neoptolemus.[12]

This is eminently respectable opposition; yet I trust that we can move past and summarize the central action of the *Philoctetes* as follows: "Neoptolemus, renouncing deception, returns the bow to Philoctetes and eventually agrees to take the outcast home to Malis." Properly speaking, it is a twin action: one peak followed by another; and it takes us far afield from Aeschylus and Euripides, where the basic action was a straightforward "Odysseus steals the bow and persuades Philoctetes to return to Troy." In fact, the Sophoclean action is so unprecedented and unprepared for by the tradition—as the reader of the first chapter of this book has seen—that the novelty in itself would have drawn the attention of his audience (which we can think of as moderately to thoroughly informed) to the bizarre doings of Neoptolemus.

Philoctetes is replete with puzzles, but wonderfully enough, they do not affect the twin action I have just named. The latter subsists whether we resolve the puzzles or not—or, if we do resolve them, whether we provide one solution or another. Like many and perhaps most poets, Sophocles allowed a degree of blurring in matters of subordinate interest to him, content to be luminous and logical with regard to the essential action.

It may be useful to list a few of the questions raised by the text.

---

12. C. M. Bowra, *Sophoclean Tragedy*, pp. 261–63; Karin Alt, "Schicksal und Physis im Philoktet des Sophokles," p. 174; Ignacio Errandonea, "Filoctetes"; B. M. W. Knox, *The Heroic Temper: Studies in Sophoclean Tragedy;* W. M. Calder III, "Sophoclean Apologia: *Philoctetes*"; T. B. L. Webster, ed., *Philoctetes;* G. H. Gellie, *Sophocles: A Reading,* p. 131; Joe Park Poe, *Heroism and Divine Justice in Sophocles' Philoctetes,* p. 22; Lesky, *Die Tragische Dichtung der Hellenen.*

Poe's book is the exception to Lesky's observation (see n. 24 below). As for Gellie's chapter on *Philoctetes,* while I do not always gree with it, its unaffected good sense and plain speaking make it one of the most attractive commentaries of the last decades.

Does Odysseus want the bow and only the bow; does he want Philoctetes with the bow; does he want one thing once and the other another time; or does he have in mind a first best and a second best?

Is Odysseus willing to use force on Philoctetes if he can get away with it? Or is he ever mindful of the oracle that forbids it?

Why is Odysseus so intent on blackening himself in the eyes of Philoctetes, especially through the Spy?

Does Odysseus bluff, or is he sincere when he turns his back on Philoctetes after securing the bow?

Why, after Odysseus has instructed Neoptolemus to seize the bow, does Neoptolemus concentrate his attention on drawing Philoctetes—fully armed!—to the ship?

Does the Spy scene serve any significant purpose in the play?

How is it that Neoptolemus seems to know so little about the oracle at the beginning, and yet is fully instructed at the end?

Is Odysseus a villain? Is he, as Karl Reinhardt believes *(Sophokles)*, part right and part wrong? Or might he be the hero, as Errandonea amusingly asserts?

Is Philoctetes perfectly right, partly wrong, or terribly wrong in his stubborn refusal to yield?

Is Heracles an emanation or representation of Philoctetes' inner consciousness, or an outside voice issuing a command? In other words, does Philoctetes finally come away of his own free will or not?

Let me repeat: however we answer these questions, the twin action at the heart of the play manifests itself without equivocations. Neoptolemus continues to be persuaded to deceive and exploit Philoctetes for the common good, continues to return to his basic nature (the *physis* so widely discussed in the critical literature), and continues to return the bow and to start back for Malis with Philoctetes. Every episode, however interpreted, contributes to this fundamental action and to the ethical thesis which it upholds.

Consider the oddity that Neoptolemus, whose primary mission is to disarm Philoctetes, says and does nothing to the purpose, instead exciting Philoctetes to his desperate prayer to be taken along at least as far as Scyros (ll. 468–506). What will the Greeks do once Philoctetes is aboard, clutching the deadly bow? Overwhelm him while he is asleep? Fall at his feet and beg? But these are tricks they can play as well in the cave. Sophocles has written an unforgettable scene, but hardly a logical one. However, it poses no thematic problems. Sophocles is intent on making Neoptolemus stoop to ignoble lying. And lie he does. He lies as if inspired by the god of lies whom Odysseus has just invoked.

Enter the Spy (l. 542). Another splendid scene in itself, but equally open to question. Odysseus has no reason to portray himself as a brute. On the contrary. Logically, the Spy should speak in glowing terms of Odysseus, of his repentance for having mistreated Philoctetes, of his admiration for Philoctetes, and of the glory awaiting Philoctetes at Troy. For if Philoctetes "bites," all is well; if he does not, nothing is lost.

As for the action as such, at the end of the Spy scene we are in some important respects precisely where we were at the beginning. Philoctetes still wants to be taken home, only more urgently—an unessential point. And still nothing has been done to disarm him. On the contrary again. For the Spy's terrifying words can only cause Philoctetes to tighten his fingers about his bow. Odysseus has no way of foreseeing that Philoctetes is about to be overcome by his fit, and that in his distress he will thrust the bow into the hands of Neoptolemus.

The action does move forward, however, for Philoctetes receives the news that the Greeks, supported by the gods, want him at the siege. A more detailed inspection of the text would show that Sophocles is right in wanting this information conveyed to Philoctetes now rather than later. But how is it to be conveyed? Here a curious point seems to have escaped the attention of critics. Neoptolemus, having imprudently blurted out to Philoctetes that he has never so much as heard of him (l. 250), is thereby incapacitated. But Odysseus wants Philoctetes to be apprised of his destiny. If we suppose, with many critics, that he has been lurking within earshot of the conversation, we can imagine his giving the necessary instructions to the Spy, whom he was holding ready for an emergency. Thus the scene makes clear sense, even though the black picture the Spy paints of Odysseus remains inexplicable.

All the same, this and other explanations for the controversial Spy scene merely grapple with incidentals which Sophocles could have handled in other ways. He might have found technically less questionable avenues to reach his destination. But what *is* his destination? It is again a double one. Neoptolemus is to grasp that even an oracular dictum will not overcome Philoctetes' opposition, and he is to be driven deeper into the net of Odyssean lies. When the Spy leaves, Neoptolemus, mortified by the lies, moved by Philoctetes' anguish, and aware that Philoctetes will hold firm, "discovers" that the wind is contrary to their departure (ll. 639–40). His education is by no means complete—he has yet to be shaken to the depths and to learn what justice requires of him—but he is on his way. In summary, the Spy scene remains logically imperfect, but dramatically breathtaking, and thematically well focused on the first fundamental action, inasmuch as a concert of sin, moral compunction, and rising compassion has been orchestrated in the soul of Neoptolemus.

Another oddity occurs at lines 1055–61 when Odysseus, now master of the bow, bids Philoctetes a curt farewell and tells him that he himself, or Teucer, will make good use of it. Is Odysseus bluffing, as the majority of critics think, or does he fully intend to leave Philoctetes behind? Even more important, how does Neoptolemus interpret his words? Does *he* give them credit? We are understandably anxious to know—such a glorious coup de théâtre!—and yet the questions are once again irrelevant to the play's essential problem, for Neoptolemus's decision to return the bow is equally valid, plausible, and significant whether Odysseus is bluffing or not, and whether or not Neoptolemus thinks he is.[13]

Only one element in the play seems to endanger the Neoptolemus

---

13. I am, however, in wholehearted agreement with the minority view according to which Odysseus is dead-serious—without, however, following B. M. W. Knox *(The Heroic Temper)*, who holds that Odysseus has been determined from the start to get rid of Philoctetes and keep all the glory for himself. Here, in brief, are my reasons for believing that, at this particular point, Odysseus means what he says. (1) The bluff hypothesis has no textual support, and conjectures should be advanced only if a text is incapable of making sense as it stands. Here it does make sense. (2) Sophocles would be seriously at fault if he left so important a trick as bluffing Philoctetes without textual support. (3) From the beginning Odysseus has harped on the bow and made only perfunctory allusions to the desirability of taking Philoctetes himself. So predisposed, furthermore made cocky by his possession of the bow, and finally angered by Philoctetes' flood of invective (ll. 1004–44), he is ready to play fast and loose with the oracle. D. B. Robinson, elaborating on R. C. Jebb: "Sophocles did not expect his audience to think that capturing the bow without its owner was an impossible response to the oracle of Helenus" ("Topics in Sophocles' *Philoctetes*," p. 45). (4) If Odysseus really wanted the man, he would have used force at this point, instead of bluff. He has told the Greeks that he is prepared to do so, and his instructions to Neoptolemus (ll. 103–34) have shown that he has so far avoided force only because it was *unsafe* to use it. (5) After the curses he has just heard from Philoctetes, and after he has seen Philoctetes ready to commit suicide, Odysseus can hardly believe that his victim will suddenly come piteously dashing after him. (6) But why has Odysseus prevented Philoctetes from killing himself? Does this not prove that he is determined to bring the outcast back to Troy? Hence that his departure is a feint? But the forty lines of imprecations occurring between the forced rescue from suicide and Odysseus's turning his back on Philoctetes amply motivate Odysseus's turnabout. This time, in other words, there is no inattention on Sophocles' part at all. Instead, he paints the powerful picture of a politician besotted with success and angrily amazed that his victim has the gall to curse him. If this is admitted, we may incidentally view the imminent return of the bow to Philoctetes as punishment sent by the gods to Odysseus for his moment of hubris. Finally, it is preferable, though not indispensable, to visualize Neoptolemus shocked into action on his way to the ship by the realization that presently, without any bluff, the oars will beat the water and it will be too late for him to repair the wrong he has done.

thesis. It will be recalled that at an early point in the play (ll. 191–200), before he has met Philoctetes, Neoptolemus speaks to the Chorus in such a way as to suggest that, in his opinion, the gods have foreordained the return of the outcast to his post. If this fatalistic note impresses itself on Neoptolemus, on the Chorus, and on the spectators, then those who, like C. M. Bowra, interpret the play as a morality on the futility of human decisions and counter-decisions are right. Indeed, the comings and goings must cease to interest us. Does Philoctetes refuse to budge? It does not matter. We know that he will and must. Does Odysseus threaten to leave him behind on Lemnos? What of it? He knows and we know that Philoctetes shall go to Troy. And why does Neoptolemus give way to anguish when, in the exodos, he yields to Philoctetes? He must be joking, or playing his best trick, for did he not imply an hour before that Philoctetes was about to return to Troy, now that the appointed time had come?

But the play is obviously not wrapped in fatalism. We have seen how hesitantly Neoptolemus gives his explanation to the Chorus (see Part I, section 11). Maria Rosa Lida diagnoses it correctly: "Neoptolemus's pompous declaration is illusory: like the others, he knows nothing" (*Introducción al teatro de Sofocles,* p. 94). Sophocles has even been careful to leave the time of Philoctetes' return vague: Philoctetes, according to the youth, has been removed from the war "till the time be fulfilled, when, as men say, Troy is fated by those shafts to fall." Therefore this particular mission might fail. But tentative or otherwise, his declaration leaves no trace in anyone's mind. This is a drama of human ethics and politics from which the gods stand aside, if only temporarily. Neoptolemus, Odysseus, and Philoctetes behave at all times like men fully convinced that their man of destiny may really be lost to the war, either by remaining obdurately on Lemnos, or by sailing home to Malis, or most decisively by committing suicide. It is true that the two men (and the Chorus) liberally invoke the oracle and the will of the gods when they are arguing with Philoctetes. But this is standard rhetoric, which relieves neither themselves nor Philoctetes of doubt.[14]

Even more to the point are the uncertainties which Sophocles has notoriously spread—or allowed to hover—over the oracle, whose fully authentic message he withholds until the end. At one crucial point, this

---

14. See for instance ll. 989–92:
    ODYSSEUS. Zeus, let me tell you, Zeus rules in this land;
    Zeus has done this—and I am but his servant.
    PHILOCTETES. Villain, what pretext will you think of next?
    By crediting the gods you make them liars!

message is vehicled to us by the most suspect character in the play, Odysseus's spy. G. M. Kirkwood's observation, "There is one original statement several times reported in the play, each time a little differently, according to the exigencies of the moment" (*A Study in Sophoclean Drama*, p. 79) is incontrovertible. For example, Sophocles is so intent on the moral decisions to which he is gradually leading Neoptolemus that he allows the Spy to tell us all but simultaneously that Philoctetes must be brought back "by winning words" *and* that Odysseus has pledged himself to use force if necessary (ll. 603–21). Exact oracular prescriptions and predictions, vital to other plays of Sophocles, do not interest him this time. For Neoptolemus will be making his decision, whether the oracle says black or white, or nothing at all.

But to top it all, Sophocles himself disregards the oracle in the end. If these "winning words" were as crucial to the return of Philoctetes as many critics think they are, if it is of capital importance to the play that Philoctetes return of his own free will, then Sophocles commits a singular error in making the Lemnian yield, not to the persuasive words of Neoptolemus (ll. 1314–47), but to the command of Heracles. What sort of free will is that? We note, in passing, that Heracles appears at this juncture altogether as divine power, and not in the role of a trusted companion of old who has therefore a better chance than Neoptolemus of convincing Philoctetes. Now some critics assert that Heracles is but Philoctetes' inner voice given a body on stage; Alt ("Schicksal und Physis") contends that the god merely foretells the future, which Philoctetes then recognizes; F. J. H. Letters does not hesitate to offer: "There is only the divine command freely obeyed" (*The Life and Works of Sophocles*, p. 276). But why do critics torture texts? When a god says "Go," men go. God *dissolves* the human will.

A useful additional clue is to be found in a remark by Neoptolemus (ll. 1338–42) to the effect that Helenus told the Greeks they were free to kill him, Helenus, if his word proved false. Clearly, an oracle *may* prove false, being but a human voice transmitting a divine message. One can never be utterly beyond doubt until the god himself, dispensing with an oracular medium, lays down the law.[15] No wonder that Odysseus is

---

15. A Euripidean fragment already alluded to is relevant: "Why do you sit on the prophet's stool," says Philoctetes to Odysseus, "and swear you penetrate the gods' decisions? Your utterances are only human. For whoever boasts that he understands the gods is nothing but a babbler." The passage is preserved by Stobaeus (*Eclogae* 2. 1. 2). The sayings of an oracle, and a fortiori the report of the sayings of an oracle, are obviously less credible than the unmediated utterance of a god.

prepared to use force, even though the oracle suggested persuasion; no wonder he is ready to drop Philoctetes altogether, even though the oracle spoke very distinctly of summoning the hero.

But the burden of my argument here is only that Sophocles has been less than consistent in his application of oracular voices to the *Philoctetes*. They are blurred and even contradicted, because a negative dramaturgical decree hangs over the play: nothing must disturb our sense, and the sense of the three personages, that they are free to choose. Like the *Electra,* this is a play in which convictions born within the soul are worked out. In the words of Heraclitus: Character is Fate.

Still, Neoptolemus's hesitant dissertation on the will of the gods is not entirely without use—otherwise Sophocles would surely have thrown it out. The hesitancy (followed by oblivion) preserves Neoptolemus's freedom; but we the spectators may, if we wish, remember that the gods have in fact determined the end. The young hero himself remains in doubt. *He* is not utterly certain that Troy will fall. The proof is that he envisions, late in the play, the Greeks ganging up on him in revenge for having foiled them of their victory (ll. 1404–1409). But the audience is reminded that all will end as the history books have said. Those who wish to make precise theological points after the performance will recognize that the gods have permitted Neoptolemus just enough objective freedom to make the two authentic moral choices which constitute the play. The sphere spins freely. It comes to a halt. Then, and only then, the gods take it in hand and move it to click with the larger sphere, that is, the Trojan War. Necessity is reimposed.

The centrality of Neoptolemus is confirmed in the mysterious finale of the play. The young warrior has restituted the bow to Philoctetes. Purged of deceit, established in Philoctetes' mind as his friend, indeed his savior, he is in a superb position to launch his grand final appeal (ll. 1314–47).[16] So eloquent is this appeal that Sophocles is at a loss to find

---

16. It is here that Neoptolemus suddenly shows a knowledge of the oracle which he seemed far from possessing at the beginning of the play. Granting Sophocles the minor liberty of ascribing an unlikely ignorance to one of his characters in order to facilitate the exposition, we can still ask why such powerful arguments were not used on Philoctetes earlier. The answer must be that inasmuch as they would have failed to sway Philoctetes then as they fail now, Sophocles would have deprived himself of a climactic episode, vital to his thesis, for nothing. Note, however, that if his strategy was dramaturgically and thematically sound, his psychological plotting was again at fault, for surely Neoptolemus would have been strongly motivated to use his best arguments much earlier.

an appropriate reply for Philoctetes. The latter turns down his friend with the flimsiest of arguments. All the same, Neoptolemus yields, and Sophocles is obliged to correct the march of the play through a *deus ex machina*.

Obviously, a child could have concluded the action without the interference of a god. Philoctetes could have surrendered to Neoptolemus with complete credibility, or he could have been nudged by Heracles right there and then. Why does Sophocles keep Philoctetes firmly rooted in his resistance? Clearly, in order to launch a supreme moral challenge at his hero, Neoptolemus. It has been argued that our attention is now directed to Philoctetes, and that we are interested in the inflexibility he shows even to a true and proven friend. But in his view, Neoptolemus had also been true and proven early in the play; and Sophocles has taken a strangely roundabout way with his plot if his exclusive purpose has been to establish and reestablish that Philoctetes is obstinate. However, the most telling feature of this episode is that Sophocles gives us no moral hint whether Philoctetes is being true to his uprightness or, on the contrary, wickedly defiant of the gods. Is his obstinacy admirable, or blameworthy? The text is mum. As a result, this question too has exercised critics; and again the answer does not matter. Sophocles allows us to choose freely among interpretations because his mind is on Neoptolemus. The dastardly work of Odysseus must be completely undone and utterly reversed; reversed must be the even dirtier actions of Neoptolemus himself—the lies, the manipulation of a helpless victim, and finally the horrible acceptance of the bow from the sick and confiding victim who has *thrust* it on him. Neoptolemus discovers that the most fluent eloquence cannot repair an injustice; justice must be *done;* it demands action.[17] A simple retreat to the *status quo ante* is not sufficient reparation. For a moment he had thought that returning the life-sustaining bow would do. But Justice is an exacting mistress. Neoptolemus must carry the injured man home: the false invitation must become a true one; and Sophocles underscores its consequences—the Greeks outraged, their cause ruined, a massive revenge threatened. When Neoptolemus makes the second and greater of his decisions, he does so fully conscious that he will

---

17. Both Aeschylus and Euripides broke Philoctetes through rhetoric; Sophocles pointedly makes eloquence futile. As Valgimigli has put it, "The *Philoctetes* of Euripides had been the triumph of Odysseus's eloquence; Sophocles' *Philoctetes* is the sharpest discomfiture of this eloquence, and of all sophistical and oratorical talent" (*Poeti e filosofi di Grecia*, p. 223).

become a hounded outcast. His moral victory is complete.[18]

Neoptolemus's words are few, but in performance the action must have been stunning. The reader should beware of giving equal stage time in his mind to all the lines he reads. After Neoptolemus has said to Philoctetes, "Bless this land, then, and depart" (l. 1408), we must allow a substantial interval before Heracles makes his appearance, though he does so at the very next line. Philoctetes bows to the earth; perhaps he gathers his goods; and we picture the old man and the young, one supporting the other, beginning to turn towards the path that will lead them to the ship—where, of course, Odysseus and the sailors will have to be cowed by the terrible weapon. Perhaps they are well on their way when Heracles majestically bars the way: "Not yet!" The scene, in sum, is not thrown away merely because few words are spoken.[19]

This Heracleian "Not yet," which appears at first sight—at first *reading*, rather—to be a reaction to the line of Neoptolemus just quoted, is in fact not addressed to him at all, but to Philoctetes: good evidence again that Sophocles intended a period of significant action to separate the two lines. But the really startling feature of Heracles' long speech is that it takes no notice whatsoever of Neoptolemus's sensationally unpatriotic decision. We can now see why. Heracles stands of course for the prosecution of the war along the lines determined on Mount Olympus. Thus he cannot be expected to praise Neoptolemus. On the contrary, he ought to reprove him. But to reprove him would place him in opposition to a master as formidable as Zeus himself, namely the author, for whom the beauty of Neoptolemus's decisions was the point of the whole play. The only issue from this dilemma would have been a

---

18. And, at this point, tragic. Indeed, both decisions of Neoptolemus which I have called the twin action of the play are tragic in the purest sense of the word, while it is evident that neither Aeschylus nor Euripides had conceived this particular legend in tragic terms. The peculiarity of Sophocles' drama, however, is that he allows but a fleeting moment to the second tragic suffering of Neoptolemus, after which he provides a happy solution, not wholly to our satisfaction. See Oscar Mandel, *A Definition of Tragedy*, chap. 7. Incidentally, *Philoctetes* is the only one of Sophocles' seven surviving plays without a single fatality.

19. The same observation applies to another passage which seems strangely curt and cold on the page. Early in the play, Neoptolemus vigorously objects to Odysseus's tactics, and then abruptly yields (l. 116). Because of the particular structure of stychomythia, or one-liners, we may get the feeling that these lines were delivered machine-gun style, each line, and each pause between lines, receiving the same unit of time. Instead, we had better imagine a longish pause for agonizing before Neoptolemus speaks his line, quite aside from the emotional emphasis which the actor will naturally supply.

rather complicated speech by Heracles in which the god would have made the subtle distinction between temporary freedom and ultimate necessity which I have discussed in this essay. But such distinctions have their place precisely in essays, not on stage, and certainly not when a huge, popular audience is ready for refreshments. Sophocles wisely took the course of silence. Perhaps too he reflected that it was the prudent course to take.

So then, at the end of the play, Sophocles has managed to uphold both the principles of justice and of historical necessity, though they were contradictory up to this point. However, as Kitto rightly remarks, "nowhere in the whole of Sophocles is there a speech less impressive than this one which he wrote for Heracles" (*Form and Meaning in Drama*, p. 105). This particular Heracles plainly does not excite Sophocles' enthusiasm. He returns us to the everyday politics of Athens, to the Sophists, to expediency, to the Peloponnesian War, to the violence of Peisander, Antiphon, and Cleophon.[20] The chief point, that there is something superior to all this, has been made outside Heracles' jurisdiction.

When Neoptolemus makes his supreme move, he is moving against the state—not necessarily because the state is evil, but because a value higher than the state has disclosed itself to his view. He has no fear of the gods when he offers to take Philoctetes home: "How can I escape the anger *of the Greeks*?" (l. 1403) And here—at the heart of the play— Sophocles emerges in brilliant contrast to the tradition we have surveyed, and particularly to Aeschylus and Euripides. The two predecessors had not evinced the slightest doubt of the legitimacy of the Greek

---

20. M. H. Jameson ("Politics and the *Philoctetes*") and others have studied the political realities surrounding *Philoctetes*. Jameson cautiously suggests a possible identification of Neoptolemus with the younger Pericles. The year 410/9 was certainly a ripe one for anyone wishing to criticize political expediency, but what year is not? The biographical approach, on the other hand, has not been tried to my knowledge—and so little is known about Sophocles that it is perhaps wiser to say nothing. Yet one is tantalized by the fact that he held several high public offices in Athens. This gives his attack on the Odysseus type, and political immorality in general, a peculiar poignancy, as coming from one who knew whereof he was speaking. If, furthermore, we combine with his civic, military, and diplomatic experiences the famous report by his contemporary Ion of Chios, in which Sophocles laughs at his own poor reputation as a general, while Ion adds, "In political affairs he was neither able nor energetic, but behaved as any Athenian aristocrat might have done," a genuinely tempting portrait limns itself in the mind, and we see the *Philoctetes* emerging in a highly natural manner during a time of intense political and military trouble. Ion's anecdote is translated in full by F. J. H. Letters (*The Life and Works of Sophocles*, chap. 2).

mission. They drew from their audiences deep sympathy for Philoctetes. But his partial isolation, his resentment, and his physical suffering served only as formidable obstacles which the legitimate mission—indeed, the divine purpose—had to surmount. They never dreamed of using this suffering and this resentment to precipitate an act of treason against the state by an attractive young hero—a son of Achilles, no less! Nor did Sophocles inspire a later generation. In our survey of the tradition, we saw that (as far as one can tell today) his shocking idea was dropped, blocked out, after his death. It begot no literature of dissent. Not a single one of all the authors we have quoted or discussed in the opening chapter so much as side-glances at the motif of the return of the bow. Sophocles is hailed, but his inconvenient, his dangerous central scene is obliterated. Nor do we discover any approach to this so splendidly visual episode in any of the surviving illustrations. Everyone joined in the conspiracy of silence.[21]

Both the *Antigone* and the *Philoctetes* affirm a virtue which takes precedence over the state; hence we know that this problem interested Sophocles throughout his adult life. But in the earlier play the state is not, so to speak, its ordinary self. In fact, we observe two states, not one, in the *Antigone*. The first is that of Creon who, though he is no monster, acts tyrannically as well as godlessly in preventing Polyneices from being decently buried. The other is that of the Chorus, Haimon, Teiresias—in short, everybody else. Antigone, far from being an isolated figure, is actually the spokeswoman for the state in this second, morally sound condition. It is true that the state does not seem to interest her. She is a fanatic for justice and sees nothing else. But a morally sound state would defer to *her* view and not to that of Creon. A morally sound state would accept a political reversal rather than commit a crime. Clearly, Antigone's position is shared by all the Thebans we hear of in the text—except Creon, of course—and her isolation derives only from her individual courage, from the fact, in other words, that only she accepts martyrdom for her convictions.[22]

Creon brazenly ignores or overrides the imperatives of religion. To condemn such evident impiety did not involve Sophocles in any extraordinary or suspect thinking. In *Philoctetes,* however—some thirty

---

21. I will take up this theme again in Part II. Aristotle's references to Neoptolemus in *The Nicomachean Ethics* (1146a, 1151b), discussed above, are probably typical. He chose to praise the boy's truthfulness, and to close his eyes to the political insubordination which is the other side of the coin.

22. Perhaps we should drop the received notion of Sophocles as a serene and moderate poet and digest his interesting proclivity to side with violent righteousness.

years later—he dared to go farther. For Odysseus does not represent a crazed aberration of the state, but the state in its everyday operations. I have said before that the Ithacan's moral stature is not defined for us—whereas we are told exactly what to think of Creon. At times Odysseus appears rather comical: in his sudden flight, for instance, or when we reflect that he is the self-made victim of a wonderfully ironic reversal, since, having chosen on purpose a youth innocent enough to serve as his tool, he is defeated by that very quality of innocence. Elsewhere, he behaves like an unprincipled brute. At other times, however, his contention that one must sometimes dirty one's hands in the public service is made to seem persuasive, so much so that some critics—Reinhardt (*Sophokles*), for example, and Martha Nussbaum ("Consequences and Character in Sophocles' *Philoctetes*")—can argue without lapsing into eccentricity that Odysseus represents a positive value in the full Hegelian sense.

In my opinion, Sophocles has blurred the picture on purpose. The state, he intimates, *is* an ambiguous creature, good and evil, serious and ridiculous. Since the text invites such indecision, I believe it would be a mistake for a director to make a Creon out of Odysseus. This would trivialize to some extent Neoptolemus's victory over the Ithacan and over himself. For in Odysseus he recognizes an opponent who is at one with the Greeks as a body, who obeys certain commands of the gods, whose ultimate goal (victory over Troy) he shares, and who therefore represents a vital portion of himself. That is why decision comes harder to him than to Antigone, who faces an arrant blasphemer, and whom Haimon and all Thebes will applaud. In short, Neoptolemus is far more truly *alone* than she. His virtue must be so extreme that it causes him to betray his own cause and to defy what we can only call the legitimate enterprises of any well-run country. So much righteousness becomes at last too much of a good thing in the eyes of the gods, and Heracles, the public servant *par excellence,* simply puts a halt to it. For, as I have said before, the double action of Neoptolemus revolves freely and loosely inside the divinely predetermined matter of Troy.

If we place *Oedipus at Colonus* at one end, *Antigone* at the other, and *Philoctetes* in the middle, a highly satisfying picture presents itself to the mind. In the *Antigone* the state is corrupted by a tyrant who, at a climactic moment, goes so far as to defy Zeus himself; in the *Philoctetes* the state exists in the background as a normal body, and Odysseus is its authentic delegate and voice; finally, there appears in Sophocles' posthumous work a truly idyllic vision of the state—and it will be remembered that one of the species of imitation mentioned by Aristotle in the *Poetics* is of things as they ought to be. The state here is Athens, of course, to which, at the moment of its all too real, historical catastrophe,

Sophocles offers a dream of righteousness both in the means and the ends, nostalgically drawn from the never-never land of the heroic past. The representative of this dream of purity, against which no revolt could be virtuous, is Theseus. Creon, we saw, was a tyrant; the character of Odysseus is complex and questionable; but Theseus is already the perfect knight-monarch of medieval fable.

It should be clear by this time why Sophocles needed to press a new actor into the Philoctetes matter. If his play had really concerned the suffering of Philoctetes, or the decision to forego, or not forego, his hatred of the Greeks, or divine providence unaltered by human decisions, he would have had no reason to seek a substitute for Diomedes. But for a delicate question of the soul, for an ethical dilemma as fine as the one he had decided to take on, the leathery hide of a Diomedes would have been a ludicrous agency.[23] Pierre Vidal-Naquet ("Le *Philoctète* de Sophocle et l'éphébie") has suggested that Neoptolemus is almost an Athenian ephebe before initiation into the ranks of the hoplites, that is, on the way to maturity. This view differs from the one commonly proposed, to the effect that Neoptolemus merely returns to his original *physis*. In a gross sense he does no more. He begins as the true son of Achilles (who is repeatedly named and invested with an aura of righteousness), he becomes untrue to the spirit of his father, and finally he recovers his purity. But has he not experienced and learned so much—traveled through a terrible night of the soul—that we may think of him, in the conclusion, as standing on higher ground? At the beginning he was righteous. At the end he is righteous, having experienced, and then conquered, unrighteousness at the core of his being. So there is considerable merit in the French critic's notion. But be that as it may, Sophocles rightly turned to a youth as yet unsoiled by excessive experience. Neoptolemus is not girlish (as in Gide's play), but he has in common with Antigone and Electra the condition of having stayed at home so far in his life—and preserved the ideals one traditionally (if cynically) associates with youth.

Nor could a figure like Diomedes have worked plausibly as a fount of compassion for Philoctetes. Compassion is the psychological basis for the grand ethical decisions that are to be made. We have seen that Sophocles' innovation in surrendering Philoctetes to perfect solitude was more than a move to overbid the pathos of his predecessors. The

---

23. He is, besides, too closely associated with Odysseus in the *Iliad* to have become a foil to the Ithacan.

claims of the state could take second place only vis-à-vis a supremely wronged figure, and this figure must awake a supreme compassion. The Chorus is moved, but not to the point of changing sides, or even giving up its tricks. Could a veteran like Diomedes have gone farther? Better, Sophocles must have thought, a new personage, a youth, a Neoptolemus fresh come from Scyros.

As for Philoctetes, unlike Neoptolemus he does not grow; he does not make any moral or intellectual discovery; his virtue is not tested. Indeed, the text allows us to say that he would have been as virtuous yielding as he is virtuous not yielding. Still—to return to a point I have made before—his character is not therefore scenically belittled. He remains *massive* throughout: the unmoving great cause of the action. Perhaps it is not stretching metaphor too far to say that Philoctetes has mass, and Neoptolemus motion.

And it is not an extravagance, I believe, to think of the *Philoctetes* as turning a new page for mankind. Only for a moment, to be sure; then the book hastily returns to the more familiar chapter. Naturally, Sophocles cannot be thought of as philosophizing in intellectual isolation, and we must imagine him in the midst of an intellectual world in which talk about morality and politics—talk constantly tested against the realities of Athenian life—was plentiful and exciting. Socrates had been in some sense the founder of systematic speculation on these subjects. Early in his career he had turned his back on questions of what we would call pure science today in order to devote himself to the duties of man on earth. In retrospect we can see that in the absence of refined instrumental technology, it was as yet too early for Newtonian triumphs in the natural sciences, and Socrates was not unwise to give up unverifiable speculations. In any event, systematic moral and political thinking seems to have made rapid progress in his lifetime—so rapid that within a decade of his own "sublime" self-sacrifice to the divinity of the state, Sophocles could propose a counter-morality to that of the much younger man suggesting that the *individual conscience* will and must sometimes rebel against the commands of a perfectly normal and legitimate political authority. This view would still be fresh, controversial, and dangerous when Thoreau voiced it again after too many centuries of silence.

The individual conscience: this concept deserves to be italicized. I have said before that the action of *Philoctetes* is unmanaged by the gods. They are concerned only with the final move on the checkerboard. Neoptolemus never refers his two great decisions to divine inspiration, as Antigone insistently and unambiguously does. Critics, we have seen, speak of his return to his *physis*, his altogether natural character. We might also say that he loses and regains his *honor*. All the while the gods are still.[24]

Furthermore, does not *Philoctetes* anticipate the Kantian concept that a man shall never be treated as an object, but always as an end in himself? This too remains a fresh and in fact, if not in theory, a controverted thesis. Indeed, *Philoctetes* is an advance over *Antigone*—and over *Electra*—because here the duty that transcends political imperatives is not to one's own kin, but to a stranger. Not yet to a complete outsider, not yet to a "barbarian," but to a person not met before and claiming no kinship. By refusing to treat Philoctetes as an object—a useful instrument—Neoptolemus takes us a step beyond Antigone defying the state for her brother, or Electra avenging her father's death.

However, finally, one reads *Philoctetes*, there is no denying that it is authentic thesis drama. Sophocles is a more philosophical playwright than, say, Shakespeare or Racine, and critics have not erred in working hard to define his thought, whether comprehensively or within the boundaries of a single play at a time. But a thesis drama like *Philoctetes* rises above the type developed in the nineteenth century and perfected by Shaw, in whose plays the action stops so that certain characters can speak well-rounded essays which the author does not trust his audiences to compose for themselves. In the higher species of thesis drama, the lifelike deeds and utterances of the characters provide a set of clues that solicit from the audience an inductive process leading to a unifying hypothetical generalization, namely the thesis. So the conceptual side is satisfied without violence to the dramatic side. This is how *Philoctetes* functions. It is both flesh and philosophy. And, like all supreme works of art, it moves us before we have time to think, though it makes us think because it moved us.

---

24. Are these gods—who preside over the fall of Troy while Neoptolemus struggles with his conscience—perhaps the same dark divinities that strike in *Oedipus the King,* and whom the Chorus of the *Antigone* perceive as battering three generations of the Labdacidae without the slightest concern for innocence or guilt, sin or righteousness, piety or impiety? Sophocles seems to have served two sets of gods, and sometimes confused us as a result: an older set representing the amoral and implacable march of the universe; and a more civilized set, punishing wrongdoers, if not always rewarding the good. See Poe *(Heroism and Divine Justice)* for a lively and stimulating discussion in which this malevolence of the gods is underscored, but (in my opinion) wrongly offered as the *subject* of the *Philoctetes*.

Part II

PHILOCTETES, 1502–1896: A Preliminary Survey

1

In principle, the tale of Philoctetes remained available throughout the Middle Ages, since it could be read in Ovid and other well-known writers; but I have found no reference to it in that period, when it might have become fair game for edifying allegories.

It is perhaps a little more surprising that it failed to impress itself on artists of the Renaissance. But, as Eugène Müntz pointed out long ago, Greek tragedy as a whole played only a marginal role in the pictorial arts of Renaissance Italy, whether early or late; and we can extend this observation to other nations and to the other arts.[1] I discussion of the reasons for this neglect, but ex post facto, several explanations might be offered. One is that the recirculation of Greek tragedy was a recent event, and occurred at a time when a tradition of mythological subjects was already fairly well established in the arts. Another, related to the first, would be that in an epoch still dominated by church commissions, the familiar pagan texts more than sufficed to absorb the ration of work-time left over from Holy Virgins and crucifixions. More important, the three major provinces of painting and sculpture outside of portraiture, which one may schematize perhaps as the divine, the heroic, and the erotic, could be amply satisfied by Hebrew and Christian texts, and by Ovid with a few other old pagan friends. What remains to be said is that if Oedipus and Antigone, if Phaedra and Hippolytus, if Agamemnon and even Helen are rare, we shall hardly expect to see Philoctetes loom in a Raphael or Titian.

---

1. Eugène Müntz's three-volume *Histoire de l'art pendant la Renaissance* (Paris, 1889–95) is excellent for its study of subject matter. Beyond Italy, it can be mentioned that neither Andor Pigler's fundamental—though admittedly selective—*Barockthemen* nor the *Decimal Index to the Art of the Lowlands* mentions Philoctetes or the particular Neoptolemus and Odysseus associated with him.

But concerning Philoctetes another remark can be made. As we saw in an earlier chapter, his special attribute was the long-lasting suffering on Lemnos that had reduced him to haggard wretchedness. This fitted into a perfectly acceptable, if somewhat less popular, class of motifs; but what need was there to search the pagans for the representation of a hermit? Innumerable Christian personages, familiar to art patrons and church congregations, begged to be chosen as exemplars of privation, isolation, and endurance. Neither Oedipus at Colonus nor Philoctetes on Lemnos was required to fill this particular slot.

Nevertheless, the existence of no fewer than four Renaissance bas-reliefs of Philoctetes proves that the blackout was not absolute. The reliefs, all variants around a single motif, are located today at the Victoria and Albert Museum in London, the Hermitage in Leningrad, the Palazzo Ducale in Mantua, and the Cleveland Museum of Art. Little is known about their history, but they appear to be connected with the court of Ferrara in the first decades of the sixteenth century, and one or more of the reliefs may have been carved by Antonio Lombardo (about 1458–1516), who was employed by Alfonso I d'Este after 1506. Until more facts, or ampler speculations, are published, we must content ourselves with a tantalizing glimpse of an ephemeral *demand* for Philoctetes images in the High Renaissance: four sculptures, and a great many unanswered questions.

All four pieces concur in exhibiting the hero in the act of fanning his wounded foot with the wing of a dove. We have seen already that this had been the subject of a remarkable cameo by Boethos (Fig. 3) two or three centuries before Christ. This cameo did not make its appearance in Europe until the first decade of the nineteenth century, when the French ambassador to Constantinople brought it to his country. But it had been widely copied, and one of the copies, possibly a Roman one, must have served as the original sculptor's model. It should be noted, though, that the imitators had misinterpreted Boethos. They had failed to see the tiny flies swarming about Philoctetes' foot—an image apparently suggested by a passage in Aeschylus's *Philoctetes*, as attested by a surviving fragment. Unlike Boethos, they showed Philoctetes merely ventilating the wound; and so he appears in the four reliefs.

An inscription at the base of the elegant Victoria and Albert version (pl. 6) implies that the artist had read Servius's commentary on Virgil to the effect that Philoctetes wounded his own foot with one of Hercules' arrows.[2] The reliefs are probably to be dated well after 1502, the year

---

2. "Vulnera Lernaeo dolet hic Poeantius Heros" ("This hero, son of Poeas, suffers from a Lernaean wound"). See Part I, sections 7, 11.

in which the Aldine Sophocles had appeared in Venice. Were it not for the inscription, the temptation would have been to postulate a combined Sophocles / Boethos inspiration for the sculptures. Under the circumstances, however, the honor goes to Servius alongside Boethos. The play was apparently not consulted—perhaps not known—and Müntz's observation concerning the neglect of the tragedians remains unchallenged.

For the rest, the four reliefs seem to have begotten no progeny. Unless other representations, with different origins, come to light—for this writer, at any rate—we are left with a single though impressive outcropping of Philoctetes icons for the entire length and breadth of the Italian Renaissance.[3]

When we turn to music, we discover that as soon as composers turned their attention away from church compositions, they struck the erotic chord even more emphatically than their colleagues in the visual arts. Once again, no one needed Greek tragedy for a supply of savory love stories. Ironically enough, the creators of opera in Italy aspired to a faithful re-creation of Greek tragedy. But their faithfulness broke at the prospect of a plot without a pair or two of ardent lovers. The direction was set by such works as Jacopo Peri's pioneering *Euridice* (1600) and two capital scores by Monteverdi: *Orpheus* (1607) and *Ariadne* (1608). The truth is that the notion of an opera—or a madrigal—concerning Philoctetes is downright comical and need not be pursued.

For sustained interest in Philoctetes and other characters from

---

3. My information concerning the reliefs comes from two works by John Pope-Hennessy: *Catalogue of Italian Sculptures in the Victoria and Albert Museum,* vols. 1, 3 (London, 1964); and *Italian Renaissance Sculpture* (2d ed. London, 1971), as well as a personal communication. The gem tradition is surveyed by L. A. Milani in his two fundamental studies (see Bibliography). Milani was aware of the existence of what he knew only as a "modern" bas-relief in Mantua; but he also mentions a print after the gem—quite possibly the same cameo Antonio had used as his model—by Enea Vico (1523–67), a notable engraver active in Ferrara, and author of a *Discourse on Medals in Antiquity* (1555). A purely fanciful scenario might go as follows. Someone brings to the court of Ferrara a supposedly antique gem, creating a certain excitement there. A learned personage explicates it in the light of several authorities (other than Sophocles). Perhaps this occurs at the time, around 1507, when a large number of mythological reliefs (now at the Hermitage) are being made for Alfonso I. Antonio Lombardo—or someone else—is asked to carve a Philoctetes after the gem. This prestigious commission begets others, including (I take the hint from Pope-Hennessy) the version, now at Mantua, for Isabella d'Este. Finally, a generation later, Vico produces his engraving, and brings to a conclusion the tale of Philoctetes at Ferrara.

Greek tragedy, we must turn to the activities of scholars and scholarly playwrights. There had been some knowledge, or rather awareness, of Greek tragedy before the invention of printing—both Dante and Petrarch write reverently of it—but we can speak of a genuine influence only after the first complete Sophocles (the seven extant tragedies) was printed in Venice in 1502. A complete Latin edition followed, surprisingly slowly, in 1543. In addition, a number of *separate* Sophoclean plays were printed in Europe in the sixteenth century, either in Greek or in Latin. It is known, for instance, that Roger Ascham translated the *Philoctetes* into Latin in 1543—no copy has survived, however—and another Latin *Philoctetes* was printed in 1586. From records which are obviously highly incomplete, it is also clear that academic performances of the Greek classics in Latin translations were not uncommon, both at the university and the secondary school level. There are traces of an *Ajax* and an *Electra* performed at Cambridge in 1564 and 1583, respectively; and the Gymnasium of Strasbourg acquired international renown from its school performances, which included a substantial number of Greek plays. I have found no hint of a production of *Philoctetes* in Western Europe in this entire epoch; but, again, it should be remembered that records of academic performances are scanty.

In 1608, the *Ajax* was performed at the Strasbourg Gymnasium in German. Long before, the high tide of humanism had brought with it the publication of a number of vernacular translations, imitations, and adaptations of Greek comedy and tragedy. *Philoctetes* is still missing, but we note an English *Electra*, a French *Electra* and *Antigone*, a Spanish *Electra*, and a German *Trachiniae* and *Ajax*. The absence of *Oedipus* from this list is worthy of a special question mark. As is to be expected, Italy led the way in all this activity. But there as elsewhere, Seneca was the venerated model to whom, strange as it seems today, both Sophocles and Euripides were required to conform. I will make no attempt here to distinguish between more or less faithful translations, looser *rifacimenti* (reworkings), and original plays containing materials from or imitating external forms of Greek tragedy, since *Philoctetes* seems never to have been italianized at all. Enough to say that every approach was tried out. Select audiences were found. And the summit was reached when the Teatro Olimpico of Vicenza was inaugurated in 1585 with an adaptation of *Oedipus tyrannus* by Orsatto Giustiniano. But it would seem that high culture can make mistakes. Trissino—Rucellai—Dolce—Alamanni—Giraldi—Speroni—Aretino—as playwrights they survive only in the history books. Either they wanted genius by accident, or the historical hour had not yet struck when writers disdainful of popular shows would know how to disentangle what is truly drama from oratorical, epic, and lyric elements. It is at any rate no accident that the Italian declamatory tradition in tragedy was to evolve into opera rather than great theater.

As humanist fervor declined and national literatures—the local product—gained in prestige, interest in Greek tragedy in its pure state diminished to a startling degree. The students at Strasbourg gave a performance of *Prometheus* (in Latin) in 1609—a curiosity in itself, as Aeschylus had lagged far behind the other three great dramatists during the sixteenth century—and thereafter little is heard of Greek tragedy on stage and even in editions, Greek, Latin, or vernacular. The grand event at the Teatro Olimpico had no tomorrow. In England and Spain, native forms eclipsed the classics altogether.

In France, of course, Greece returned in full glory under Louis XIV. But it returned to *influence* playwrights, not to impose its own masterpieces. In the sixteenth century, serious French dramatists had begun to use Senecan and Greek models in emulation of the Italians. At first they made the same mistakes. But by the 1630s the French descendants of Trissino had acquired an accurate sense of the nature of drama. As a result, neoclassical tragedy (indebted more to Euripides than to Sophocles) was able to attract a public which it has not lost to this day. But at no time was any Greek tragedy produced as such during the reigns of Louis XIII and Louis XIV—not even in the schools run by the Jesuits, where theatrical activity was intense. And no one imitated or adapted *Philoctetes*. Indeed, as far as *Philoctetes* is concerned, it is fair to say that in spite of editions and translations, and a few visual representations, he and his coagonists had gone down with the Roman Empire and all but ceased to exist as functioning cultural realities.

2

The revival came from an unexpected direction—not from the theater, nor from closet drama, nor yet through a painting, a sculpture, or a musical composition, certainly not from some pioneering critical work, but by way of a chapter in a prose fiction. In 1699, François de Salignac de la Mothe-Fénelon, archbishop of Cambrai, brought out his *Suite du quatrième livre de l'Odyssée; ou, Les aventures de Télémaque*. The twelfth chapter of this political romance is, broadly speaking, a retelling of the tale of Philoctetes as Fénelon found it in Sophocles, with small helpings from Seneca, Virgil, and Servius. Whether or not Fénelon knew that Philoctetes had lain dormant all these centuries, his paraphrase of Sophocles did in fact bring the hero back to life.

Telemachus quickly became a classic in itself, and remained a much-translated and oft-reprinted favorite well into the nineteenth century.

It was the irreproachable book to place into the hands of deserving youths and maidens. As we see it now, this noble, chaste, sweet, humane, smooth, reasonable, sentimental, and soporific sermon in fictive form, which is to letters what Poussin is to painting, marks the end of the trumpeting art of the baroque and introduces us to the era of neoclassicism. And indeed, though Fénelon seems at first browse to keep faith with Sophocles, it does not take a reader long to discover that he cannot cope with Sophoclean harshness; he must tame the Greek. Neoclassicism is in fact classicism with its teeth drawn.

Telemachus meets Philoctetes in the latter's old age, as ruler of Petelia in South Italy. Though put off for a moment by the notion of fraternizing with the son of his former enemy, Philoctetes eventually gives an account of his tribulations highly favorable to Odysseus. Fénelon retouches Sophocles very lightly, but one light touch suffices to overturn the entire Sophoclean conception: it is Odysseus himself who returns the bow to Philoctetes—and who does so without cunning afterthought—even though he knows that Troy cannot fall without it. And he offers to leave Philoctetes alone on Lemnos—with his bow—out of pure magnaminity. The Sentimental Age is upon us, and Goethe's *Iphigenia in Aulis* already incubates in *Telemachus*. Enemies are reconciled; tears of sympathy are shed.

Still, there comes a moment mid-story when Philoctetes does threaten Odysseus with instant death. In Sophocles this is the point at which Odysseus breaks and runs. It is again typical of neoclassical art that Fénelon's Odysseus stands firm—a detail which opens for us the immense distance that separates Periclean art from the Winckelmann code of "noble simplicity and calm grandeur."[4] Only in the final episode does Fénelon show that his place is at the opening rather than the height of an epoch: though filled with admiration for Odysseus, Philoctetes fails to throw down his bow—won over by so much virtue—to embrace his former enemy; Sophocles' Heracles must still appear and *command* a reconciliation. As soon as he does so, however, Philoctetes cries out "in a transport of joy: The night is past! The dawn breaks upon me!" and the new age reasserts itself.[5]

---

4. Jakob Winckelmann's *History of Art in Antiquity* appeared sixty-five years after *Telemachus*. It constitutes a confirmation, not an innovation.

5. The same significant tug-of-war between tough classicism and soft neoclassicism reveals itself in the conclusion: Philoctetes cannot forget and forgive, even after winning many victories upon his return to the field; *but,* because he loves Telemachus, his aversion to Odysseus does give way. We seem to catch Fénelon astride two horses going off in contrary directions.

As for Neoptolemus, Fénelon takes little notice of him, since he has used the return of the bow as his spectacular example, not of how idealists should rebel against ruthless politics, but of how mercy should reign in the hearts of monarchs. In any case, to present an attractive picture of a youth who sets his personal sense of right above the demands of the state would have been unthinkable for Fénelon or anyone else enjoying the light of life under the Sun King. As it was, the mild murmurings against bellicose monarchs which Fénelon dared write into the *Telemachus* alienated him from Louis XIV for the rest of his life.

3

The eighteenth century saw the first great wave of Sophoclean translations into modern languages, after limited stirrings in the sixteenth and all but complete inactivity in the seventeenth century. To England goes the honor both of the first complete Sophocles—in 1729—and the first *Philoctetes*—namely that of Thomas Sheridan, dated 1725—in a post-classical language. The French followed with a complete Sophocles in 1730. In 1742, Louis Racine (the playwright's son) translated some seventy lines of the first encounter between Philoctetes and Neoptolemus for his *Réflexions sur la poésie* (6. 2). German versions of *Philoctetes* were printed in 1760 and 1763, while the first complete Sophocles in German appeared in 1787. An Italian *Philoctetes* was published in 1767, and a complete Italian Sophocles in 1823. I have found three Spanish translations of *Philoctetes* before 1780, and a Dutch one in 1793. Meantime, Winckelmann had mentioned Philoctetes, and Lessing had discussed him at length in the *Laokoon*. The Lemnian hero was circulating again.

Whether or not Sophocles was regularly performed at schools and universities in this period I do not know. It is certain, however, that there was still no demand for authentic Greek tragedy on the professional stages of Europe. Poets continued to rewrite the classics in order to make them palatable to their audiences: complicating the intrigues; making them "reasonable" (for instance, the Thebans in Dryden and Lee's *Oedipus* pointedly comment on the age difference between Oedipus and his wife); filling the plots with self-sacrifices and other un-Greek actions; and above all, supplying the sentimental interest so deplorably neglected by Sophocles.

In 1659 Corneille had inserted a romantic episode into *Oedipus*. In 1718, Voltaire decided to use the name of Philoctetes in his own *Oedipus,* and proceeded to make him a suitor to Jocasta! Audiences were unfailingly warm to these "improved" classics. If *Philoctetes* was destined to be revived on stage, after its resurgence on the printed page, it would be, it would necessarily be, with the assistance of a marriageable virgin.

This happened in 1755 at the Comédie-Française, where the *Philoctète* of Jean-Baptiste Vivien de Chateaubrun held the stage for seven performances, followed by a revival (for which I do not have a date) of five more. The chevalier de Mouhy, writing in 1780, succinctly reports "a great success."[6]

Lessing's attack on the play in his *Laokoon* is obviously just—it was an easy target—but Chateaubrun's version, besides its purely historical merit of being the first *Philoctetes* ever staged in postclassical Europe, has its modest virtues. Philoctetes' virginal daughter, inevitably named Sophie, and inevitably "killing" poor Neoptolemus at first sight, must be firmly pushed into the wings so that they can be considered.

For Chateaubrun as for Fénelon, Neoptolemus is a dead-end figure. Typically neoclassical, he is too pure to steal the bow and arrows or tell lies. In fact Philoctetes remains in possession of his weapon to the end. Furthermore, Neoptolemus fully agrees with Odysseus that the state comes first; but, alas, he is in love with Sophie, and his heart aches for Philoctetes. It is the old conflict between reason and feeling, and not the Sophoclean one between a lower and a higher reason, and this means that if Neoptolemus were to yield to Philoctetes (and Sophie), he himself would view this as a defeat. But he is not allowed to act at all. His dilemma is solved *for* him. The playwright removes him from the action and clears the stage for a debate between Odysseus and Philoctetes. Odysseus, fully as noble as Fénelon's hero, bares his breast to Philoctetes' arrow if doing so will assuage his fury. Failing to placate him, he offers to take Philoctetes' place as an outcast on Lemnos. However, though sympathetic to the offended hero, he has a correct sense of the hierarchies:

> Je sais ce que je dois aux pleurs des malheureux,
> Mais l'État a sur nous des droits plus rigoureux.
>   [3.2]
>
> (I know what I owe to the tears of the unfortunate;
> But the state has more exacting rights over us.)

---

6. Charles de Fieux, chevalier de Mouhy, *Abrégé de l'histoire du théâtre françois*. Whether this hack and parasite can be trusted is an open question. Chateaubrun (1688–1775), once obscure and now forgotten, was elected to the Academy to succeed Montesquieu in the same year the *Philoctète* was produced. He also wrote a *Trojan Women* and an *Astyanax*.

The debate between the two protagonists is eloquent, and Chateaubrun rises to some admirable poetry here—so much so that Philoctetes melts, recognizes that he has been too rancorous, and reconciles himself to Odysseus without the interference of a god.[7]

Philoctetes' change of heart—

> Le ciel m'ouvre les yeux sur la vertu d'Ulisse
> [5.3]
>
> (Heaven opens my eyes to the virtue of Ulysses)

—is pure eighteenth century kitsch. But in an earlier scene Odysseus presents an argument to Neoptolemus which hints of things to come in the world:

> Et vous ne plaignez pas vos amis qui périssent,
> Dans un camp resserré nos soldats qui languissent?
> [3.2]
>
> (And you do not pity your friends who are dying,
> Nor in a narrow camp our suffering soldiers?)

Here, for the first time in the history of the Philoctetes legend, a thought is addressed, however fleetingly, to the common soldier in the field.

Chateaubrun also places some new and telling arguments in Neoptolemus's mouth when the young man is trying to win over Philoctetes. If you hate the Atrides so much, he says, what could be more enjoyable than having them grovel at your feet? And how can a warrior like you be willing to die in a desert instead of on a battlefield?

In his reply, Philoctetes sounds another modern note:

> Eh! quelle est cette guerre où l'on nous fit courir,
> Où vingt rois aveugles s'obstinent à périr?
> Fatal événement dont la cause est si vaine!
> Tous les Grecs à grands cris redemandent Hélène.

---

7. As far as we know, straightforward persuasiveness also vanquished Philoctetes in Aeschylus's and Euripides' versions. Chateaubrun confirms for us the suspicion that this is a poor dramatic device. The audience inevitably feels that it is being manipulated by the author. It is strange but true that an outright miracle like Sophocles' deus ex machina is a more acceptable maneuver. It tells us frankly that there is no human solution.

Honte éternelle aux Grecs de la redemander,
Et malheur aux Troyens de la vouloir garder!
Eh! laissons la, Seigneur, cette guerre frivole,
Trop peu digne du sang des Guerriers qu'elle immole.
                                                                [2.3]

(What is this war to which they made us rush,
Where twenty blind kings insist on perishing?
Fatal event whose cause is so vain!
All the Greeks are shouting for the return of Helen.
Eternal shame to the Greeks for demanding her again,
And woe to the Trojans for wanting to keep her!
Come, my lord, let us not meddle with this frivolous war,
Not worth the blood of the warriors it has swallowed.)

Unfortunately, this argument, worthy of Shakespeare's Thersites, is quickly swept aside, and the very same scene ends with an absurd though short-lived pact between Philoctetes and Neoptolemus to conquer Troy by themselves after the Greeks have been forced to lift the siege.

4

Chateaubrun's play came and went. For a genuine landmark we must turn to Jean-François de La Harpe, who, in 1780, read before the Academy the first two acts of his translation of *Philoctetes* and was greeted with "universal applause" by the Immortals. In 1781 the full text was printed. As we have seen, Sophocles' play had been translated earlier in the century into several modern languages; but La Harpe's version—omitting the spy episode and the choral sections—is important as the first to have reached the stage. Indeed, it is very nearly the first play by Sophocles to have received a professional production since the great event at Vicenza in 1585. La Harpe's translation was performed at the Comédie-Française in June 1783. The previous December, Guillaume Dubois Rochefort's translation of *Electra* had been staged at Versailles. We may note it as another curiosity of history that neither the *Oedipus* nor the *Antigone* took the honor of launching Sophocles once more upon the European stage.

The significance of La Harpe's effort does not lie in its modest literary merit, but in the fact that it received a great deal of exposure. According to H. C. Lancaster, it was performed fourteen times in 1783–84, acted again in 1786, "and in most of the years that followed down to 1816, and again in 1825 and 1826. The troupe of the

Comédie-Française played it in all eighty-six times."[8] La Harpe's translation was widely discussed, favorably and unfavorably. And it was reprinted at least seven times from 1781 to 1843—perhaps an even more important fact. By contrast, an "imitation" of Sophocles' drama by A. F. C. Ferrand, printed in 1786, seems to have made no lasting impression.[9]

The revival of Philoctetes brought about by Fénelon, Chateaubrun, and La Harpe was a specifically French phenomenon; for the translations into other languages had caused no memorable stir in their respective countries.[10] In England interest in producing Greek plays was sluggish. A letter by Dryden on 26 November 1699 mentions an *Iphigenia* by John Dennis, "imitated from Eurypides," and about to be produced at Lincoln's Inn Fields by Betterton; "and another play of the same name, is very shortly to come on the stage in Drury Lane."[11] But nothing further is heard of either. In 1714, a performance of *Oedipus Tyrannus* in Greek was staged in London "by Mr. Low's scholars"— possibly a hint that one could unearth a few school performances of Sophocles in Greek or Latin in England in the eighteenth century. But all other classical plays were *rifacimenti* such as the *Oedipus* by Dryden and Lee already mentioned (a long-lasting favorite) or James Thomson's *Agamemnon*. In February 1773 a letter signed "Cantab" appeared in the *Gentleman's Magazine* lamenting that no play by Sophocles had ever been acted at Drury Lane and predicting that "this new species of drama" would be well received. Many years were to pass before anything so *new* as an unadorned Greek tragedy would be seen in a British playhouse.

Germany seems to have been equally unreceptive. Goethe oversaw a production of a very freely translated *Antigone* in 1809, and then again in 1813. But these were two isolated events; I have uncovered no trace of any performance of a Sophoclean play in the German-speaking world before the *Antigone* just named. It is only from the year 1841, when Ludwig Tieck produced a highly acclaimed *Antigone* at the

---

8. H. C. Lancaster, *French Tragedy in the Reign of Louis XVI and the Early Years of the French Revolution, 1774–1792* (Baltimore, Md.: Johns Hopkins University Press, 1953) p. 41.

9. I have not read this work.

10. However, I cannot positively assert that translations or adaptations or re-creations of the play were unknown to the stages of Italy, Spain, and Holland.

11. William Van Lennep, ed., *The London Stage 1660–1800*, part 1 (Carbondale: Southern Illinois University Press, 1965), p. 517.

Potsdamer Schlosstheater before the king of Prussia, that Greek drama found a permanent place in the Germanic theater.[12]

Goethe, however, gave deep thought to the *Philoctetes*. On 31 January 1827, he confided to Eckermann that if time enough were granted him, he would turn the Philoctetes fragments of Aeschylus and Euripides into a play of his own. On 21 February, Eckermann recalls another conversation in which both he and Goethe—but Eckermann more fully than Goethe—drew up an impressive list of parallels between the figure of Philoctetes and that of Oedipus at Colonus. It has never been improved upon. Yet the direction which this conversation took suggests that Goethe too would have overlooked the great and forgotten theme of Sophocles' play in order to dwell on the reconciliation between Philoctetes and Odysseus. Goethe was obviously not the man to promote subversion of the state.

Two short poems of this period should be mentioned here: a lyric lament—"Philoktet"—by Johann Mayrhofer (1817) made into a song by Schubert,[13] and "When Philoctetes in the Lemnian isle," a mediocre sonnet by Wordsworth (1827) in which a bird, instead of being shot and eaten as the tradition will have it, alights on the grieving hero to prove

> that no Bastile
> Is deep enough to exclude the light of love,
> Though man for brother man has ceased to feel.

5

Parallel to the resurgence of Philoctetes in the domains of literature and the stage, a remarkable display of interest in the long-suffering hero occurred on the part of painters and sculptors.[14] The chronologi-

---

12. Mendelssohn wrote the choral music for Tieck's production, which was presently transferred to the Berlin Hoftheater, and thence to several major cities in Germany. I have found references to subsequent professional productions—still in the nineteenth century—of *Medea, Oedipus at Colonus,* and *Hippolytus,* but none to *Philoctetes.* Here as elsewhere I hope that further information will come to light.

13. This song—not one of Schubert's most distinguished—was brought to my attention by Maria Feder.

14. I am deeply indebted to the French art historian Suzanne Gutwirth for opening my eyes to the field of Philoctetes representations in the neoclassical age—a field, indeed, which no one had seriously inspected before. Madame Gutwirth continued to provide valuable facts and hints in the sequel. In the Preface I have acknowledged the help of other generous scholars in the United States, France, and England.

cal list of works of art set out in the following pages, covering almost exactly a century of activity, is meant to raise the curtain on this subject, not to exhaust it. I have not—for instance—consulted the numerous illustrated editions of Homer, Fénelon, and others that would have lengthened the roll. But I am also persuaded that many a painting, sculpture, drawing, watercolor, and print has escaped my notice. Furthermore, no aesthetic analysis is attempted here. That not a single artist in this period achieved the pure, poised excellence of the Victoria and Albert bas-relief, I silently take for granted. In these pages I am concerned only with the conceptual element, though fully aware that in a reputable aesthetic analysis this element would and must play a capital role.

Three approaches may be distinguished. The first and dominant one—unfortunately so from our point of view—was to depict Philoctetes filling the "page," full-size and alone, nude or partly dressed, and caught making one or another operatic gesture. In most of these representations Philoctetes is in effect a model in an academic life-class, and the artist a dutiful virtuoso of flesh, muscle, and bone.

A second approach was to treat Philoctetes—alone or otherwise— from a distance as an element in a landscape.

The third approach—most interesting to us—was to illustrate a dramatic incident from the hero's life, involving interaction with other characters.

1770. Once again the story seems to begin with an Englishman, to wit James Barry (1741–1806), who, inspired by the epigram on Parrhasios quoted in the first chapter of this book, painted a full-length pathetic "portrait" of the unhappy Philoctetes (pl. 7), which he donated to the Accademia Clementina in Bologna, where it hangs to this day. A drawing on the same subject is in the Oppé collection in London.

Lessing's *Laokoon* had appeared in 1766. While Barry's portrayal is true to Parrhasios, and in debt to his protector Edmund Burke's essay on the sublime (1756), it conforms significantly to the German critic's notion of authentic classicism. Lessing had rejected Winckelmann's opinion that Greek artists severely reined in expressions of suffering. According to Lessing, Greek poets saw no conflict between wild outcries of pain and greatness of soul. It was true, Lessing argued, that the Greeks did not, and that no one ever may, show an open mouth on a hero in a painting or a sculpture; but aside from this detail, "the civilized Greek could be brave at the same time that he wept." For the rest, Lessing agreed with Winckelmann that nothing must impair the *beauty* of the figure.

Barry's Philoctetes fully obeys Lessing. He weeps (we see a tear under each eye), but his expression is undaunted to the point of fierceness. He is handsome, athletic, and healthy-looking. An innocent viewer could not guess that he has been on short rations for ten years. His wound seems altogether separate from the rest of his body, an impression sustained by his vigorous physique. The bandage around his foot is scrupulously tidy and fresh. His rags are ragged in the best of taste; his quiver suggests a recent and advantageous purchase; the dead bird on the ground looks adorable. Barry's composition is academically harmonious. He pays special homage to ancient Greece by seating Philoctetes on a stone fragment into which two Greek figures have been delicately chiseled.[15] Nevertheless, our gaze returns to the scowl that accuses the gods: "Behold your work!" says the scowl, while the victim's display of his wound, which is clearly addressed to the Olympians, repeats the indictment. A cloud-swept sky bears witness. However, unbeknownst to Philoctetes, Odysseus and Neoptolemus are approaching in their sailing vessel. As with most anecdotal paintings, the spectator is asked to carry in his memory a heavy load of information, but if he does so in this particular case, he will conclude that the sailboat is the gods' reply to Philoctetes' accusation—a reply soon to become manifest and to restore their honor.

1774–75. Barry's emulsion, if I may so call it, of the fierce and the neat can legitimately be read as pointing either toward the yet more lucid neoclassicism of the Davidian school, or on the contrary toward outright Romanticism. No such ambiguity marks our next representation of Philoctetes. In contrast to Barry, and in refutation of both Winckelmann and Lessing, the Dane Nicolai Abildgaard (1744–1809), working in Rome, painted a Philoctetes (pl. 8) in which Sturm und Drang prevails over the ideals of calm fortitude and virile beauty. This work is now at the State Museum of Copenhagen. A preliminary study for it also survives. Abildgaard's Philoctetes, nude, ugly, contorted, hunched over, clutches his foot with a massive hand (whereas Barry's hero daintily unrolls his neat bandage)—and *opens his mouth*. I have seen no more exciting visual representation of the marooned hero than this Philoctetes, who, throwing neoclassical dignity to the winds, anticipates the *terribilità* of the later Goya.

What follows, however, is a predominantly French period of interest in Philoctetes during which the neoclassical ideals of a grave purity and

---

15. Professor Fehl has plausibly suggested to me, in a private communication, that one of the two figures may be that of Iphigenia, another sacrifice to the Greek cause. For the tears, see the epigram concerning Parrhasios (Part I, section 17), where the "dry" tear may reasonably be interpreted as a tear frozen in its track. True to his time and temper, Barry chose to lean on the most polite of the three epigrams I have quoted. The other two are distinctly more brutal.

luminous polish are firmly illustrated. Much of the work listed below can be connected with the influence and sometimes the direct tutorship of Jacques Louis David, and then again with the École des Beaux-Arts, the Académie des Beaux-Arts, and the Académie de France à Rome, to which the winners of the Grand Prix de Rome were sent. These artists were expected to explore new and sometimes obscure mythological and historical subjects—not so obscure, however, as to be unavailable in a variety of handbooks and other aids to flagging memories. It is not easy to guess at the precise source or sources of their Philoctetes paintings and sculptures: the handbooks, Homer, Ovid, Dio, Hyginus. . . . As everyone knew his *Télémaque,* and as Fénelon's work was in general a favorite source, we may surmise that several artists took their Sophocles through this intermediary. One hopes that some went more directly to the Greek master through the translations of Brumoy or La Harpe. One or two may have read Sophocles in Latin or even Greek. However, an article by Henry Bardon suggests that Greek tragedy, then as two centuries before, still lagged far behind other classical sources as a stimulant to artists.[16] And it is not excluded that an artist here and there simply filched the subject of Philoctetes from another without further ceremony of any kind!

1784. *Ulysse et Néoptolème enlèvent à Philoctète les flèches d'Hercule (Odysseus and Neoptolemus Take the Arrows of Hercules from Philoctetes)* by Jean-Joseph Taillasson (1745–1809). This was Taillasson's reception piece on the occasion of his election to the Académie, and was exhibited at the Salon of 1785 (pl. 9).[17] Taillasson's operatic work—the term imposes itself again—illustrates neither Sophocles nor Fénelon directly, since neither of these authors allows Odysseus to be present when Philoctetes wakes from his swoon—for I take this to be the episode narrated by the painter. We may instead consider the picture as a composite of two or three episodes. Once again we note the outcast's athletic vigor. The contrast here is not between good health and decay, but between near nudity and the splendid regalia—as if out of a baroque entertainment

---

16. Henry Bardon, "Les peintures à sujets antiques au dix-huitième siècle d'après les livrets de salons," *Gazette des beaux-arts,* April 1963, pp. 217–50. Bardon notes that the library of the Académie in Rome owned *Télémaque* (as indeed goes without saying), but he does not mention La Harpe, and I cannot ascertain from his article whether the library held a set of the Greek tragedians, either in the original or in translation. A recent investigation by Dr. Anne Wagner suggests that it did not, or, if it did, that the tragedies were seldom if ever consulted (private communication).

17. Every year since 1737 the Academy organized a vast exhibition of works of art, selected by a jury.

on some Roman theme—of Philoctetes' interlocutors. Neoptolemus, we gather, is pointing towards Troy and glory to come, while Odysseus appears to be explaining and justifying. This painting is at the museum of the small town of Blaye, near Bordeaux, Taillasson's birthplace.

1788. *Philoctète accusant les dieux (Philoctetes Accuses the Gods)* by Jean-Germain Drouais (1763–88), who painted this work in Rome, where he spent the last three years of his short life. It is now at the museum of Chartres (pl. 10). Drouais's picture is strongly influenced by Barry, whose intentions the French painter obviously read much as I have.[18] For good measure, however, Drouais threw in the Boethos motif—the fanning of the wound—which he could have seen in one of the Lombardo reliefs, or in a copy of the gem.

1789. *Pyrrhus apercevant Philoctète dans son antre, à l'isle de Lemnos (Neoptolemus Discovers Philoctetes in His Cave, on the Island of Lemnos)* by Pierre-Henri de Valenciennes (1750–1819), a painter known in his day as "the David of landscape art." This picture, shown at the Salon of 1789, was sold in Paris in 1933. Its present location is unknown. A comment from a contemporary critic—"How crude and mannered is the form of that sky! And how that sea is sharply broken at the horizon!"—tells us that this was in fact essentially a landscape with small figures, similar to the Michallon to be discussed below.

The subject of Philoctetes lay neglected during the "hot" years of the revolution, when Roman history was the prevailing source of patriotic inspiration. But a new start was made in the last years of the Directory.

1798. *Philoctète dans l'île déserte de Lemnos, gravissant les rochers pour avoir un oiseau qu'il a tué (Philoctetes on the Desert Island of Lemnos, Scaling the Rocks in Order to Reach a Bird He has Killed)*, a vast canvas by Lethière (Guillaume Guillon, 1760–1832), exhibited at the Salon of 1798, latterly at the Musée Ochier in Cluny, but now transferred to the Louvre, where this sadly worn painting is currently in restoration.[19] A variant of this work was once in the collection of Lucien Bonaparte. It is lost, but an engraving made after it can be seen in the *Galerie de Lucien Bonaparte*, printed in London in 1812.

Lethière's great merit is to have represented Philoctetes without cosmetics, unprettily, as a wild, disheveled hunter. C. P. Landon asserts that the artist took his subject from La Harpe's translation of Sopho-

---

18. I saw Drouais's work *after* writing the interpretation of Barry's work printed here; hence it constitutes a useful independent corroboration.

19. A photograph of the picture made as workers were preparing it for delivery to the Louvre has been kindly given me by Mr. J. Foucart.

cles, and quotes the passage which is being illustrated.[20] Lethière's willingness to be rugged is in itself evidence that he allowed Sophocles rather than Fénelon to inspire him. Or to do so, at any rate, for the two works I have mentioned so far. For a third version, a small preliminary painting at the Musée municipal of Brest (pl. 11) suggests that Lethière did some hurried reading between this initial version (a splendid one, to be sure) and the two definitive works; for the Brest version shows us a Lear-like Philoctetes—as haggard and ragged as we can wish him to be, but quite old enough to be the prince's father, if not his grandfather. While rejuvenating his figure for the definitive paintings, Lethière also substituted a dead bird for the goat of the Brest version, although a flight of birds does cross the sky in the latter. Sophocles, it will be remembered, emphasizes the hunting of birds, and though he mentions mountain animals in general, he does not specify goats. Be that as it may, the respective positions of goat and hunter in the Brest version give Philoctetes good cause to despond. How can he ever reach the beast? Whether or not Lethière intended to raise this question, his is an exemplary work in that "pathetic classicism" which was shortly to evolve in France into full-blown romanticism.[21] It also escapes from the threefold distinction I have made, in that figure and landscape are evenly balanced here: the exchange between them is a dramatic one of matched antagonists.

1800. *Neoptolemus et Ulysse enlevant à Philoctète les flèches d'Hercule (Neoptolemus and Odysseus Take the Arrows of Hercules From Philoctetes)*, by Francois-Xavier Fabre (1766–1837). This large-scale painting, at one time in the collection of Charles X, was transferred in 1980 from the French embassy at the Vatican to the Louvre.[22] While Fabre chose the same subject as Taillasson, the spirit is antithetical both to Taillasson and to Winckelmann idealism, and true to the character of Sophocles' work: classicism as practiced by the classics themselves. For Fabre's Philoctetes is genuinely eaten-up by his suffering. For once, the very ribs show through the flesh. Lethière, instead, had been unable to forego the customary heroic build. Fabre's personage stretches a pair

---

20. *Annales du Musée et de l'école moderne des beaux-arts*, 2d ed., *École française moderne*, vol. 2, (Paris, 1833). Landon's discussion is supported by an engraving (pl. 19) which he mistakenly refers to the Cluny-Louvre version, but which is actually based on the Lucien Bonaparte version.

21. Lethière's two or three Philocteteses must have enjoyed some notoriety, for as late as 1814 a caricature was sold as a colored print exhibiting Napoleon relegated on *his* Lemnos, the island of Elba.

22. A clear photograph was not obtainable at the time of this writing.

of bony hands toward his tormentors. But Odysseus has grasped Neoptolemus by the wrist to drag him toward the ship making ready to sail nearby. Neoptolemus, holding the stolen quiver, casts a pitying glance at the desperate wretch who implores him. This comes closer to Sophocles' keystone scene than any other visual representation known to me. Still, Fabre's brush does not hint that Neoptolemus will yank his arm from his master's clutch. We are left with pure pathos rather than moral daring. A preparatory drawing exists in a private collection in Brescia.

1806. Philoctetes was the subject that year for the Prix de Rome in sculpture. The Grand Prix was won by P. F. G. Giraud (1783–1836) with a *Philoctète quittant l'île de Lemnos pour aller au siège de Troie (Philoctetes Leaving the Island of Lemnos to Go to the Siege of Troy)*. A bronze copy was shown at the Exposition Centenniale de l'Art Français in 1900. A photograph preserved at the Musée d'Orsay in Paris reveals that Philoctetes is standing bent over, one hand holding his leg just below the knee, and leaning with the other against his bow. The only noteworthy feature of this routine creation is that not the foot but the lower leg is bandaged, a minor solecism which does not seem to have caused any alarm.[23]

Like the other prizes that will be listed below—Philoctetes posed as a subject until 1873—Giraud's work was placed in the Salle des Grands Prix de Sculpture of the École des Beaux-Arts in Paris, a hall that was sacked by the young iconoclasts of 1968—perhaps the finest compliment these all too respectable monuments had been paid in a century. The fragments and surviving works are now collected in the school's basement, waiting to be sorted out.[24]

1807. A statue of Philoctetes by the Austrian artist Johann N. Schaller (1777–1842) is in the Oesterreichische Galerie in Vienna. I have not seen this work.

1807. *Philoctète*, painted by Pierre-Paul Prudhon (1758–1823), located at the art museum of Ponce, Puerto-Rico. This academic life-

---

23. There is a line drawing in Landon's *Annales du Musée et de l'école moderne des beaux-arts*, vol. 12 (Paris, 1815), pl. 68.

24. While this volume was in press, Professor H. W. Janson kindly communicated to me the Philoctetes entries which have emerged from the subject index for Stanislas Lami's *Dictionnaire des sculpteurs de l'école française au dix-neuvième siècle*, 4 vols., (Paris: E. Champion, 1914–21) currently being compiled under his direction. It appears that the École des Beaux-Arts set the subject of Philoctetes for its sculpture prizes as early as 1797, for Lami reports that a bas-relief by F. Milhomme showing the theft of the hero's weapon won the second prize in that year. Later prizewinners mentioned by Lami are Cortot

study par excellence of a most virile youth (pl. 14) can be recognized as a Philoctetes only because he holds a bow in one hand and because of a bandaged foot which the painter has, however, moved into the background. Sinning in reverse of Lethière, Prudhon has made Philoctetes too young—young enough to be Neoptolemus. One is tempted to wonder whether the artist had consulted any source at all.[25]

1810. *Philoctète dans l'île de Lemnos* by Nicolas-André Monsiau (1754–1837), exhibited at the Salon of that year. Its content and location are unknown.

1810. Also lost is another painting bearing the same title, this one by Louis-Pierre Baltard (1764–1846). The catalogue of the exhibition calls it an "historical landscape." It may be supposed that the Monsiau and Baltard were both in the tradition that will be illustrated below by Michallon.

1810. At the same Salon, Louis-Marie Dupaty (1771–1825) exhibited a statue of Philoctetes which can be seen today in the gardens of the Château de Compiègne (pl. 16).

1812. Edmé Gois (1765–1836) exhibited a statue of Philoctetes at the Salons of 1812 and 1814. I have not seen the line drawing, which appears in C. P. Landon's *Salon de 1812*.

1812. Another entry at the Salon was a study of *Philoctète dans l'île de Lemnos* by one Hyppolite Pochon, reported as "active" between 1810 and 1819.

1812. Giacomo Spalla (1755–1834) made a sculpture, no longer extant, of the wounded Philoctetes for the king of Bohemia.

1812. *Philoctetes and Neoptolemus at Lemnos,* a watercolor by William Blake (1757–1827) now at the Fogg Museum, Harvard (pl. 12). I believe it is the only illustration of a play by Sophocles in Blake's entire body of works. As is to be expected, stylistically it lies wholly outside the academic tradition. Moreover, as far as subject is concerned, Blake's representation is the only one known to me in which members of the chorus are portrayed, and in which Philoctetes is beardless. But did Blake intend to illustrate a particular passage in the play? If so, it is

---

(1806), Pradier, Flatters and Lebon (1813), and Roguet and Maniglier (1848). Outside the École, Lami mentions three Philoctetes sculptures, namely by Pollet (before 1836), Ménard (1872), and Peinte (1873). The reader will easily coordinate this belated information with my survey in the text. No innovative conceptions of Philoctetes seem to occur.

25. In a private communication, Dr. René Taylor, director of the museum, has expressed his doubt whether the painting, though signed, is really by Prudhon.

difficult to determine which one. A catalogue description unhesitatingly informs us that Philoctetes is pointing the arrow at his own breast, and that Neoptolemus looks on in horror.[26] I, however, cannot tell at whom this toy-shop instrument is being aimed (if at anyone), nor what precise emotion is stirring Neoptolemus. Whatever one's interpretation, Blake's watercolor ("but lightly tinted, almost entirely in grey") seems rather a composite—like Taillasson's version—than an illustration.

1814. A mosaic, *Philoctète dans l'île de Lemnos,* by Francesco Belloni (1772–1845) appeared at the Salon.

1816. The French royal house ordered a statue of Philoctetes from the sculptor Jean-Joseph Espercieux (1758–1840). This subject may have been particularly attractive to a monarch who had just regained his throne after a long exile. Like Dupaty's work, Espercieux's statue stands today in the gardens of the Château de Compiègne (pl. 17).

1819. *Philoctète dans l'île de Lemnos* by Jean-Charles-Joseph Rémond (1795–1875). The catalogue for the Salon of 1819 calls this painting a "paysage historique," but no description is available and its location is unknown. However, Rémond's own invocation is printed, and it gives us a sense of his work: "O rugged cliffs, it is to you that I send my complaints; you are accustomed to my groans; I harbor a wound that devours me, and hope lies dead in my heart." It may be inferred from this outcry that Rémond had painted an idle Philoctetes.

1822. It was otherwise with Achille-Etna Michallon (1795–1822), whose *Philoctète se traînant sur les rochers de Lemnos pour ramasser une colombe qu'il a percée de ses flèches (Philoctetes Crawling on the Rocks of Lemnos to Pick Up a Dove He Has Pierced with His Arrows)* gave Philoctetes his customary activity, but seen from a distance so as to permit a view of an idyllic landscape in the best neoclassical manner (pl. 13). One might well envy Philoctetes in such a setting. Were it not for the ominous *se traînant* in the title, our innocent viewer could easily interpret the picture as that of some happy noble savage—almost an American Indian as he was rhapsodized by sentimentalists. For Michallon has also kept faith with the academic tradition by depicting an immaculately robust Philoctetes. On the other hand, if the flora hardly looks Lemnian, was Michallon really untrue to the spirit of the place which Sophocles evokes in his epilogue, "O my streams and my Lycian spring. . . ."?

---

26. For a Blake exhibition held at the Philadelphia Museum of Art in 1939. *William Blake: A Descriptive Catalogue.* . . . (Philadelphia: Museum of Art, 1939), p. 128.

1825. The museum of Angers has a large *Philoctète dans l'île de Lemnos* by Auguste-Hyacinthe de Bay (1804–65). While de Bay has no improvement to offer on the tradition of muscle and tendon (pl. 18), he puzzles by making Philoctetes gesture toward the vessel riding at large. The shape of the sail suggests that the ship is leaving Lemnos behind, and this view is seconded by the rather fanciful flow of our hero's cloak, indicating the wind's direction. It follows that we are seeing Philoctetes at the time he was shipped by Odysseus from Chryse to Lemnos, and there abandoned. It follows too that Philoctetes is asking the gods to witness the perfidy and cruelty of the Greeks. For once, too, we can accept the sturdy, well-dieted body, for Philoctetes has not yet begun to starve. Unfortunately, the ship's prow is headed *toward* the island! Did de Bay intend after all to portray the return of Odysseus, and thus the *last* days of the hero's ordeal? But if this is admitted, his attitude becomes equivocal. We cannot tell whether he is thankful, irritated, fearful, or merely perplexed.

Around 1830. *Philoctète blessé dans l'île de Lemnos* by Antoine-Jean Gros (1771–1835), at the museum of Marseille. In the Baron Gros's huge oil no ship at all is visible, but David's faithful partisan drearily repeats that facile eloquence of the arm flung out toward the gods.

1833. An unfinished sculpture of Philoctetes by Pierre-Charles Simart (1806–57), location unknown; but a correspondent, writing to Simart, cited Ingres's interesting critique: "All you saw in Philoctetes was an ordinary wounded man who had been suffering for ten years. You were wrong to make him thin and emaciated, even *uncombed* [mal peigné]. Why did you dwell on this detail? This is a hero; he knows how to bear up under pain. He is not of the same kind [du même sang] as other men; he must be handsome."[27] One's curiosity about Simart's sculpture is whetted by this remorselessly Winckelmannic attack.

1833. The École des Beaux-Arts assigned five stanzas from Sophocles—they concern Philoctetes bewailing the theft of his weapon—as the subject for its local Concours de Composition—a sketching competition for sculpture students. The students were allowed to choose the specific moment of the hero's tirade for their sketch. I do not know whether any of these drawings survive.

1840. The volume is raised, so to speak, by David Scott (1806–49) in his Promethean *Philoctetes Left in the Isle of Lemnos*, owned by the National Gallery of Edinburgh. His is still the life-class manner, but this

---

27. Quoted from Gustave Eyriès's *Simart* (Paris, 1860) by Madame Le Normand in a private communication.

time Géricault and Delacroix have contributed their sensationalism to the concept. Our warrior is writhing on a rocky ledge, one leg plunged into the Aegean and his head thrown back, while half a dozen outbound sails line up on the horizon.[28]

1844. The subject for the sketching competition at the Ecole des Beaux-Arts was a conventional *Philoctetes Abandoned on the Island of Lemnos.*

1848. The Grand Prix de Rome in sculpture was awarded to Gabriel-Jules Thomas (1824–1905) for another *Philoctète partant pour le siège de Troie.* Thomas's work vanished with the rest in 1968, but a surviving photograph shows Philoctetes vigorously striding, though with bandaged foot.

Around 1849. A picture of Philoctetes sitting on a rock, leaning on one hand while the other, inevitably, stretches into space, was painted by Alejandro Cicarelli (1811–74), a Neapolitan who had become drawing master to the empress of Brazil, where he created this work before moving to Chile to assume the post of director of the recently created Academia Chilena de Pintura. I do not know whether this Philoctetes is to be found in Brazil or Chile.[29]

1852. Again Philoctetes appeared at the École des Beaux-Arts as the subject for the Prix de Rome in sculpture. The first prize went to a *Philoctète à Lemnos* by Alfred Lepère (1827–1904). Although this too disappeared in 1968, a drawing in *L'illustration* (1852, no. 2, p. 252) reveals the usual woebegone figure sitting on his rock. Lepère added a wave or two lapping at the stone. The hero's left hand clutches his brow. His face shows intense suffering. Helmet and quiver lie on the ground.

1852. The second prize was given to a far more important artist, namely Jean-Baptiste Carpeaux (1827–75), whose *Philoctète blessé s'abandonnant à sa douleur (The Wounded Philoctetes Surrenders to His Pain)* can still be seen at the museum of Valenciennes (pl. 15). Interestingly, Carpeaux drew on a tradition going as far back as Pythagoras of Rhegium (see "The Tradition," n. 26) to give Philoctetes a stick to lean on—though admittedly the thought might have come to him unaided.

---

28. Scott's painting is reproduced in several texts, among them Graham Reynolds's *Victorian Painting* (London: Studio Vista, 1966).

29. This exotic item is mentioned by Robert Rosenblum in his *Transformations in late Eighteenth Century Art* (Princeton, N.J.: Princeton University Press, 1967), pp. 13–14. A poor photograph can be seen in Juan de Contreras, Marqués de Lozoya, *Historia del arte hispanico,* vol. 5 (Barcelona: Salvat, 1949), p. 573.

In any event, the required slickness and vigor of the body trivializes this element. Philoctetes looks like a blooming warrior temporarily disabled by having stepped on a thistle. Instead, a much smaller plaster provides a more powerful evocation of our hero.[30]

1873. The prize this year was awarded for a bas-relief rather than a "rond de bosse" ("in the round"—a statue). As a result, it was possible to set a more dramatic subject, to wit *Philoctète ramené au camp par Ulysse et Neoptolème, pansé par Machaon (Philoctetes Brought Back to Camp by Odysseus and Neoptolemus, and Bandaged by Machaon).* Jean Idrac (1849–84) received the first prize.

1873. The second prize was awarded to Jean Hughes (1849–1930). A photograph of his creditable bas-relief survives at the Musée d'Orsay in Paris (pl. 19). Both the Idrac and Hughes vanished in 1968.

Around 1874. *Der verwundete, auf der Insel Lemnos ausgesetzte Philoktet (The Wounded Philoctetes Relegated to the Island of Lemnos),* a pencil drawing by Friedrich Preller (1804–74) intended for an edition of the *Iliad* which never appeared. It belongs to a private collection.[31]

Other German or Austrian representations than the two I have found undoubtedly exist, or existed, but even though German artists flocked to Rome as eagerly as the French, they seem to have shown only sporadic interest in Greek mythology. The massive catalogue for an exhibit, held at Darmstadt in 1914, of German baroque and rococo art from 1650 to 1800, offers the occasional *Diana and Actaeon, Amor and Bacchus, Aurora,* and even an *Iphigenia;* but—and a large number of other catalogues I have consulted confirm this impression—German art seems to have jumped, by and large, from Christian subjects to idyllic or ecstatic landscapes, domestic scenes, and romantic narratives, with only exceptional pauses for Graeco-Roman subjects on the way. I doubt therefore that a host of Germanic Philoctetes works will be uncovered, or, furthermore, that many such representations will be forthcoming from the Low Countries or even Italy, where mythological subjects had rapidly fallen behind Christian, Biblical, historical, novelistic and domestic motifs, besides portraits and landscapes.

Our panorama of representations reveals that the Philoctetes legend

---

30. It is reproduced—along with the full-size sculpture—in the *Catalogue des peintures et sculptures de J. B. Carpeaux à Valenciennes* (Valenciennes: Musée des Beaux-Arts, 1978).

31. This drawing is listed but not reproduced in *Gedächtnis-Ausstellung zur 150. Wiederkehr des Geburtstages F. Preller d. Ä* (Heidelberg: Kurpfälziches Museum, 1954). The reader may be reminded at this point that I have not made a search of text illustrations, either for Homer or any other author.

was but timidly explored by artists. Variety is not altogether lacking, and even a touch of drama appears now and then. But in general, painters and sculptors continued to dwell, like the ancients, on the sheer pathos of Philoctetes' plight. Now that interest in saints had declined, the holy eremite or the martyr could be replaced by Philoctetes on Lemnos, just as the Virgin and Child had been secularized into ordinary family groups. Moreover, the idyllic predilections of the times usually kept Philoctetes from appearing truly weather-beaten and devastated, and the island from looking genuinely barren. Almost every dramatic confrontation provided by Sophocles was ignored. If the evidence so far available stands, neither the fury of Philoctetes, nor the bluster and cowardice of Odysseus, nor the agony of Neoptolemus— here Fabre is the honorable exception—nor the solemn though aborted departure of the two new allies, nor even the appearance of Heracles, impressed themselves on neoclassical artists. A more dramatic and ethically active approach might have recommended itself to the school of Delacroix, but the Romantics were yielding Greece and Rome to their foes and conquering the Near East instead.

Most significant of all, no one sought out the heart of Sophocles to portray the pivotal scene—magnificently pictorial—of Neoptolemus returning the bow to Philoctetes. Once again I note the astonishing blotting out of this scene from the consciousness of those who tangled with the Philoctetes matter from the time of Sophocles himself (if the surviving evidence is representative) to the second half of the nineteenth century. We have seen that Fénelon and Chateaubrun eliminated it altogether. Sophocles' translators could not do this, of course; but they could and did blind themselves to its true meaning. Brumoy, for instance, introducing the play to his readers in the 1730 translation of the complete Sophocles, merely pointed to the contrast between the political cunning of Odysseus and the *sincerity* and *generosity* of Neoptolemus; and La Harpe quoted his remark approvingly, without additional comment, in 1781. The notion of a betrayal of the Greek cause in the name of a higher ideal never hove into view.

As far as painters and sculptors are concerned, allowance must be made for the possibility, already noted, that a few of them had not read Sophocles to begin with. But once this discount has been granted, I think it is not bombastic to speak of "mass repression," even if the mass—of artists, of poets, of scholars—is on the whole a small one, and even if the repression affected a secondary hero like Philoctetes or Neoptolemus. Thought repression occurs in corners as well as center-stage, and we are sometimes signaled to the realities of a civilization through a revelatory incident in a back street. The incident which our

PLATE 1. Back of Etruscan mirror. Philoctetes is healed. *Museo Civico, Bologna. Photo Giraudon, Paris*

PLATE 2. Hermonax, Vase painting. Philoctetes is bitten by the serpent. Mid-fifth century B.C. *Musée du Louvre, Paris. Photo Giraudon, Paris*

PLATE 3. Hermonax. Vase painting. Agamemnon kills the serpent. *Musée du Louvre, Paris. M. Chuzeville Photo*

PLATE 4. Silver cup (the Hoby cup). Odysseus and Diomedes steal the bow from Philoctetes. Rome, Augustan age. *Nationalmuseet, Copenhagen. Reproduced by permission of the Danish National Museum. Photo by Lennart Larsen*

PLATE 5. Silver Cup (the Hoby cup). *Nationalmuseet, Copenhagen. Reproduced by permission of the Danish National Museum. Photo by Lennart Larsen*

PLATE 6. Antonio Lombardo (?). Bas-relief of Philoctetes. After 1506.
H. 41 cm. *Victoria and Albert Museum, London*

PLATE 7.   James Barry. *Philoctetes.* Oil. 1770. H. 228 cm, w. 157 cm. *Accademia Clementina, Bologna*

PLATE 8. Nicolai Abildgaard. *Philoctetes.* Oil. 1774–75. H. 123 cm, w. 173 cm. *Statens Museum for Kunst, Copenhagen. Photo by Hans Petersen*

PLATE 9. Jean-Joseph Taillasson. *Odysseus and Neoptolemus Take the Arrows of Hercules from Philoctetes.* Oil. 1784. H. 277 cm, w. 211 cm. *Musée d'Histoire et d'Art du Pays Blayais. Photo by J. Rochin*

PLATE 10.   Jean-Germain Drouais. *Philoctetes Accuses the Gods.* Oil. 1788.
H. 225 cm, w. 176 cm. *Musée des Beaux-Arts, Chartres. Photo by Igor Delmas*

PLATE 11. Lethière (Guillaume Guillon). *Philoctetes on Lemnos.* Oil. 1798(?). H. 34 cm, w. 44 cm. *Musée Municipal, Brest. Cliché des Musées Nationaux, Paris*

PLATE 12. William Blake. *Philoctetes and Neoptolemus at Lemnos.* Water-color. 1812. H. 31 cm, w. 42 cm. *Fogg Museum, Harvard University. Photo courtesy of the Fogg Art Museum, Harvard University. Bequest of Grenville L. Winthrop*

PLATE 13. Achille-Etna Michallon. *Philoctetes Crawling on the Rocks to Pick Up a Dove He Has Pierced with His Arrows.* Oil. 1822. H. 67 cm, w. 98 cm. *Musée Fabre, Montpellier. Cliché des Musées Nationaux, Paris*

PLATE 14. Pierre-Paul Prudhon. *Philoctetes.* Oil. 1807. H. 160 cm, w.
127 cm. *Museo de Arte, Ponce, Puerto Rico*

PLATE 15. Jean-Baptiste Carpeaux. *The Wounded Philoctetes Surrenders to His Pain.* Sculpture. 1852. H. 127 cm. *Musée des Beaux-Arts, Valenciennes Photo A. Wagner*

PLATE 16. Louis-Marie Dupaty. *Philoctetes*. Sculpture. 1810. H. 220 cm.
*Musée National du Château de Compïègne. Cliché des Musées Nationaux,
Paris*

PLATE 17. Jean-Joseph Espercieux. *Philoctetes*. Sculpture. 1816. H. 240 cm. *Musée National du Château de Compiègne. Cliché des Musées Nationaux, Paris*

PLATE 18. Auguste-Hyacinthe De Bay. *Philoctetes on the Island of Lemnos*. Oil. 1825. H. 220 cm, w. 270 cm. *Musée des Peintures, Angers. Cliché Musées d'Angers*

PLATE 19. Jean Hugues. *Philoctetes Brought Back to Camp by Odysseus and Neoptolemus, and Bandaged by Machaon*. Bas-relief. 1873. *Formerly at the École des Beaux-Arts, Paris. Photo courtesy of Documentation du Musée d'Orsay*

PLATE 20.   Production of *Philoctetes* at the University of California at Irvine, 1978, directed by David MacDonald. *Photo by Philip Channing*

study of Philoctetes has brought to light is a consistent, perhaps unconscious deflection from a perilous scene by the later Greeks, the Romans, and the men who rediscovered Philoctetes in modern times, even though the scene in question was standing out bold and clear as nothing less than the climax of the masterpiece they were interpreting.

When other representations of our legend are reported—for I must emphasize the preliminary status of this survey—they will undoubtedly cluster for the most part in the period between 1770 and 1830. By the mid-nineteenth century, Greek mythology and Roman history were gasping out their last breaths in European art. The authentic "voice" is not that of the École des Beaux-Arts clinging to Philoctetes as late as 1873, but, a few years afterwards, that of Odilon Redon, in one of whose finest works we watch Apollo dissolve into a dream of Apollo, as an immense tradition falls asleep forever. Illustrations for classical texts will always be made, of course, but it is hardly believable that Greek mythology will ever be fashionable again in ateliers and galleries.

6

Throughout the nineteenth century, editions and translations of *Philoctetes* multiplied. In Germany alone, besides nine or ten translations of the complete Sophocles, no fewer than seven separate translations of *Philoctetes* were published between 1750 and 1832, and the flow continued unabated in the following decades. No wonder that the beginnings and a first maturity of specific Philoctetes scholarship and criticism occurred in Germany. As we have seen, no corresponding effervescence is to be found in the theatrical world.

It would seem, however, that *Philoctetes* and other Greek plays were produced at universities like those of Berlin and Leipzig.[32] These events influenced a notable translation and performance by students of the Petit Séminaire of Orléans in 1855. It took place under the direction of Monsignor Dupanloup, bishop of Orléans and a distinguished humanist, at the Chapelle Saint-Mesmin, with music by Mendelssohn.[33] There is even a printed account of this apparently excellent production. Academic performances of *Philoctetes* were given in the following years in Marseilles, Agen, and Mortain, and then again

---

32. This valuable hint is in H. L. Nostrand's informative *Le Théâtre antique et à l'antique en France de 1840 à 1900* (Paris: Droz, 1934). I have had access to no similar study concerning German academic productions.

33. I do not know whether the *Antigone* music was adapted. Mendelssohn had also written incidental music for *Oedipus at Colonus*.

at the Petit Séminaire de Notre-Dame-des Champs in Paris in 1877. Translations made for these performances were regularly published, appearing beside translations of *Philoctetes* brought out independently of the stage.

Tieck's production of *Antigone* triggered similar efforts in London in 1845 (Covent Garden), 1850 (Drury Lane), and 1895 (Hampstead Conservatory)—each time with Mendelssohn's music; and another *Antigone* was produced at the Crystal Palace in 1890—not to mention the inevitable British burlesque, namely in 1845. But this seems to exhaust the subject of Greek drama in the professional theaters of London in the nineteenth century. Once again we must turn to the schools. Such plays as *Ajax, The Eumenides, Oedipus Tyrannus,* and *Iphigenia in Tauris* were mounted at Cambridge between 1882 and 1894; and it may well be that further search will unearth even a *Philoctetes*.

We reach the *Philoctète* of André Gide after crossing a last bridge. Sophocles' drama was performed at the Odéon, in Paris, on 19 November 1896, as one in a series of "matinées classiques" offered by the theater. The translation was by Pierre Quillard (1864–1912), Symbolist poet, classical scholar, journalist, and political activitist on behalf of the oppressed, from Dreyfus to the Macedonians. I cannot prove that Gide was in the audience, but the likelihood is strong, for the two men had been on friendly terms since at least 1891. They had probably met in or around Paul Fort's Théâtre d'Art, a stage on which the good battle against Naturalism was being fought. Fort's *Mémoires* indicate that Gide was present at a performance in December 1891 and a vigorous supporter of Fort against the philistines. In March 1892 Fort produced a playlet by Quillard. It was a small world, and the inference that Quillard and Gide had met by that time is a safe one. As it happens, it is known that the two writers saw each other at Mallarmé's legendary Tuesdays in the same period. Thereafter Gide embarks on his travels; but in April 1896 he reappears in Paris, hungry for the cultural life of the capital. He may just have missed Quillard's second Symbolist mini-drama, but as an old acquaintance and intellectual ally of Quillard's, we readily picture him at the November performance of *Philoctetes*, or at least as being acquainted with the translation. If he sat in the audience, was he stimulated by the oddity that the part of Neoptolemus was played by a girl? His own Neoptolemus is nothing if not girlish; but as Gide required no external guidance to make him so, this particular coincidence remains inconclusive. Be that as it may, the hitherto unexplored Gide-Quillard connection leads us to the interesting conjecture that it was a Sophocles revived on stage who inspired the young writer.

Quillard's translation was austerely pedantic. The play was called *Philoktètès*, Achilles was referred to as "Akhilleus," and words like *moira* were delivered in Greek. The reviewer for the *Figaro* expressed his particular admiration for "the *turnabout* of Neoptolemus, incomparably grand," calling it "an invention of Sophocles' exquisite soul"—proof that by the end of the century the repression I have spoken of had been lifted from men's minds. Another phrase suggests that even though Paris had probably seen no professional production of *Philoctetes* since 1826, the efforts of scholars, translators, editors, and artists had not failed of some effect: "As everyone will remember," wrote the critic, "this beautiful play is a very simple one." A casual phrase like "dans la mémoire de tous" is significant precisely because it is casual; it could not have slipped out if the reviewer had been discussing a Noh drama. It tells us, at any rate, that when Gide took up the story of Philoctetes, he knew that many and probably most of his readers would recognize his characters and recall the main features of Sophocles' story with or without an afternoon spent at the Odéon.

Part III

THE MODERN PHILOCTETES

Introduction

A cultural curiosity of our century is that the virtual extinction of Greek mythology in the visual arts has been offset by a renewed mythological vitality in all sectors of literature. In the theater, worldwide, Greek tragedies are enacted and reenacted as never before. Even Aeschylus, all but dead to the stage since ancient times, is regularly revived. At the same time, new playwrights retell the ancient tales for new purposes of their own. And others make up modern analogues to Greek myths.

I take it that all these manifestations—revivals, re-creations, and analogues—form but one phase of the larger phenomenon of experimental theater, literary quarterlies, avantgarde cinema, ensembles dedicated to the performance of medieval music—in short, the entire fabric of high-brow art, of eclectic intellectual elitism, which is a singular feature of our times, related to the world's exploding population of educated and quasieducated men and women.

But why did painters and sculptors abandon subjects which their literary comrades found so stimulating? Clearly, it is much easier to refresh a myth with new significances through words than by means of pictures. This is another way of saying that literature is a more philosophical art then either painting or sculpture, and it is precisely for philosophical purposes that writers have chosen to reinterpret Greek myths. But in addition, it will be remembered that many, if not most, contemporary visual artists have renounced, and indeed denounced, "anecdote" altogether in favor of the purely sensory. For them, Greek myths are excluded a priori.

Speculation aside, Philoctetes can be found in the literature of our times under each of the heads I have named. A special issue of the Athenian magazine *Thespis* (June 1966) reports productions of Sophocles' play in France, Great Britain, Sweden, and Japan, all in the 1960s.

153

I have no doubt that a diligent searcher would uncover other productions, before and since, especially in the universities. One performance of which I am aware was mounted by Professor David McDonald at the University of California at Irvine in 1978 (pl. 20), "as if directed by Machiavelli for the Florentine Academy at the Medici Palace of Careggi" and *also* as if Artaud had conceived the production—perhaps as fair an illustration as any of elitism at work![1]

On 11 December 1968, the British Broadcasting Corporation televised a Philoctetes analogue, namely a script by Tom Stoppard called *Neutral Grounds*.[2] A summary appeared in the May 1974 issue of *Theatercraft*:

> [*Neutral Grounds*] involves the attempt of a British agent Charles Acherson to bring Philo (a broken, ageing, ex-secret agent) back to England after he has been exiled by the secret service when suspected of being a double agent. He befriends Philo and offers to help him return to his home, a Russian-occupied territory, where he may live out his days. Just before Philo boards the train that will carry him not home, but back into the hands of the British secret service, Acherson confesses that it has all been a trick, and that he cannot betray Philo after he has suffered so many injustices by the British government. However, Philo, realizing the danger to Acherson if he does not go now that Acherson has warned him, resigns himself to his fate, leaving Acherson safe but disillusioned and guilt-ridden.

This script has not, to my knowledge, been printed.

Three modern re-creations of the Sophoclean tale, each with its own dramatic and thematic constitution, are presented in the following pages, and separately introduced. But two earlier versions should be mentioned here. *Der Bogen des Philoktet* [Philoctetes' bow] by Karl von Levetzow appeared in 1909. Here, after Neoptolemus has returned the bow to the wounded hero, a transfigured Philoctetes returns it to him. No one has been able to stretch it before (a touch from the *Odyssey*, perhaps); that prowess is reserved for the man who does a deed worthy of Heracles. This the generous Neoptolemus has performed by surrendering the bow. The weapon now obedient in his hand, the young

---

1. This adaptation was given five performances in 1978–79, among them one at Stanford University and another at the Santa Cruz campus of the University of California. A different adaptation, with a contemporary perspective, was performed under Professor McDonald's direction on three occasions in 1980. Instead of limping, for instance, Philoctetes was confined to a wheelchair, and the play was pointed at the Vietnam War.

2. I am indebted to Professor Ruby Cohn for bringing this play to my attention.

man departs for Troy and victory, while Philoctetes hurls himself into the sea!

A *Philoktet* by Rudolf Pannwitz (1913) is briefly and none too auspiciously described by Karl Heinemann in the second volume of his *Tragischen Gestalten der Griechen in der Weltliteratur* (Leipzig, 1920). This brings to six the number of new Philoctetes versions I have located. Finally, however, notice must be taken of the unprecedented wealth of editions and translations, and of the scholarship and criticism lavished on *Philoctetes* in our times—some of which I have touched upon in the first part of this volume. A comprehensive bibliography remains to be undertaken.

André Gide

PHILOCTETES OR THE TREATISE ON THREE ETHICS (1898)

Translated by Jackson Mathews
from *Philoctète; ou, Le traité des trois morales*

André Gide (1869–1951) wrote a dozen plays in his long and fertile career, beginning with *Saül* in 1897–98 and ending with *Robert; ou, L'intérêt général*, composed from 1934 to 1940 and first published in 1944–45.[1] *Philoctète* was his second attempt at drama. Originally announced under the title *Le traité de l'immonde blessure* [Treatise of the foul wound], it appeared under its present title in the *Revue Blanche*—one of the most notable journals of letters and graphics of its time—on 1 December 1898. Its first publication in book form occurred in 1899, when it was printed together with several other works by Gide. In an anthology of his writings published in 1948, Gide remarked in a note that he had not intended his play for the stage. J. C. McLaren reports three performances, however: the first in a private theater in Paris in 1919; the second, a reading at the Comédie des Champs-Elysées in 1937; the third, a reading with drawings of the three protagonists projected on a screen, again in Paris in 1921. These were all one-time performances.

We have seen that by 1898 a writer could recuperate the long-neglected central thought in Sophocles' work without anxiety and indeed without a sense of conquest, and firmly subordinate patriotism to some other value of his choosing. Gide's subtitle invites us to look for alternatives in his text.

In the figure of Ulysses, Gide follows the lead of Sophocles, inasmuch as his Ithacan is a noble representative of the ethic of patriotism, but loses the argument against his betters. Presently, however, Gide begins to diverge from the Greek. His second ethic seems to make its appearance in act 4, when Neoptolemus betrays Ulysses' plot to

---

1. For further background on Gide and *Philoctète*, see James C. McLaren, *The Theater of André Gide, Evolution of a Moral Philosopher* (Baltimore, Md.: Johns Hopkins University Press, 1953); and Helen Watson-Williams, *André Gide and the Greek Myths* (Oxford: Oxford University Press, Clarendon Press, 1967).

Philoctetes. "I love you and am trying to save you," he cries. And he asks Philoctetes, "Do you love me? Say, Philoctetes, is that what virtue is?" The love of one's country is here displaced by personal love. This differs from Sophocles, who, in a more severe voice, speaks of honor; yet it should be remembered that in the Greek text a powerful compassion—love, if we so wish to think of it—is the psychological force which awakens the young man's vision of his real duty. The divergence remains a genuine one, but Gide's second ethic does not remove us to another planet.

His third ethic does. The inverted pyramid comes to a point: from broad social love to individual love and then finally to self-love. "My only care is to be," says Philoctetes. He relishes his fine phrases and his deep thinking (art and intellect) all by himself. He is that familiar figure of Symbolism, the lone prince in his castle. His "acte gratuit" of drinking the potion insures that the bow will be removed and that he will be left alone. That is when the flowers break through the ice and the birds come down to feed him. This almost Christian embroidery to Gide's Symbolist fervor is not inappropriate, for Philoctetes has become the perfect anchorite. It hardly needs to be added that praising a life cut off from the polis would have seemed to Sophocles and any other Greek pure madness.[2]

---

2. A similar distrust of love is perceptible in *Saul* and the slightly later *King Candaules.* In the first of these, the Witch of Endor warns the hero against love, and in the second, the monarch makes the mistake of lovingly sharing his happiness with someone else, and is stabbed to death for his reward.

CHARACTERS

NEOPTOLEMUS
ULYSSES
PHILOCTETES

Act 1

A level waste of snow and ice; a low gray sky.

SCENE 1

[ULYSSES *and* NEOPTOLEMUS]

NEOPTOLEMUS. Everything is ready, Ulysses. The boat is moored. I left it in deep water, sheltered on the north, for fear the wind might freeze the sea around it. This island is so cold it seems to be inhabited by nothing but birds along the sea cliffs; but I took the precaution to tie up the boat in a spot where no one passing along the coast could see it.

My mind too is made up; it is ready for sacrifice. Speak now, Ulysses, and tell me; all is ready. For fourteen days, you have been leaning on the oars or the tiller, perfectly silent except for the sharp words of command needed to steer us out of danger of waves. Faced with your obstinate silence, I soon ceased to ask questions; I understood that a great sadness was oppressing your dear spirit, because you were taking me toward death. And I fell silent too, feeling that all our words were too quickly swept away by the wind over the immensity of the sea. I waited. I saw the beautiful shore of Skyros falling way behind us, beyond the horizon of the sea; then the islands of golden sand or stone, which I loved because I thought they were like Pylos; thirteen times I saw the sun go down in the sea; and each morning it rose from paler waves, mounted less high, more slowly, until at last, on the fourteenth morning, we waited for it in vain; and ever since then we have been living, as it were, beyond night and day. We have seen ice floating on the sea, and were unable to sleep because of the constant pale glimmer; the only words I heard from you then were

163

those that signaled icebergs to be avoided by the stroke of an oar. But speak now, Ulysses! My spirit is prepared, not like the goats of Bacchus led to the sacrifice covered with festal ornaments, but like Iphigenia advancing to the altar, simple, decent, and unadorned. To be sure, since, like her, I wish to die for my country without complaint, I should have preferred to die among the Greeks, in a land bright with sunshine, and to show, by accepting death, all my respect for the gods and all the beauty of my spirit; it is valiant and has not fought. It is hard to die without glory. Yet, O gods! I hold no bitterness; though reluctantly, I have left everything, men, sun-warmed shores . . . and now, coming to this inhospitable island, with no trees, no sunlight, where every green thing is covered with snow, where everything is frozen, and the sky so blank, so gray, it is like another plain of snow stretched above us, far away from everything . . . this seems like death already, here; every hour my mind has been growing so much colder, and purer, all passion gone, that now nothing is left but for the body to die.

Ulysses, at least tell me that Zeus, mysterious Zeus, will be appeased by my faithful death and will give victory to the Greeks; at least you will tell them, won't you, Ulysses! tell them that is why I died without fear . . . you will tell them. . .

ULYSSES. Child, you are not here to die. Don't smile. Now I can tell you. Listen to me and don't interrupt. Would that the gods might be satisfied simply by the sacrifice of one of us! What we have come here to do, Neoptolemus, is not so easy as dying. . . .

This island that looks deserted to you is not so at all. It is inhabited by a Greek; his name is Philoctetes, and your father loved him. Long ago he set sail with us in the fleet that left Greece for Asia, full of hope and pride; he was the friend of Hercules, and one of the noblemen among us; if you had lived in camp before now, you would already know his story. In those days everyone admired his courage; later on they all called it rashness. It was what moved him once when we rested our oars at an unknown island. The shore had a strange aspect; bad omens had undermined our courage. The gods had ordered us to make sacrifice on this island, so Calchas told us, but each one of us was waiting for some other to make the first move; then Philoctetes volunteered, with a smile. On the shore of the island a treacherous snake bit him. Philoctetes was still smiling when he came back on board and first showed us his little wound, just above his foot. It grew worse. Philoctetes soon stopped smiling; his face turned pale, then his troubled eyes filled with an astonished anguish. After a few days his swollen foot stiffened; and he, who had never complained, began to groan pitifully. At first everyone gathered around, eager to console and amuse him; nothing could do so, except to cure him; and, when it was proved that the art of Machaon had no power over his wound, since his cries were likely to weaken our courage, and since the ship was approaching another island, this one, we left him here, alone with his bow and arrows, which are our business today.

NEOPTOLEMUS. What, Ulysses! You left him? Alone?

ULYSSES. Of course, if he had been going to die, I think we might have kept him a little while longer. But no: his wound is not mortal.

NEOPTOLEMUS. But even so?

ULYSSES. Well, do you think the courage of a whole army should have been subjected to the suffering and wailing of a single man? It is easy to see that you never heard him!

NEOPTOLEMUS. Were his cries frightful?

ULYSSES. No, not frightful: plaintive, dampening our souls with pity.

NEOPTOLEMUS. Couldn't someone at least stay and take care of him? What can he do, sick and alone here?

ULYSSES. He has his bow.

NEOPTOLEMUS. His bow?

ULYSSES. Yes: the bow of Hercules. And then I must tell you, child: his rotting foot filled the whole ship with the most unbearable stench.

NEOPTOLEMUS. Ah?

ULYSSES. Yes. And he was obsessed with his illness, incapable ever again of any devotion to Greece. . . .

NEOPTOLEMUS. Too bad. And now we have come, Ulysses. . . .

ULYSSES. Listen again, Neoptolemus: you know Troy has long been condemned; you know how much blood has been spilled, how much virtue, patience, and courage spent there, far from home and our dear land. . . . Well, none of all that has sufficed. Through the priest Calchas the gods have finally declared that the bow and arrows of Hercules alone, in one final test of virtue,[1] could give the victory to Greece. That is why we two have come; blessed be the fate that chose us! And now it seems that on this distant island, all passion put behind us, our great destinies at last are to be resolved, and our hearts, here, more completely dedicated, are at last to achieve the most perfect virtue.

NEOPTOLEMUS. Is that all, Ulysses? And now, after such a fine speech, what do you plan to do? My mind still refuses to understand your

---

1. "Par une dernière vertu." That is to say, the victory over Troy will be their final show of excellence. (All notes are by the editor.)

words completely. . . . Tell me: why have we come here?

ULYSSES. To take the bow of Hercules; now do you understand?

NEOPTOLEMUS. Is that your idea, Ulysses?

ULYSSES. Not mine; it is one the gods put into me.

NEOPTOLEMUS. Philoctetes will not want to let us have it.

ULYSSES. Therefore we shall take it by trickery.

NEOPTOLEMUS. Ulysses, you are detestable. My father taught me never to use trickery.

ULYSSES. It is stronger than force; force doesn't know how to wait. Your father is dead, Neoptolemus; I am alive.

NEOPTOLEMUS. Weren't you saying that it is better to die?

ULYSSES. Not better; it is easier to die. Nothing is worse for Greece.[2]

NEOPTOLEMUS. Ulysses! Why did you choose me? Why did you need me for this act? My whole soul disapproves it.

ULYSSES. Because I cannot do it myself; Philoctetes knows me too well. If he sees me alone, he will suspect some trick. Your innocence will protect us. You must be the one to do this act.

NEOPTOLEMUS. No, Ulysses; by Zeus, I will not do it.

ULYSSES. Child, do not speak of Zeus. You don't understand me. Listen. Do you think I am less sad than you because my tormented soul is masked, and accepts? You do not know Philoctetes; he is my friend. It is harder for me than for you to betray him. The gods' commands are cruel; they are the gods. I did not talk to you in the boat because my great saddened heart no longer even dreamed of words. . . . But you flare up as your father used to and no longer listen to reason.

NEOPTOLEMUS. My father is dead, Ulysses; do not speak of him; he died for Greece. Ah, to struggle, suffer, die for her! Ask whatever you will of me, but not to betray my father's friend!

ULYSSES. Child, listen and answer me: are you not the friend of all the Greeks rather than the friend of a single one? Or, rather, isn't our country greater than one man? And could you bear to save one man if, to save him, Greece must be lost?

NEOPTOLEMUS. It is true, Ulysses, I could not bear it.

ULYSSES. And you agree that, though friendship is a very precious thing, our land is still more precious? . . . Tell me, Neoptolemus, what is virtue?

NEOPTOLEMUS. Teach me, wise son of Laertes.

ULYSSES. Calm your passion; put duty above everything. . . .

NEOPTOLEMUS. But what is duty, Ulysses?

---

2. "Rien n'est trop malaisé pour la Grèce." Nothing one does for Greece should be thought too hard.

ULYSSES. The voice of the gods, the order of the city, giving ourselves to Greece; just as we see lovers looking about them for the most precious flowers as gifts for their mistresses, and wanting to die for them, as if the unhappy things had nothing better to give than themselves, what is there too dear for you to give to your country if it is dear to you? And didn't you agree awhile ago that friendship came next after your country? What did Agamemnon have dearer than his daughter, except his country? You must sacrifice, as on an altar . . . but now, in the same way, what does Philoctetes have, living all alone on this island, what does he have more precious than this bow to give to his country?

NEOPTOLEMUS. Well, in that case, Ulysses, ask him.

ULYSSES. He might refuse. I do not know what mood he is in, but I do know that his abandonment angered him against the leaders of the army. It may be he has angered the gods with his thoughts and, shockingly, no longer wishes us victory. And maybe the offended gods have decided to punish him again, through us. If we force virtue upon him by obliging him to give up his weapons, the gods will be less severe with him.

NEOPTOLEMUS. But, Ulysses, can deeds we do against our will be praiseworthy?

ULYSSES. Don't you think, Neoptolemus, that what is most important of all is that the gods' orders be carried out? Even if it must be done without everybody's consent?

NEOPTOLEMUS. All you said before, I approve; but now I no longer know what to say, and it even seems to me—

ULYSSES. Shsh! Listen. . . . Don't you hear something?

NEOPTOLEMUS. Yes: the sound of the sea.

ULYSSES. No. It's he! His frightful cries are just beginning to reach us.

NEOPTOLEMUS. Frightful? On the contrary, Ulysses, I hear singing.

ULYSSES [*listening closely*]. It's true, he is singing. He's a good one![3] Now that he's alone, he sings! When he was with us, he screamed.

NEOPTOLEMUS. What is he singing?

ULYSSES. I can't yet make out the words. Listen: he's coming nearer.

NEOPTOLEMUS. He has stopped singing. He is standing still. He has seen our tracks in the snow.

ULYSSES [*laughing*]. And now he is beginning to scream again. Ah, Philoctetes!

NEOPTOLEMUS. It's true, his cries are horrible.

ULYSSES. Look, run put my sword on that rock, so he will recognize a

---

3. "Il est bien bon!" Good man!

Greek weapon and know the tracks he has seen are those of a man
from his own country.—Hurry, he is getting near.—Good.—Now
come; let's post ourselves behind this mound of snow, so we can see
him without being seen. How he will curse us! "Beggars," he will say,
"perish the Greeks who abandoned me here! Commanders of the
army! You liar, Ulysses! You, Agamemnon, Menelaus! May they all
be devoured by my disease! Oh, death! Death, I call on you every day,
will you not hear my complaint? Will you never come? O caves!
Rocks! Promontories! Mute witnesses of my suffering, will you
never—"

[*Enter* PHILOCTETES; *he sees the helmet and weapons placed in the center of the
stage.*]

SCENE 2

[PHILOCTETES, ULYSSES, NEOPTOLEMUS]

PHILOCTETES: [*He is silent*]

Act 2

SCENE 1

[ULYSSES, PHILOCTETES, NEOPTOLEMUS]

[*All three are sitting*]

PHILOCTETES. I tell you, Ulysses, only since I have lived apart from men
do I understand what is called virtue. The man who lives among
others is incapable, believe me, incapable of a pure and really disin-
terested action. You, for instance—came here—for what?
ULYSSES. Why, to see you, my dear Philoctetes.
PHILOCTETES. I don't believe a word of it, but no matter; it is a great
pleasure to see you again, and that is enough. I have lost the talent for
seeking the motives of what people do, since my own are no longer
secret. To whom would I need to appear what I am? My only care is
to be. I have stopped groaning, because I knew there was no ear to
hear me; I have stopped wishing, because I know that I could get
nothing by it.

ULYSSES. Why didn't you stop groaning sooner, Philoctetes? We might have kept you with us.

PHILOCTETES. That is just what should not have happened, Ulysses. In the presence of others my silence would have been a lie.

ULYSSES. Whereas here?

PHILOCTETES. My suffering no longer needs words to make itself known, being known only to me.

ULYSSES. So, you have been silent ever since we left, Philoctetes?

PHILOCTETES. Not at all. But since I no longer use my complaint to manifest my suffering, it has become beautiful, so beautiful that it consoles me.

ULYSSES. Good, my poor Philoctetes.

PHILOCTETES. Above all, don't pity me! I stopped wishing, as I was telling you, because I knew that I could get nothing by it. . . . I could get nothing from others, it is true, but a great deal from myself; it was then that I began to desire virtue; my spirit is now wholly occupied with that, and I am at peace, despite my pain. At least I was at peace when you came. . . . Why do you smile?

ULYSSES. I see that you have been busy.

PHILOCTETES. You listen but do not understand me. Don't you love virtue?

ULYSSES. Yes: my own.

PHILOCTETES. What is it?

ULYSSES. You would listen but would not understand me. . . . Let's talk about the Greeks instead. Has your solitary virtue made you forget them?

PHILOCTETES. So as not to be angry with them, yes indeed.

ULYSSES. You hear, Neoptolemus! So our success in the battle which—

PHILOCTETES. —made you leave me here—what do you expect me to think of it, Ulysses? You left me here so as to conquer, didn't you? Then I hope for your sake that you are conquerors. . . .

ULYSSES. And if not?

PHILOCTETES. If not, then we have believed Hellas greater than she was. On this island, you know, I have become every day less Greek, every day more a man. . . . Yet when I see you, I feel—Is Achilles dead, Ulysses?

ULYSSES. Achilles is dead; my companion here is his son. Why, you are sobbing, Philoctetes? . . . Where is the calm you have been seeking? . . .

PHILOCTETES. Achilles! . . . Child, let me stroke your fine forehead. . . . It has been a long time, a long time since my hand touched a warm body; even the birds I kill fall in the water or the snow, and when my hands reach them, their bodies are as cold as those upper regions of the atmosphere where they fly. . . .

ULYSSES. You express yourself well for one who is in pain.

PHILOCTETES. Wherever I go, always, I am a son of Greece.

ULYSSES. But you have no one to talk to here.

PHILOCTETES. Didn't you understand me? I told you that I express myself better now that I no longer talk with men. Except for hunting and sleeping, my whole occupation is thinking. In this solitude nothing, not even pain, interferes with my ideas; and they have taken a course so subtle that I follow them sometimes myself only with difficulty. I have come to understand more of the secrets of life than all my teachers ever revealed to me. I tried telling myself of my suffering, and if the sentence were beautiful, I was comforted accordingly; sometimes I even forgot my troubles in telling them. I learned that words are more beautiful when they ask for nothing. With neither ears nor mouths around me, I used only the beauty of my words; I called them out to the whole island, along the beaches; and the island listened and seemed less solitary; nature seemed the image of my distress; it seemed that I was nature's voice and that the mute rocks were waiting for my voice to tell their illnesses; for I learned that everything around me is sick . . . and that this cold is not normal, for I remember Greece. . . . And I gradually got the habit of crying the distress of things, rather than my own; that seemed better, but how can I explain to you? Anyway, their distress and mine were the same and I was comforted. It was in speaking of the sea and the interminable wave that I made my finest phrases. Do you know, Ulysses—O Ulysses!—some were so beautiful that I sobbed with sadness because there was no man to hear them. It seemed to me his soul would have been changed by them. Listen, Ulysses! Listen. No one has heard me yet.

ULYSSES. I see you got the habit of talking without interruption. Come, recite for us.

PHILOCTETES [*declaiming*]. The numberless smiling waves of the sea—

ULYSSES [*laughing*]. Why, Philoctetes, that's from Æschylus.

PHILOCTETES. Perhaps. . . . Does that bother you? [*Continuing*] Numberless sobbing waves of the sea— [*Silence*]

ULYSSES. And then—

PHILOCTETES. I don't know any more. . . . I am mixed up.

ULYSSES. Too bad! But you can go on another time.

NEOPTOLEMUS. Oh, please go on now, Philoctetes!

ULYSSES. Well! The child was listening to you! . . .

PHILOCTETES. I don't know how to talk, any longer.

ULYSSES [*rising*]. I will leave you for a moment to collect your thoughts. Good-by, Philoctetes. But tell me: no captivity is so hard that it doesn't allow some repose, some forgetfulness, some respite, is there?

PHILOCTETES. True, Ulysses; one day I shot a bird and it fell; my arrow had only wounded it, and I hoped to revive it. But how could it keep the airy emotion that made it fly, down here on this hardened earth where the cold fixes even upon water, when it freezes, the form of my logical thought.[4] The bird died; I watched it die in a few hours; to warm it again, I smothered it with kisses and warm breath. It died of the need to fly. . . .

It even seems to me, dear Ulysses, that the stream of poetry, as soon as it leaves my lips, freezes and dies because it cannot be repeated, propagated, and that the intimate flame that animates it is steadily shrinking. I shall soon be, though still alive, quite abstract. Dear Ulysses, the cold is invading me, and I am frightened, for I find beauty in it, even in its rigor.

I walk securely over things, over frozen fluids. I never dream any more; I only think. I can no longer taste hope, and for that reason I am never elated. Here, where everything is hard stone, when I set anything whatever down—even a seed—I find it again long afterwards, just as it was; it has never sprouted. Here, Ulysses, nothing becomes: everything is, everything remains. In short, here one can speculate! I kept the dead bird; here it is; the freezing air keeps it ever from rotting. And my acts, Ulysses, and my words, as if they were frozen in permanence, surround me like rocks arranged in a circle. And because I find them there every day, all my passion is quieted, and I feel the Truth always firmer—and I should wish my actions likewise always sounder and more beautiful, Ulysses, as those crystals of clear frost through which the sun, if the sun ever appeared, could be seen whole. I do not wish to stop a single ray of Zeus; let him transpierce me,Ulysses, like a prism, and the refracted light make my acts lovable and beautiful. I should like to achieve the greatest transparency, the clarification of all my opacity; and I should like for you, watching me act, to feel the light yourself. . . .

ULYSSES [*leaving*]: Well, good-by. [*Pointing to Neoptolemus*] Chat with him, he's listening. [*Exit*]

---

4. "Où le froid donne à l'eau même, gelée, la forme de mes logiques pensées." Gide may mean that even the water is frozen—as frozen as his pure thought.

SCENE 2

[PHILOCTETES AND NEOPTOLEMUS]

NEOPTOLEMUS: Philoctetes! Teach me virtue. . . .

Act 3

SCENE 1

PHILOCTETES [*entering; overcome with surprise and grief*]. Blind Philoctetes! Recognize your error, weep for your folly! That the sight of
Greeks should have stolen your heart. . . . Did I hear rightly? To be
sure: Ulysses was sitting there, and near by was Neoptolemus; they
didn't know I was there, they didn't even lower their voices; Ulysses
was advising Neoptolemus, teaching him to betray me; telling
him—You are cursed, Philoctetes![5] They came only to steal your
bow! How they must need it! . . . Precious bow, my only possession,
without it—[*Listening intently*] They are coming! Defend yourself,
Philoctetes! Your bow is good, your arm is sure. Virtue! Virtue I
cherished so much when I was alone! My silent heart had grown calm
before they came. Ah, now I know what it's worth, the friendship
they offer! Is Greece my country, detestable Ulysses? And you,
Neoptolemus. . . . And yet how he listened to me! So gentle!
Child—as fair, oh, fairer than your father was fair. . . . How can so
pure a forehead conceal such a thought? "Virtue," he said, "Philoctetes, teach me virtue." What did I tell him? I don't remember
anything but him. . . . But what does it matter now, whatever I told him!
. . . [*Listening*] Footsteps! . . . Who is it coming? Ulysses! [*Seizing his bow*]
No, it's—Neoptolemus.
[*Enter* NEOPTOLEMUS]

SCENE 2

[PHILOCTETES AND NEOPTOLEMUS]

NEOPTOLEMUS [*calling*]. . . . Philoctetes! [*Coming, nearly fainting*] Ah! I'm
sick.

---

5. "Malheureux Philoctète!" Wretched Philoctetes!

PHILOCTETES. Sick?

NEOPTOLEMUS. You are the cause of my trouble. Make me calm again, Philoctetes. All you told me has taken root in my heart. While you were talking, I did not know what to answer, I listened, and my heart opened naïvely to your words. Ever since you stopped, I have kept on listening. But now I am troubled, and waiting. Speak! I have not heard enough. . . . What were you saying? A man must devote himself—

PHILOCTETES [*unresponsive*]. —devote himself.

NEOPTOLEMUS. But that is what Ulysses teaches me too. Devote himself to what, Philoctetes? He says, to one's country—

PHILOCTETES. —to one's country.

NEOPTOLEMUS. Ah, tell me, Philoctetes; you must go on now.

PHILOCTETES [*evasive*]. Child—do you know how to draw the bow?

NEOPTOLEMUS. Yes. Why?

PHILOCTETES. Could you string this one?

NEOPTOLEMUS [*disconcerted*]. You mean— I don't know. [*Trying it*] Yes, perhaps.—You see!

PHILOCTETES [*aside*]. What ease! He is like—

NEOPTOLEMUS [*uncertain*]. And now—

PHILOCTETES I have seen all I wanted to see. [*He takes the bow*]

NEOPTOLEMUS. I don't understand you.

PHILOCTETES. No matter, alas! . . . [*Changing his mind*] Listen, child. Don't you believe the gods are above Greece, more important than Greece?

NEOPTOLEMUS. No, by Zeus, I don't believe it.

PHILOCTETES. But why not, Neoptolemus?

NEOPTOLEMUS. Because the gods I serve serve Greece.

PHILOCTETES. So! You mean they are subject?

NEOPTOLEMUS. Not subject—I don't know how to say it . . . But look! You know they are unknown outside Greece; Greece is their country as well as ours; by serving her, I serve them; they are no different from my country.

PHILOCTETES. Yet, look, I have something to say, there;[6] I no longer belong to Greece, yet—I serve them.

NEOPTOLEMUS. You think so? Ah, poor Philoctetes! Greece is not so easily shaken off . . . and even—

PHILOCTETES [*attentive*]. And even—?

NEOPTOLEMUS. Ah, if you knew. . . . Philoctetes—

---

6. "Moi je puis t'en parler." I am able to talk to you about the gods.

PHILOCTETES. If I knew—what?

NEOPTOLEMUS [*recovering*]. No, you, you must talk; I came to listen, and now you question me. . . . I see plainly that Ulysses' virtue and yours are not the same. . . . You used to speak so well, but now when you have to speak, you hesitate. . . . Devote oneself to what, Philoctetes?

PHILOCTETES. I was going to say: to the gods. . . . But the truth is, Neoptolemus, there is something above the gods.

NEOPTOLEMUS. Above the gods!

PHILOCTETES. Yes. I will not act like Ulysses.[7]

NEOPTOLEMUS. Devote oneself to what, Philoctetes? What is there, above the gods?

PHILOCTETES. There is— [*Taking his head in his hands, overcome*] I don't know any longer. I don't know. . . . Ah! Ah, oneself! . . . I don't know how to say it any longer, Neoptolemus. . . .[8]

NEOPTOLEMUS. Devote oneself to what? Tell me, Philoctetes.

PHILOCTETES. Devote oneself—devote—

NEOPTOLEMUS. You are weeping!

PHILOCTETES. Child! Ah, if I could only *show* you virtue. . . . [*Standing up suddenly*] I hear Ulysses! Good-by. . . . [*Going*] Shall I ever see you again? [*Exit*]

NEOPTOLEMUS. Farewell, Philoctetes.

[*Enter* ULYSSES]

SCENE 3

[ULYSSES AND NEOPTOLEMUS]

ULYSSES. Did I come in time? What did he say? Did you talk well, my scholar?

NEOPTOLEMUS. Thanks to you, better than he. But what does it matter? Ulysses—he gave me his bow to string!

ULYSSES. His bow! What irony! Well, why didn't you keep it, son of Achilles?

NEOPTOLEMUS. What good is a bow without arrows? While I had the bow, he wisely kept the arrows.

ULYSSES. Our friend is clever! . . . Does he suspect, do you think? What did he say?

NEOPTOLEMUS. Oh, nothing, or almost.

ULYSSES. And did he recite his virtue to you again?

---

7. "Puisque je n'agis pas comme Ulysse." Since I do not act like Ulysses.
8. "Je ne sais plus parler." I can no longer speak.

NEOPTOLEMUS. He talked so well awhile ago; but when I questioned him, he shut up.[9]

ULYSSES. You see! . . .

NEOPTOLEMUS. And when I asked him what else there is to devote oneself to except Greece, he said—

ULYSSES. What?

NEOPTOLEMUS. He didn't know. And when I said that even the gods, as you taught me, are subject to Greece, he answered: then, above the gods, there is—

ULYSSES. What?

NEOPTOLEMUS. He said he didn't know.

ULYSSES. Well! Now you see, Neoptolemus! . . .

NEOPTOLEMUS. No, Ulysses, it seems to me now that I understand it.

ULYSSES. You understand what?

NEOPTOLEMUS. Something. Because, after all, on this solitary island, when we were not here, what was Philoctetes devoted to?

ULYSSES. Why, you have already said it: to nothing. What good is solitary virtue? Despite what he believes, it was dissipated, to no use. What good are all his phrases, however fine? . . . Did they convince you? Nor me either.

The reason he was left here, alone on this island, as I have already proved to you, was to rid the army of his groaning and his stench; that is his first devotion; that is his virtue, whatever he may say. His second virtue will be, if he is so virtuous, to be consoled when he loses his bow, by remembering that it was done for Greece. What other devotion, if not to one's country, is imaginable? He was waiting, you see, for us to come and give him the chance. . . . But since it is possible he might refuse, we'd better force his virtue, impose the sacrifice on him—and I think the wisest course is to put him to sleep. You see this bottle. . . .

NEOPTOLEMUS. Ah, don't talk so much, Ulysses. Philoctetes was silent.

ULYSSES. That was because he had nothing to say.

NEOPTOLEMUS. And that was why he was weeping?

ULYSSES. He was weeping because he was wrong.

NEOPTOLEMUS. No, he was weeping because of me.

ULYSSES [*smiling*]. You? . . . What begins as nonsense, we later call virtue, out of pride.

NEOPTOLEMUS [*bursting into sobs*]. Ulysses! You don't understand Philoctetes. . . .

---

9. "Il s'est tu." He fell silent. (The French expression is formal).

Act 4

SCENE 1

[PHILOCTETES AND NEOPTOLEMUS]

[PHILOCTETES *is sitting, alone; he seems overcome with grief, or in meditation*]

NEOPTOLEMUS [*enters, running*]. I must find him in time! . . . Ah, it's you, Philoctetes. Quick, listen to me. What we came here for is shameful; but you must be greater than we are and forgive me. We came—oh, I am ashamed to say it—to steal your bow, Philoctetes!

PHILOCTETES. I knew.

NEOPTOLEMUS. You don't understand me—we came to steal your bow, I tell you. . . . Ah, defend yourself!

PHILOCTETES. Against whom? You, dear Neoptolemus?

NEOPTOLEMUS. Certainly not against me; I love you and am trying to warn you.

PHILOCTETES. And you are betraying Ulysses. . . .

NEOPTOLEMUS. And I am in despair. . . . It's to you I'm devoted. Do you love me? Say, Philoctetes, is that what virtue is?

PHILOCTETES. Child! . . .

NEOPTOLEMUS. Look what I bring you. This phial is meant to put you to sleep. But I give it to you. Here it is. Is that virtue?—Tell me.

PHILOCTETES. Child! Superior virtue is attained only step by step; you are trying to make it at a leap.

NEOPTOLEMUS. Then teach me, Philoctetes.

PHILOCTETES. This phial was to put me to sleep, you say? [*Taking it, looking at it*] Little phial—you, at least, do not miss your aim! Do you see what I am doing, Neoptolemus? [*Drinks*]

NEOPTOLEMUS. What! This is awful, it is—[10]

PHILOCTETES. Go and tell Ulysses. Tell him—he can come.

[*Exit* NEOPTOLEMUS, *terrified, running, shouting*]

SCENE 2

[PHILOCTETES *then* ULYSSES *and* NEOPTOLEMUS]

---

10. "Quoi! Malheureux, mais c'est. . . ." The French words are formal.

PHILOCTETES [*alone*]. And you shall admire me, Ulysses; I want to compel
you to admire me. My virtue rises above yours and you feel yourself
diminished. Be exalted, my virtue! Be content with your own beauty!
Neoptolemus, why did you not take my bow at once? The more you
loved me, the more difficult that was for you: you were not devoted
enough. Take them. . . . [*Looking about him*] He's gone. . . .

That drink had an awful taste; it turns my stomach to think of it;[11]
I wish it would put me to sleep faster. . . . Of all devotions the craziest
is to be devoted to others, for then you become their superior. I am
devoted, yes, but not to Greece. . . . I regret but one thing, and that is
that my devotion serves Greece. . . . Yet, no, I don't even regret it. . . .
But don't thank me: I am acting for myself, not for you.—You will
admire me, won't you, Ulysses? Won't you admire me, Ulysses?
Ulysses! Ulysses! Where are you? You must understand: I am devoted, but not to Greece—to something else, you understand, to
something—what? I don't know. Will you understand? Ulysses! You
will probably think I am devoted to Greece! Ah, this bow and these
arrows will help you to think that! . . . Where can I throw them? The
sea! [*He tries to run, but falls overcome by the philter*] I am too weak. Ah,
my head whirls. . . . He is coming. . . .

Virtue! Virtue! Let me find in your bitter name some exaltation.
Could it be I have already drained it all? My sustaining pride totters
and gives way; my life is leaking out on every side. "Don't leap; don't
leap," I told him. Whatever we try beyond our strength, Neoptolemus, that is what we call virtue. Virtue—I don't believe in it any
longer, Neoptolemus. Listen to me, Neoptolemus! Neoptolemus,
there is no virtue.—Neoptolemus! . . . He can't hear me.

[*Overcome, he falls and sleeps. Enter* ULYSSES *and* NEOPTOLEMUS]
ULYSSES [*seeing* PHILOCTETES]. And now leave me with him, alone.
[NEOPTOLEMUS *greatly moved, hesitates*]

Yes! Go, anywhere; run and get the boat ready, if you wish.
[*Exit* NEOPTOLEMUS. ULYSSES *approaches* PHILOCTETES, *bends down*]
Philoctetes! . . . Can't you hear me, Philoctetes?—You will never hear
me again?—What can I do? I wanted to tell you—you have convinced
me, Philoctetes. I see virtue now; it is so beautiful that in your
presence I no longer dare to act. To me, my duty seems crueler than
yours, because it seems less dignified. Your bow—I can't, I no longer
want to take it: you have given it.—Neoptolemus is a child: let him
obey. Ah, here he is! [*In a tone of command*] And now, Neoptolemus,

---

11. "Le breuvage avait un goût affreux; d'y penser, mon coeur se soulève."
The French words are again formal.

take the bow and the arrows and carry them to the boat.

[NEOPTOLEMUS *approaches* PHILOCTETES *in grief, falls to his knees, kisses his forehead*]

I order you to do it. Isn't it enough to have betrayed me? Do you wish to betray your country as well? Look how he has devoted himself to his country.

[NEOPTOLEMUS *obediently takes the bow and arrows; exit*]

And now farewell, harsh Philoctetes. Did you despise me very much? Ah, I should like to know. . . . . I should like him to know, I think he is admirable—and that—thanks to him, we shall win.

NEOPTOLEMUS [*calling from a distance*]. Ulysses!

ULYSSES. I'm coming. [*Exit*]

Act 5

PHILOCTETES *is alone, on a rock. The sun is rising in a perfectly clear sky. Over the sea, in the distance, a boat is moving away.* PHILOCTETES *looks at it, long*

PHILOCTETES [*murmuring, very calmly*]. They will never come back; they have no more bows to seek. . . . I am happy.

[*His voice has become extraordinarily mild and beautiful; around him flowers are showing through the snow, and birds from heaven come down to feed him*]

Oscar Mandel

THE SUMMONING OF PHILOCTETES
A Tragedy
(1961)

The Summoning of Philoctetes appeared in a first version under the title *Island* in the Winter 1961 issue of the *Massachusetts Review*. Dramatic readings were given in the same year at Amherst and Smith colleges. In 1962 a group of actors, including Harold Innocent, Barry Atwater, and Harold Gould staged a concert reading in the studios of radio station KPFK in Los Angeles. This was subsequently broadcast, and frequently rebroadcast, by that station and its affiliates in San Francisco (KPFA) and New York (WBAI). Similar concert readings by the same group were given in 1962 at Los Angeles City College and the California Institute of Technology. A revised version of the play appeared in the first volume of my *Collected Plays* (Santa Barbara, Calif.: Unicorn Press, 1970). It is still further revised under its present title.

Isolation from mankind, celebrated by Gide, becomes problematic in *The Summoning of Philoctetes*. Heracles provides the original postulate, to wit, that social man is man at war with man: *homo homini lupus*. The play proceeds to illustrate his point through two acts of atrocity. On the other hand, the blessings of civilization are given their due as well. The mesh of good and evil becomes inextricable. And the central exhibit is the unclarifiable ambiguity of the man Odysseus: the great civilizer, but also, and inevitably, the ruthless blood-letter.

Philoctetes and Demodocus are both brought face to face with this ambiguity in the man, which is also the ambiguity of the state. Shall a man be pure? He can be so only in perfect solitude. Does a man want human companionship? He must accept the pollution that goes with it.

Demodocus has the last word on this dilemma, but if I read the text correctly, the last word in this case is not necessarily the best word. Even though the state—through Odysseus—is painted in a far darker light than what we find in Sophocles, we are no longer so sure that the values embodied by the Ithacan leader should be, or can be, subordinated to some higher value. The play ends upon a doubt.

The solitude which Demodocus chooses in the end should not be confused with the solitude of Philoctetes in the beginning. Philoctetes

181

has Medon. Here is dialogue, not soliloquy. Philoctetes lives and operates in a family way, somewhat like people today who take their kith and kin to live in the wilderness. It must be added, as an aside for our times, that sexual considerations are grossly impertinent in this context. The point is that we see Philoctetes from the start as—unbeknownst to himself—a sanguine and companionable soul. No wonder that when he is shown perfect solitude—as Galileo was shown the instruments—he breaks, and discovers that, like most human beings, he is willing to pay the price for human warmth.

The structure of the play is a chiasm—an X crossing, since Demodocus takes the place on Lemnos left empty by the older man. I have said already that the two solitudes are by no means the same. Now it must be added that the choice of authentic solitude is made by Demodocus the man, not Demodocus the poet. The play does not suggest, I think, that art, unlike engineering, is a solitary activity. Bereft of Medon, Philoctetes would undoubtedly have ceased to work and experiment. (That is perhaps why the pictorial tradition represents him, in his absolute solitude, as barely surviving and doing nothing else). But will Demodocus compose lyrics on Lemnos? By no means. The text tells us unequivocally that he will fall silent. The imperative voice for Demodocus has been that of ethics, not aesthetics.

While both science and art are seen as communal enterprises, it is clear that the community gives them quite distinct estimates. The play indicates that society welcomes the poet, and will miss him if he vanishes. But it *requires* the scientist / technologist. There will be no oracle in Agamemnon's army warning that without Demodocus the war will be lost, or Greek society will go to pieces. But Philoctetes must be harnessed. At worst, his services must be denied to the enemy. It turns out, therefore, that the choice between companionship and solitude was one which Philoctetes, all too useful to the state, would never have been allowed to make. As soon as the oracle sniffed out the existence, somewhere, of an ultimate weapon, the cleverest of the generals was sent to buy it, steal it—or neutralize it.

CHARACTERS

HERACLES
ODYSSEUS
PHILOCTETES
DEMODOCUS
MEDON
CHORUS of ten soldiers

The action takes place before the cave of PHILOCTETES *on the island of Lemnos*

PROLOGUE *with drum*

HERACLES. Philoctetes! My voice fills this island, you do not hear it, yet
soon you shall. Heracles returns to earth: your master and companion when I too knew the warm and cold of life; but now become
among the Gods another God, and still your master. And my word as
God remains my word when I was man: War!

Philoctetes! Let it fall away that Odysseus banished you long ago to
Lemnos ringed by the sea: a warrior, lord of seven ships, but useless
to the Greeks, your foot swollen with the serpent's venom, a coarse
stench polluting the holy sacrifice, and your cries unbearable to the
soldiers. Let it fall away, for your banishment must end. Troy stands
unbowed. Its princes strut upon the unbroken battlements, and shall
not perish until pierced by the strong strange arrows you fashioned,
Philoctetes, in the long hours we the Gods emptied for you, foreseeing it all.

Philoctetes! Unite with your brothers! On the plains of Ilium the
son of Achilles, beautiful and brutal Pyrrhus, waits for you. His the
hand that cracks the city open. Yours the weapon in his hand. Come,
come from the hunting of birds. Hunt Troy! Two heroes have
landed on Lemnos, charged by the oracle to summon you. You do
not hear them, but they take possession of you. They are trampling
the beach, resolute. They have scaled the hill towards your cave,
while elsewhere the string of your bow thuds and the wild birds,
premonitory, die in the sky. You do not hear yet you shall hear the
human word, the god-sent word: War!

To be is to do. To do is to fight. To fight is to be. Such is the law of
Heracles, obedient to his master: Zeus the Olympian. [*He vanishes*][1]

---

1. Both here and in Scene 4 Heracles may be suggested rather than shown.
Contrary devices—a strong light, or a gigantic shadow—could be equally
effective.

185

SCENE 1

FIRST SOLDIER. No one is here, Odysseus. Follow me.

ODYSSEUS. The old horrible stench. I remember it. All but unbearable. Soldiers, spread out and look for our man, each in a different direction.

[*The* EIGHTH, NINTH, *and* TENTH SOLDIERS *leave*]

DEMODOCUS. Are we really on the spot, Odysseus?

ODYSSEUS. On the spot or near it. The darkness of Lemnos under the heavy trees. The stairway of rocks and caves. The inhuman silence. Here, Demodocus, I myself brought the unhappy man ten years ago at the command of Agamemnon.

FIFTH SOLDIER. Men! Here's a cave, and the remains of a fire!

DEMODOCUS. Would this be his shelter?

ODYSSEUS. Go in, my friend. Take your sword in hand. Caution!

DEMODOCUS [*within*]. It *is* the cave, men! Furnished. Almost a house.

ODYSSEUS. What do you see?

DEMODOCUS. Strange. Two couches covered with skins—Medon is still alive. Wooden utensils—table, benches, a few knives—bronze basins and pots—

ODYSSEUS. More than we left him!

DEMODOCUS. [*emerging*]. Stone tools. A hearth. Sunlight penetrates from a high opening in the rock. But why do you hang back, Odysseus with your hand on your sword? Go in yourself.

ODYSSEUS. Soldiers, keep looking about. Too many trees for comfort here. A man might be concealed anywhere with a bow in his hands.

DEMODOCUS. Do you think he will be hostile to us, Odysseus? After ten years?

ODYSSEUS. Ten years may have made him forget, or they may have deepened his hatred. That is why my hand is on the sword.

DEMODOCUS. Still, capturing the bow may be easy; but taking him back with us—

ODYSSEUS. And voluntarily! Freely offering us his skill!

DEMODOCUS. I see great difficulties in that, Odysseus. Volunteer to join the atrocious miseries of the war?

FIRST SOLDIER. Don't dwell on difficulties and miseries, Demodocus; it's the wrong approach for a soldier. After all, if he won't come back of his own free will, I suppose we'll tie him up and argue with him later.

DEMODOCUS. Force him back with us, like an enemy; but I'm afraid he'll never reveal his secrets to us if we do.

ODYSSEUS. And yet force him back we must if he refuses to come. Have you considered, my friends, that the Trojans are sailing towards Lemnos too?

FIRST SOLDIER [*deeply alarmed*]. The Trojans? How would *they* know about his weapon?

ODYSSEUS. Why, have the Trojans no oracles of their own? Are not the same Gods in their sky as in ours? The danger is greater than you think. Perhaps they have landed already; perhaps they have made friends with Philoctetes, and learned from him how to make the bow.

SECOND SOLDIER. Odysseus, what are you saying?

ODYSSEUS. Calm yourselves. While we are here, the rest of our forces are quietly scouring the island, with instructions of their own. But I trust that we have landed first. And we too have our instructions. We must persuade Philoctetes to return with us. But what if he refuses? Shall we allow him to be approached by a Trojan delegation? In his bitterness against us he might yield to them, traitor, without so much as a bribe.

SEVENTH SOLDIER. What must we do, Odysseus?

ODYSSEUS. Persuade him if we can, compel him if he resists, kill him if we must.

THIRD SOLDIER. Kill him?

ODYSSEUS. The man has a murderous weapon in his hand or in his brain. Who made him contrive it? He himself compels us either to attach him to us, or to destroy him.

DEMODOCUS. This was kept from us till now.

ODYSSEUS. Are you ready, each one of you, to carry out Agamemnon's orders?

SECOND SOLDIER. If we must, Odysseus, if we must.

FIFTH SOLDIER. Who can blame us for keeping this weapon out of the enemy's hands?

THIRD SOLDIER. God knows we are loyal. Yet God forbid we should pour out the blood of a fellow Greek.

FOURTH SOLDIER. God forbid. Yet you know best what fighters we have been, always at your side; and how else is this endless, sorrowful war to end?

[*Enter the* EIGHTH SOLDIER]

EIGHTH SOLDIER. Odysseus, I found footprints!

ODYSSEUS. How far from here?

EIGHTH SOLDIER. About two hundred yards away; on a sandy spot; but leading down from the cave, not returning to it.

ODYSSEUS. One or two men?

EIGHTH SOLDIER. Two.

ODYSSEUS. Good. Medon is with him. Old or fresh?

EIGHTH SOLDIER. Fresh, Odysseus, fresh!

ODYSSEUS. Splendid! Go back, soldier, and look sharp. Give us a warning the moment you see him. [*Exit the soldier*] Men, are we ready to disappear at the snap of a finger?

FIRST SOLDIER. We are, sir.

ODYSSEUS. Now, Demodocus, the rest is yours. Here he will find you, a poor lonely shipwrecked Greek.

DEMODOCUS. I know my part, Odysseus.

ODYSSEUS. You were not chosen for this mission without good reason. Me and the other chiefs Philoctetes hates, as though we and not the serpent had bitten his ankle. But you are a lieutenant: noble in your own right, a man I have always placed near myself at my table, among my dearest companions, young as you are; though not yet in the highest authority. You are a stranger to Philoctetes. He can hate you only as a Greek, but you will easily persuade him to like you as a man. Furthermore, you are skilled with your speech. To whom else do we turn, after the fighting or during a feast, for a love ditty, or a hymn to battle, or a ballad of old heroes? Though even as a spearsman you are by no means a man whom the enemy would ignore. Your role it will be, therefore, to enchant the heart of Philoctetes with sinuous, inveigling words and strong appeals. Invoke the glory that shall come to him when Troy falls. Paint for him the suffering of the Greeks: and here you will stir in his heart the emotion of kinship, the longing for one's own which makes even their sins bearable. Speak to him of prizes and rewards, and particularly the gift of young women. Praise the balm of human companionship: what man can desire this terrible solitude? Who does not long now and then to hear the cozy gossip of a marketplace, the hubbub of a tavern, the cries of children at play, the soft, unique word of a woman in love, the advice of a cautious friend? Bring these to his mind, Demodocus, make him weep.

DEMODOCUS. But what if he suddenly reproaches us for abandoning him on Lemnos?

ODYSSEUS. Swear to our innocence and our good will. Did we plot the serpent's bite? Did we bribe the oracle? He was one of ours, we loved the man! No; counter with a solemn chord: duty, Demodocus, duty to our nation and to our cause: the call to arms. What man shall disobey? Troy, sitting like a harpy across the Hellespont, cramming down our ships, our goods, our sailors, Troy must be, shall be cut down!

SIXTH SOLDIER. Grant it, oh Gods!

ODYSSEUS. This is war! Not a children's game. Impress him with this, Demodocus: that you are serious; that there is no room in these matters for selfish resentments and private quarrels. You yourself are here on a mission, under orders—not on a holiday in the islands: a Greek, not a rootless outlaw or a savage. Let him indulge his tastes and his antagonisms and his appetites; but only, I say, only after having done his duty to Greece.

FIRST SOLDIER. This is soundly spoken, Odysseus. What a pity Philoctetes is not here now. You would have persuaded him already.

DEMODOCUS. Yes, your words carry a great deal of weight, as always, Odysseus. You are a king. It is only human to have misgivings, of course, but I will do my best to follow your instructions. Shall I let Philoctetes know that his father is dead, and that his son, like your own Telemachus, reigns while he waits for his father's return?

ODYSSEUS. What do you think?

DEMODOCUS. I should like to. How moved he will be! And then thankful to us, which is important.

ODYSSEUS. Nevertheless, I have to overrule you. No doubt he will ask you for news; but you will pretend to know nothing of his affairs. This will whet his appetite for a return among those of us who know. Perhaps you can say that you have heard rumors, but are they about him or about somebody else? You don't know. *You* would give him security, even the security of misery; *I* will play on his anxiety.

DEMODOCUS. It will be hard for me.

[*Enter the* NINTH SOLDIER]

NINTH SOLDIER. Odysseus, away from here!

ODYSSEUS. Is he coming?

NINTH SOLDIER. Yes! I saw two men from my hill—still in the distance, but coming this way; one limping, carrying the bow—the bow, do you hear? The other walking two steps behind. Philoctetes and Medon, as sure as there is water in the sea!

ODYSSEUS. Good work. Recall the other men. Run. Demodocus, stand before the cave. Speak boldly to him. When he grows soft, suddenly I appear. I disclose the oracle's revelation. You and I, astonished to meet. Have we left traces here?

FIRST SOLDIER. I think not.

[*The* NINTH *and* TENTH SOLDIERS *return*]

TENTH SOLDIER. We've signaled the other man, Odysseus; he'll be here in a minute.

ODYSSEUS. Good. Remember: not a word about the bow, the prophecy, and the Trojans. They're for me to manage. [*The last man arrives*] Hurry up, fool. All present? No one missing?

FIRST SOLDIER. All present, Odysseus.

ODYSSEUS. Withdraw to a safe distance but without leaving Demodocus exposed. [*To the* TENTH SOLDIER] You, follow me to the ship. [*To the* FIRST SOLDIER] You, deploy your men and send runners to report to me. Demodocus, good luck.

DEMODOCUS. Depend on me. [ODYSSEUS *and the* TENTH SOLDIER *leave*]
Friends, I think I will stand a little farther off, and choose the best
moment.
[*He leaves*]

[*The* CHORUS *speaks with flute and drum*]

SECOND SOLDIER. Does your heart beat like mine, comrades?
FIRST SOLDIER. Zeus! Be with us. Zeus! Now this man comes, and already the stench of him sickens us. Zeus! Make him pliant, bend him
to us, let him shift his ways like the stream when it parts and yields before the commanding rock. Zeus! Sharpen the words of Demodocus,
let each syllable be a hook to catch the soul of this man. Zeus! We are
your people. Will you forsake us? Are we to die in the futile plain
where bones of our brothers lie, men once ordinary, men once reasonably content, lying now where the oak, the tamarisk, and the
myrtle grew, become a barren country, yellow with war, pocked with
spears and rusted swords and shreds of armor, while the vultures
scrape in the skulls for meat. Zeus! Give us this man and his weapon,
and the end of this abomination!
SEVERAL. So be it!
THIRD SOLDIER. Men, do you know how old I was when I enlisted for the
war? Twenty years old, having barely tasted the pleasure of being a
man, of attracting a woman's sly glances, of taking my place in the Assembly, uttering my first words there, surprised almost that I was
taken seriously, no longer a boy, beginning the best years of a man;
and these years, oh my friends, these strong years in which I should
have found a kind wife, in which I might have established a house
and grown in wealth and reputation, I have spent them like a beast
among beasts in the sand; yes, my mouth filled with sand when we
crawled on the beach and drove back the Trojans in the first
onslaught, like a beast sweating and growling, muck-covered,
swearing over dice, scratching the blood off the rings I stole from the
dead—me, the son of a good man, Schedios of Pronnoi, before
whom even now I would blush to say a foul word.
FOURTH SOLDIER. This is my story too.
FIFTH SOLDIER. Fifteen years we are children, fifteen years we are old
men; and the little space between, must we spend it howling in the
attack, luckless if we die, luckless if we live, life either killed or
wasted? And why? Why? What is it to us, I ask, though timidly?
SIXTH SOLDIER. Why are we driven and driven?
SEVENTH SOLDIER. Because.
EIGHTH SOLDIER. Because.

NINTH SOLDIER. Because.
[*Three drum-beats*]
FOURTH SOLDIER. Zeus, give us quick victory!
SEVENTH SOLDIER. Give Philoctetes and the mysterious bow to us who
are dumb, we confess it, to us who fight as our fathers did, who can-
not devise and invent, whose minds cope day by day; good people,
effective enough, and loyal even when we grumble, but needing help
when troubles grow outrageous.
SECOND SOLDIER. Help is near, my friends.
NINTH SOLDIER. Oh the beaches of Troy, though we sail home at last,
will hold our shadows as if engraved on the sand.
SIXTH SOLDIER. Even the living have epitaphs.
[DEMODOCUS *appears*]
DEMODOCUS. He's coming! Scatter! Back to the ships!
FIRST SOLDIER. We'll move a little way off, Demodocus, as Odysseus
commanded.
[*All leave*]

SCENE 2

PHILOCTETES. Let me stop awhile, Medon. The wheel of pain turns
again. We could sit down awhile. [MEDON *offers to help him*] No no; sit
farther off. Why should you suffer my suffering? This stench oozes
into my very sleep and pollutes my dreams; and you so patient, with a
divine pretense of not noticing. Let me rest. The breeze cools my
wound and sings like an old nurse. Clean Lemnos. I feel better.
Medon, I'll help you pluck our catch for the day. No masters and
servants here. Philoctetes works with his hands. Look. Thick. Hard.
Efficient. I am now, good sir, become worthy of being a slave, having
learned to work. Did you see how I shot the wild geese? I hardly
aimed. Oh, I could have been Troy's horror—all Troy a giant boar,
and my uncanny arrow—now!—dying it falls, moaning, and then my
knife violent in its belly. How did this ugly thought come to
me? . . . How cool it is. If only I could smell the fragrance that must
be here. Yes, I know, the birds must be plucked. I am so tired. Why
should I lie to you? The venom is mounting again. God, what is the
purpose of such pain? Go into the cave by yourself, Medon. Leave
me. I must be alone.
[MEDON *enters the cave.* PHILOCTETES *sits moaning, his bow across his knees,
and loses consciousness.* DEMODOCUS *appears. He stands motionless at a
distance from* PHILOCTETES. *Gradually* PHILOCTETES *regains consciousness. He opens his eyes and sees* DEMODOCUS. *He leaps up and aims an
arrow*]

PHILOCTETES. Medon! Your sword! Men on the island!

[MEDON *rushes out of the cave, armed*]

PHILOCTETES. Stand back!

DEMODOCUS. Peace, my friends. I am a man who can do no harm. A castaway.

PHILOCTETES. A liar, maybe. Stay where you are. Who is here with you?

DEMODOCUS. No one. I am alone. No one else survived.

PHILOCTETES. You were shipwrecked?

DEMODOCUS. Yes.

PHILOCTETES. Your clothes are dry. You don't look exhausted.

DEMODOCUS. I had a calm journey of it on my raft for a whole day. And I slept a full night in a tree by the beach.

PHILOCTETES. Take his dagger, Medon.

[MEDON *does so*]

DEMODOCUS. You are welcome to it, my friends, whoever you are.

PHILOCTETES. What's your name?

DEMODOCUS. Demodocus, son of Terpius.

PHILOCTETES. A Greek!

DEMODOCUS. A citizen of Ithaca. But your voice fills me with fear. Will you treat me as a guest, or will you injure me? I have neither money nor goods.

PHILOCTETES. Money! The Greek says money! You'll come to no harm unless you look for it. How did your ship go down? An enemy? A storm?

DEMODOCUS. A storm. Will you not tell me where I am? Did I land on an island? Tenedos, perhaps?

PHILOCTETES. This is Lemnos.

DEMODOCUS. Lemnos! Then you—is it possible? You are Philoctetes! Alive!

PHILOCTETES. [*lowering the bow*]. You know my name.

DEMODOCUS. Who doesn't? Philoctetes! Unbelievable! How many times your story has been retold around the campfire—you—lord of Malis—bitten in the foot on that cursed island of Chryse—and I live to see you! Oh we have wondered and wondered, are they alive, he and his companion?

PHILOCTETES. What campfire is this? Not before Troy, surely?

DEMODOCUS. Troy too surely. Lucky man, not even to know. Yes, before Troy. Still before Troy.

PHILOCTETES. Amazing. And you are one of the Greeks? An officer?

DEMODOCUS. I am.

PHILOCTETES. I don't remember you.

DEMODOCUS. I was never among the first, and then ten years ago,

Philoctetes, I was a mere boy. You couldn't know me then. And even now I am better known among the Greeks for my singing than for my fighting, though even as a fighter I am not helpless.

PHILOCTETES. And was it for singing a false note, my friend, that the honest Greeks set you on a ship and sent you off?

DEMODOCUS. No, I am not an exile. I was sent to levy a thousand men in Messenia—laggards!—but the storm wrecked our ship, and I, perhaps, am the only survivor.

PHILOCTETES. The war is hungry.

DEMODOCUS. Too, too hungry. Last year—

PHILOCTETES. Tell me no stories. Keep your nightmares to yourself, and take advantage of your accident; explain it as intended by the Gods. Come, sit down; stretch your limbs, and feel what peace is like.

[MEDON *brings a bowl of water and a dish of fruit*]

DEMODOCUS. I feel it already in every bone, kind Philoctetes. The change is so sudden, I keep wondering, is it myself talking here? And to Philoctetes! Who would have thought it! Chatting under the trees. Trees! If you saw the plain before Troy. Scarred, sacked, cracked, every leaf and every blade of grass blasted. The heather uprooted. Bones and sand and mud. And now I sit here drinking clean water and eating figs.

PHILOCTETES. Tonight you will eat a curd of boar's milk and honey we call "the gift of Meleager." Other dishes too, oddities I promise you'll enjoy. Not a bad place is it, for a man who was drowning this morning?

DEMODOCUS. Yesterday, Philoctetes. Oh, this is Elysium.

PHILOCTETES. Later we'll walk halfway up a cliff to watch the night drifting in. Night without ambush. Night without blood. Take it: the island is yours. It lies in the Aegean like a pillow for the weary sailor.

DEMODOCUS. You are infinitely courteous. Ten years of solitude have not coarsened you. But tell me. I suppose that other men have landed here, recently perhaps.

PHILOCTETES. Perhaps.

DEMODOCUS. Who. When?

PHILOCTETES. I don't know. We've seen no one.

DEMODOCUS. No one? In all the years?

PHILOCTETES. Why do you ask so suspiciously?

DEMODOCUS. Not suspiciously, my friend, only with surprise. The Trojans, we understand, sail freely among these islands.

PHILOCTETES. They are welcome if they land here.

DEMODOCUS. The enemy?

PHILOCTETES. You are my enemy too. Mankind is my enemy.

DEMODOCUS. Why such a cruel word, Philoctetes?

PHILOCTETES. Why such a cruel word! Medon, did you hear this? I thank you of course—you made a gesture—oh, I notice!—yet you mastered yourself. But your fellow Greeks did not make the effort. Let me tell you what they did. They manacled me. Me, Philoctetes, like a slave caught stealing a herring. Your master Odysseus—you know it!—dragged me here manacled and threw me on the ground like a sack of garbage and hoped I would die. But I didn't die. I live to enjoy their dying. That's justice of a kind.

DEMODOCUS. Forgive me, Philoctetes. My words were rash.

PHILOCTETES. Peace. I flare up too easily. Besides, I have no grievance. This island has been my happiness. Never did I dream when I was a boy, wishing I could be another Heracles, that I should find this perfection. Yet I hate the Greeks who brought it to me. Take the paradox.

DEMODOCUS. I understand. It was not perfection they meant for you. And yet—let me ask you—is there not a thrust in your flesh toward your own brothers? Do you ever wonder, do you ever feel a small questioning ache, would you not like me to tell you whether your old companions are still alive, or how they fare—Agamemnon and pitiful Menelaus, the mountainous Ajax, Meriones, audacious Diomedes, old Nestor, Achilles perhaps, and his companion the generous Patroclus, or even, even my own master Odysseus?

PHILOCTETES. Your master Odysseus! That ragged, thirsty, patched-up king of Ithaca! Ithaca—excuse me—where people eat stones for supper! Ithaca had a king! Go on, be offended, my lad, but don't I remember him in the early days, when he saw himself sitting in Troy on a red cushion, a leg of mutton in each hand, and ten coffers of gold stowed away in his ship! And Agamemnon—no fool, I'll grant him that—invincible Agamemnon had visions of himself Emperor of Asia, he envied the centipedes because he had only two feet for people to kiss. I was more modest. A little gold, a little reputation, a few slave girls, I didn't ask for much, I was a villain of the tenth rank.

DEMODOCUS. You are a hard man, Philoctetes. Are we all bandits? Wasn't there a shred of justice in our going against Troy?

PHILOCTETES. Of course there was! Plenty of justice, my boy, Troy was a nest of pirates. An avalanche of justice! There's the beauty of your human affairs, crime and justice are bosom friends, famous allies; why, nothing's more deadly than a cause stinking with justice; but I, Philoctetes, I shook it all off the way a dog shakes the water off his back after a dip in the sea. A man stops being a bandit only when he's alone.

DEMODOCUS. Your anger burns through me. It convinces me that I should not tell you anything about these men, these criminals. Not even who died.

PHILOCTETES. Ah? Some of them died? Some of the great ones, I hope.

DEMODOCUS. Can you expect otherwise, after ten years?

PHILOCTETES. I will ask you one question. I had a father at home, a wife, a son—a son eight years old—and two younger brothers. . . .

DEMODOCUS. I don't know anything, Philoctetes. If only I did. Bad news is better than none. If you were among us again, you would find out, your son, your wife, your father. . . .

PHILOCTETES. I can live without news. My question was a formality. I've become another man. I will show you my world by and by what I and Medon have accomplished. *You* will ask the questions, believe me. Mine was a formality. I've captured the sun's rays; a river moves wheels for me; I made this bow, which can do—God knows what; I have an orchard; the hedgehog and the mole give me their hides; I have hemp for my nets; the porcupine supplies me with needles. The wild olive grows here, and wild barley too. I gather saffron on the hillsides for spice. We baked our first bread from crushed acorns, will you believe it? Sometimes we kill a boar. From the sea we catch mullet, bass, bream, and tunny; from the air and ground pheasants, quail, geese, rock-doves. But greatest wonder of all, here where men left me to rot, in this silence I can think at last. I ask questions of the stream and the tree leaf, of the spider and the seashell. Shall I tell you? I send my spirit prowling the night sky among the stars, like a child in dark streets who sees lights in the windows and puzzles at who and what is within. You, poor fools, your claptrap notions, as soon as they go outdoors, they stumble over "I am not paid enough!" or "Will the neighbors sneer?" or "My wife is growing fat!" Pah! Give me no news. Rid yourself instead of those "Messenian laggards" who are eating at your eyes and mouth. Oh, I notice!

DEMODOCUS. You notice my perplexity, Philoctetes, my admiration, my envy. We don't hear words like yours from Agamemnon! [*Silence*] Agamemnon is still alive, you see.

PHILOCTETES. Ah?

DEMODOCUS. And Menelaus too.

PHILOCTETES. Achilles defending them, of course, with a great bluster.

DEMODOCUS. No more, Philoctetes.

PHILOCTETES. Impossible. Achilles could die? Who killed Achilles?

DEMODOCUS. Hardly believable, but Paris did, with an arrow, by ignoble chance.

PHILOCTETES. And another chance shall kill Paris. But you, I imagine, are still hungry. Medon! Bring our young soldier a loaf of bread and a dish of plums. I talk like a lord! No wine, alas; but we do have bread of a kind. [MEDON *serves and reenters the cave*] Barley, you see, unleavened, not fit for a young nobleman.

DEMODOCUS. Excellent. Excellent. I marvel at you. The longer I am here—no, I daren't say it.

PHILOCTETES. Dare! Dare! I am perfectly meek.

DEMODOCUS. Then I will dare and tell you that I have a great wish, in spite of your anger, to lure you to Ilium with me—even on a raft. We need your hundred skills, your godly genius. At every council you, Philoctetes, are openly missed. And think of it—Achilles dead, Patroclus dead, Idomeneus dead, Leucus dead, Orsilocus dead, Creton dead, Menestheus dead—

PHILOCTETES. Yes yes yes yes, slaughter, dead dead dead. Enough, you are trying to make me weep; and I do, I do. Scoundrels! Yet there they lie on the sand, their brains smashed, their guts filling with maggots. But your Odysseus, is he still alive? No, tell me no more; what is it to me?

DEMODOCUS. He is still alive, God be thanked, and Diomedes too; but the glory is gone, and we remain on the plain of Ilium by a kind of habit, as if we had lost every other talent.

PHILOCTETES. Come, Demodocus, forget Troy. We have been two in this colony these many years, and now we'll be three.

DEMODOCUS. How is this possible? I was sent on a mission.

PHILOCTETES. I spit on your mission. Digging a grave for a thousand men. Look about you, my friend, and thank God he has delivered you. There's room on Lemnos for another man. You shall refresh us.

DEMODOCUS. Ah, if I were free, Philoctetes. . . . The truth is that I am sick of the noise and smell of other men, the hearty and disgusting comradeship, the bellowing in unison. Not even a privy to oneself. Fifty pallets on the ground in a row. A table where a hundred eat together. No thought without a chorus. Finally, you begin to confide over a cup of wine to a dozen bearded, swilling solitudes—out go your dearest secrets—you hate it afterwards; you are emptied into a gutter. Am I a man, you cry, am I a man or am I the cell of a polyp?

PHILOCTETES [*in pain*]. The cell of a polyp. My friend—don't stop—I hear it all—welcome now—

DEMODOCUS. You're ill! What can I do?

PHILOCTETES. The pain again again again. Look at me! A prince plagued by a foot! No—don't call Medon. I have troubled him enough.

DEMODOCUS. Tell me what I can do.

PHILOCTETES. Nothing. The wheel can't be stopped. Hold me. No. Stay away. [*Demodocus is averting and covering his face*] My friend—pity me—the Gods have cursed me. I don't know why. I was innocent!

DEMODOCUS. Is there no relief?

PHILOCTETES. No. I fall down and die for awhile and foul my cave. Wait for me. I can bear it.

DEMODOCUS. The bow is heavy. Let me hold it for you. I shall be waiting here.

[*Philoctetes gives him the bow*]

PHILOCTETES. You are kind. Medon! Medon!

[*He stumbles into the cave*]

DEMODOCUS. The bow in my hands! Kindness is rewarded. . . .

[*The* CHORUS *speaks with drum*]

SIXTH SOLDIER. Demodocus!

DEMODOCUS. Yes.

SECOND SOLDIER. Not so loud.

FIRST SOLDIER. We heard everything. Masterfully done!

SECOND SOLDIER. Masterfully!

FIRST SOLDIER. At first we worried. "Why doesn't he obey his instructions?" we asked each other. And suddenly you call out to him— "Give me the bow"—and he gives it to you like a child.

SECOND SOLDIER. You have to remember that he doesn't know how important it is.

[*Enter the* THIRD SOLDIER]

THIRD SOLDIER [*to the* FIRST SOLDIER]. We've sent the man, sir.

DEMODOCUS. Where have you sent what man?

FIRST SOLDIER. One of our men to inform Odysseus.

DEMODOCUS. Of what, busybody? Is it your duty to spy on me?

FIRST SOLDIER. No sir. My duty is to execute my orders. But why wait for Odysseus to come? We've got the bow.

THIRD SOLDIER. Now's the time to bolt.

FOURTH SOLDIER. But is this the bow we want?

FIFTH SOLDIER. Of course! Oh, I could dance and shout!

DEMODOCUS. Hands off! What I do with the bow concerns me.

FIRST SOLDIER. Do with the bow? What *can* you do with the bow? We have it! Have it!

SEVENTH SOLDIER. Why stand and wait here, Demodocus? Let's go and meet Odysseus halfway.

EIGHTH SOLDIER. I know why he hesitates.

SECOND SOLDIER. Why?

SIXTH SOLDIER. He has made friends with Philoctetes.

EIGHTH SOLDIER. No, I didn't mean that. Don't you remember that we really want Philoctetes himself? Who knows whether we can copy this bow? Whether we can handle it? What's it made of? Why does it have that curious knob in the middle? What kind of arrows does it take? I wouldn't dare use it. With this bow, the oracle said, we are doomed to win the war. But it's come into our hands too easily, that's all.

FOURTH SOLDIER. Are we sure this is really the bow itself?

FIFTH SOLDIER. Always a doubter in the crowd. Always a questioner.

FIRST SOLDIER. Demodocus, no more of this—let's take the bow to the ship and reason with Philoctetes afterward.

SECOND SOLDIER. From a position of strength.

THIRD SOLDIER. A bird in hand.

DEMODOCUS. A man who trusted me in the middle of my lies gave me the bow to safekeep for him.

FIRST SOLDIER. You asked and took it.

DEMODOCUS. He gave it to me! What if I walked into the cave while you stare at me and placed it in his companion's hand, scoundrel that I am?

FIRST SOLDIER. And the war?

FIFTH SOLDIER. We've got orders, Demodocus.

SIXTH SOLDIER. The whole army!

SECOND SOLDIER. Demodocus has made friends with Philoctetes.

SIXTH SOLDIER. That's what I said before.

SEVENTH SOLDIER. Why not? Philoctetes is a Greek.

SIXTH SOLDIER. A Greek! Did you hear him talk about the Greeks? He would eat us all boiled and salted if he could. And Demodocus was supposed to win him over. Instead it was Philoctetes who won *him* over.

FIFTH SOLDIER. The Trojans will get the bow! I see it!

SEVERAL. Quiet! God forbid! What next?

THIRD SOLDIER. Yes, the Trojans! Why not? They'll send Pandarus or another one of their professionals, somebody who won't mind a few lies and a length of dagger in the back if that's the way to purchase the bow.

FIRST SOLDIER. Demodocus, come with us, orders must be obeyed.

THIRD SOLDIER. Don't hesitate.

FIFTH SOLDIER. In another few minutes it will be too late.

SIXTH SOLDIER. Odysseus is your master.

SEVENTH SOLDIER. You'll repent it if he gets wind of this.

EIGHTH SOLDIER. And if you anger him.

SECOND SOLDIER. Stop! I hear steps.

[*Enter, running, the* NINTH SOLDIER]

NINTH SOLDIER. Here is Odysseus! Stand ready!

SCENE 3

[*Enter* ODYSSEUS, *accompanied by the* TENTH SOLDIER]
FIRST SOLDIER. Odysseus, we've got the bow!
ODYSSEUS. Childishness. Where is Philoctetes?
DEMODOCUS. He became sick. He's in the cave, unconscious.
ODYSSEUS. Medon is with him?
DEMODOCUS. Yes.
ODYSSEUS. What did you tell him?
DEMODOCUS. I served him the lie about the raft; I shrewdly aroused his
    longing for home and companionship; I successfully concealed your
    presence; I secured his sympathy by envying his manner of life; and I
    skillfully extracted the bow from his fingers. No, I did so well he
    foisted it on me.
ODYSSEUS. What have we here?
FIRST SOLDIER. See for yourself, Odysseus.
ODYSSEUS. An attack of sarcasm! What's the meaning of this? Hand me
    the bow.
DEMODOCUS. Why?
ODYSSEUS. Am I to give reasons? Hand me the bow!
DEMODOCUS. Odysseus, let me wait here until Philoctetes recovers. With
    your permission I shall reveal the truth to him and ask his pardon for
    my lies. I will even return the weapon to him. Then man to man,
    openly and clearly, you can summon him to Troy. This will be the
    real glory for us: to win over the man by honest persuasion.
FIRST SOLDIER. Don't stand for this, Odysseus. If you'd heard Philoc-
    tetes as we did, you'd know nothing will make him fight on our side.
    He says "Greek" the way a tiger growls.
ODYSSEUS. Is this true?
DEMODOCUS. Let me speak with him again. Give me more time. Think
    of his gratitude when we return—
ODYSSEUS. No. The man is obstinate. I know him well. The oracle's
    message must be conveyed to him without more preambles. I am
    glad you have the bow, however. I like him better disarmed. Take it
    back to the ship, my son. I'll wait here, talk to him as quietly as I am
    talking to you, and persuade him to return with us.
DEMODOCUS. And if he refuses? Now that I have made him helpless?
ODYSSEUS. Go back to the ship.
DEMODOCUS. What if, in his anger, he prefers the Trojans?
ODYSSEUS. Go back to the ship.
DEMODOCUS. I wish to stay here.
FIRST SOLDIER. This is open mutiny, Odysseus.
SECOND SOLDIER. I'm not surprised. Always two steps behind every-

body, and arguing, arguing, arguing.

THIRD SOLDIER. Argue Troy down if you can!

FOURTH SOLDIER. One man leaps up a battlement, sword in hand; another argues whether swords are fair weapons.

FIFTH SOLDIER. He acts as though he were the only man tired of war.

SIXTH SOLDIER. Ten years of bloody filth and now we're to lie down and die because we're too delicate!

EIGHTH SOLDIER. Give us the bow!

ODYSSEUS. Patience, my friends. All will be done gently. I myself, as it happens, do not question the loyalty of Demodocus. I understand his scruples. And yet, I don't know, I am no weakling; and we are many against one. We might have a scrap, shed some blood, but we could subdue him.

DEMODOCUS. What are you saying? Would I fight you? Never! No, I ask you simply as a man—

ODYSSEUS [*changing his tone*]. Ask me nothing. Men, draw your swords. Demodocus, I order you to take the bow to the ship. If you refuse, I advance on you myself. As I do, let the rest of you rush against him; if I die, take the bow, kill him, and kill Philoctetes.

DEMODOCUS. You're not serious!

ODYSSEUS. We'll see. You take me for a coward or a clown. [*He draws his sword.* DEMODOCUS *half raises the bow.* ODYSSEUS *throws his sword to the ground and slowly advances on the puzzled* DEMODOCUS. DEMODOCUS *retreats as far as he can*]

DEMODOCUS. Stop! Stop! [*He leaps away and disappears in the direction of the beach.* ODYSSEUS *picks up his sword and sheathes it. The others do likewise*]

ODYSSEUS. The bow is ours. But it's Philoctetes himself we want.

SEVENTH SOLDIER. And Demodocus? Surely you are not going to forgive him!

THIRD SOLDIER. He is a traitor, Odysseus. Will you not arraign him before the Assembly?

ODYSSEUS. I, not you, shall decide who is a traitor.

NINTH SOLDIER. The point is: we have the bow!

FIRST SOLDIER. And now for Philoctetes.

ODYSSEUS. Now for Philoctetes. Stand aside, men. I shall take my place here.

FIFTH SOLDIER. In the open?

ODYSSEUS. Man to man.

[*The* CHORUS *withdraws, except for the* TENTH SOLDIER]

ODYSSEUS. Stay.

TENTH SOLDIER. Yes, sir.

ODYSSEUS. I learned from Demodocus what I sent him for: how bitter the man is against us. I expected the worst; the worst is what I found.

TENTH SOLDIER. Yes.

ODYSSEUS. I will beg him again.

TENTH SOLDIER. God grant you success.

ODYSSEUS. I may fail. [*The soldier looks down*] Are you, are you all ready?

TENTH SOLDIER. My lord—

ODYSSEUS. Are you ready? God strike you!

TENTH SOLDIER. We are.

ODYSSEUS. Look out for my signal. If Zeus is merciful, I will not give it. If I give it, be prompt. The blood is on my head, not yours; but yours will answer if you disobey.

TENTH SOLDIER. You are the master, Odysseus. I am ready.

The CHORUS *speaks with harp and flute*

FIRST SOLDIER. Let us speak in praise of our lord Odysseus. To speak his praise is a lovely task, because whatever the brain shapes privately concerning this man, the mouth is glad to utter, and not only in the house, to father or wife or children, but in the market place, in the Assembly, to all men. It makes a man happy when he means his praise, when he bows because of the veneration he truly feels, when he presses a hand because he loves. Now, as is fitting, I will be the man to begin.

SECOND SOLDIER. What will you praise in Odysseus?

FIRST SOLDIER. I will praise his rank among the Greeks. Though he rules a harsh land, Ithaca, which has not grain enough to feed itself, and where few trees grow among the many-colored rocks, he is the man most honored by Agamemnon. Achilles was the stronger man; but he was proud, fierce, and factious. Menelaus is Agamemnon's brother, but he is a weak soldier, one who always leans against another. Diomedes is supreme in the battlefield; but he fights even in his dreams, even in his tent at supper, even in the Assembly. To every concern brought forward in the Assembly, he answers, "Fight!" Idomeneus was the richer man; he was king of Crete; he could plunge a hand into the treasury of magnificent Egypt; his palaces were thick and strong, with deep foundations; he called us rustics; yet because of all this, half of his mind stayed at home and only with the other half did he attend to our war. And still he died. No. Agamemnon's true brother is Odysseus, though Odysseus came to him with only twelve ships—he had no more. Odysseus is strong, wise, loyal: in the fight a fighter, in council a counselor, and, I will add, at supper a merry man. Agamemnon has said in public, "While Odysseus remains at my side, I will not lift the siege of Troy, I will never be disheartened. But if Odysseus chose to despair and withdrew from us, I too would give up." So much has Agamemnon himself said.

SECOND SOLDIER. Now let me speak of Odysseus the ruler of Ithaca. How did he come to rule? By means of conquest? By sly murder of his betters? By bribing the old men? By promising the riches of the Hesperides to our poor country? Not so. But by unanimous applause and election, promising nothing, threatening no one. And I ask you all, my friends, to tell his achievements.

THIRD SOLDIER. He taught us to build houses as fine as those of proud Argos.

FOURTH SOLDIER. He cleared the roads of bandits by hanging some and giving work to others.

FIFTH SOLDIER. He gave the poor bread without robbing the rich.

SIXTH SOLDIER. He proclaimed the festival of Pallas Athene, at which the young compete in the chariot race and the wrestling and the spear-throwing while the whole island, assembled, relaxes, takes sides, and is refreshed by idleness.

SEVENTH SOLDIER. He rescued the debtors from prison and proclaimed a full remission of all unpaid taxes.

EIGHTH SOLDIER. He gave us courts of justice and made an end of private revenge and family vendettas.

THIRD SOLDIER. He gave us peace without sloth—

FOURTH SOLDIER. And prosperity without vice.

FIFTH SOLDIER. Let me speak in my turn of Odysseus the master. I was a smith in his household before I became a soldier. And you too, my friend—

SEVENTH SOLDIER. I was a farmer.

FIFTH SOLDIER. You shall witness the truth of what I say. Did he ever speak brutally to any of us? He did not. Did he work us half to death, so that we lacked the living life on which to spend our earnings? He did not. Rather he came among us, taught us what he knew, and amazing to us, the poor, he asked to be shown; took the hammer in his own hands, spat like one of us, rolled back his sleeves, and worked.

SEVENTH SOLDIER. Once when my leg was lame he took the plow from me and turned the soil behind the ox all day long under the sun.

FIFTH SOLDIER. Singing—do you remember?—singing all the while! So that we glowed brighter than the hot iron and worked like Cyclops to please him.

SEVENTH SOLDIER. And he gave us sudden holidays. "Go, my lads," he said, "it's been a month since the harvest feast; time for a twelve-hour carouse!" Laughing as he talked, and going about boxing with the boys of the village.

EIGHTH SOLDIER. Now I will speak of Odysseus the husband and father. Noble Telemachus, his son, walks gravely by his side as he visits his people, or sits close by when he delivers judgment. He is less strong, less lively than his father; more sober, perhaps more delicate, more studious. But strong love binds these two men together. Have you seen Odysseus lean toward his son, whisper a question into his ear, receive a reply, and nod in approval? Wise is the father who knows how to flatter his son; who takes, or seems to take, advice from him. And from the day Telemachus was born, Odysseus himself raised him. He did not fear smiles by entering the nursery and seeing that the linen was washed. He was the boy's tutor, playmate, guide, and father; until it happened that, although Telemachus was only in his seventeenth year when his father left, Odysseus gave him the rule of Ithaca with peace and trust in his soul.

SIXTH SOLDIER. While Penelope his wife, glad and proud, having loved no man before and no man since, waits for the kindest husband who ever lived, in mourning and solitude. And even as she weeps, she is happy in her unhappiness, because the weight of her present misery is the measure of her former joy. Luckless woman, whom the loss of a husband cannot make unhappy! And by this I judge the goodness of Odysseus, that those who knew him best lament his absence most.

THIRD SOLDIER. And in the camp, my friends? Whose tent is empty? That of Odysseus. A man without handy concubines, without purchased whores, without soft-lipped slaves. The others quarrel over a captive and threaten civil war for the sake of a naked woman. They wake at noon from their debauches too destroyed to fight. Only Odysseus keeps faith with his wife. He rises from the banquet gay but clearheaded: even-tempered, his mind firm, his body controlled, his gaze like a prong of light into the dense world.

NINTH SOLDIER. See him now, sitting patiently. His fingers hold the strings of destiny.

FOURTH SOLDIER. Almost a god.

FIRST SOLDIER. Almost a god.

SCENE 4

ODYSSEUS. My friends, I hear a stirring in Philoctetes' mansion. Be vigilant. Philoctetes!

[PHILOCTETES *appears. He gives a shrill cry.* MEDON, *armed with his sword, stands next to him*]

ODYSSEUS. I am Odysseus.

PHILOCTETES. An army of Greeks. I should have known! [*He restrains*
MEDON *with his hand*]

ODYSSEUS. I greet you, and I greet Medon, with affection and respect. I
thank the Gods who have kept you full of strong life. Give me a
hearing, Philoctetes. Do not condemn us before we have spoken. We
come as your brothers.

PHILOCTETES. Odysseus: the same old fox. He sends me a young hypocrite to disarm me, he stalks me with a brace of tall ruffians, he stands
before me with his sword out, he murders, and as he murders he
cries out Brother!

ODYSSEUS. More gently, Philoctetes. We arrived in a strange land. Who
could predict what we should find? We are accustomed to war. But I
am reassured and I return my sword to its scabbard.

PHILOCTETES. Always the fox. What are you looking for?

ODYSSEUS. You.

PHILOCTETES. Has the oracle told you that Philoctetes must die?

ODYSSEUS. Far from it. Our solemn mission is to take you back to our
ranks.

PHILOCTETES. That is what your accomplice hinted. How affable to
poor Philoctetes! Fancy the Greeks at their Assembly one night, the
place stinking with corpses. Agamemnon strokes his beard and says,
"How I pity Philoctetes! Never has he had his chance of a nobly torn
belly or a gloriously broken skull."

ODYSSEUS. Let me speak.

PHILOCTETES. Then Diomedes takes the staff in his hand. "Oh my comrades," he brings out with tears of pity, "let us fetch the poor man
back among us to share in our sour wine, our stony bread, our broken bones, and our evening walks among the graves." Then they
send Odysseus off with a friend, and all for pity and affection they lie
to him, trick him, rob him of his weapon, and trap him in his cave.
Now Odysseus, speak up, good and blunt, and if it's blood you want,
spare me your apologies.

ODYSSEUS. You treat me, Philoctetes, as though I were childish enough
to treat you as a child. I have not come for pity of you. If circumstances require me to liquidate you, I shall do so. This we both know;
no fooling between us. As it happens, the oracle pronounces that
your good fortune is ours, and ours is yours. A common interest
binds us. Will you hear what it is? Or will you bite before the hand is
even stretched?

PHILOCTETES. Speak.

ODYSSEUS. The sentence came from Calchas the soothsayer. "Not by strength alone shall the Greeks overcome Troy, but by strength allied with immortal cunning. Let Pyrrhus, the son of Achilles, be our strength. Let Philoctetes, King of Malis, be our cunning."

PHILOCTETES. King of Malis? King?

ODYSSEUS. Your father is dead and you are king. And in the summer Troy will be toppled. Listen again. Calchas saw your bow in a dream: strong, far-shooting, unerring: its arrows deadlier than those of Crete or Thrace: your secret. Armed each one of us with this bow, we shall send into the bowels of Troy a panic like the trample of a falling mountain. And you, Philoctetes, you will live; you glorious to the end of time: cherished by Greece, your wound forgotten, a sage among men, one of us, Philoctetes, Greek again.

CHORUS [*low*]. One of us.

PHILOCTETES. He saw the bow in his dream?

ODYSSEUS. Yes, my friend. Let this persuade you of the truth of all I have told you. How could I have known that such a bow existed? Who knows except you, your companion, and the Gods?

PHILOCTETES. I can't answer you. I've become too simple here, I can't untwist your words.

FIRST SOLDIER. Noble Philoctetes, he speaks the truth.

PHILOCTETES. Well, the bow is in your hands. Demodocus stole it, if that's his name.

ODYSSEUS. Be indulgent with us, Philoctetes. The bow fell into our hands; we should have returned it to you; but we have been soldiers in the field too long; my men would not relinquish it.

PHILOCTETES. Keep it then, my friends, see if you can handle it, go back to your ships, let the pinewood oars fly, and good riddance to you all.

ODYSSEUS. And you?

PHILOCTETES. We stay here. I have my world. I need no other.

ODYSSEUS. Return with us, Philoctetes. Let the bow be your gift to us. Let us receive it from you, the man himself, and allow us to acknowledge you our friend, benefactor, and savior.

PHILOCTETES. I am satisfied here. You took the bow. Go back to Agamemnon.

ODYSSEUS. The bow is not enough, Philoctetes.

PHILOCTETES. I thought not! Away! Forget me!

ODYSSEUS. Ten years of loneliness is enough. Who can bear such loneliness? Medon may die.

PHILOCTETES. God forbid! I am the older man. I will be the first to die.

ODYSSEUS. Perhaps not. God may not forbid. And then what will become of you? You will howl on your knees and go mad. A man must live among his kind.

PHILOCTETES. Ruffian! Back to Troy! You are not my kind!
FIRST SOLDIER. Odysseus! I hear somebody running.
SEVENTH SOLDIER. There! There!
ODYSSEUS. Demodocus!
CHORUS. Stop!
[DEMODOCUS *rushes up to* PHILOCTETES *and thrusts the bow into his hands*]
DEMODOCUS. Your bow, Philoctetes! Forgive me!
PHILOCTETES [*aiming at* ODYSSEUS]. Back Odysseus, back! All the arrows, Medon!
ODYSSEUS. Back, men!
CHORUS. Oh God, help us!
PHILOCTETES. Stand back! Medon, look sharp. Back! Back!
ODYSSEUS [*to the Greeks*]. No violence, my friends. All in good time. I admire Demodocus in a way. I deplore what he did; I who thought he was speeding to our ships! But I admire him. It was his conscience.
DEMODOCUS. Why do you always jeer, Odysseus?
PHILOCTETES. Hands off your swords, all of you! Eyes open, Medon. Odysseus, don't stand there. Call your gang together and clear the island. The wind will be rising soon.
DEMODOCUS. Odysseus, this is our war, not his. Or his if he sees fit. And besides: I am no boy for dirty errands.
ODYSSEUS. We shall sit here and wait till nightfall.
PHILOCTETES. But if by nightfall you're not sailing in your ship, I will shoot you straight and happy through the heart.
ODYSSEUS. Let that be as it may. Patience. [*He sits on a rock and gives a discreet sign with his hand. The tenth soldier whispers into the ears of the* NINTH, EIGHTH, *and* SEVENTH, *and the four quietly leave*]
DEMODOCUS [*to* PHILOCTETES]. I will try to protect you.
PHILOCTETES. What are you doing?
DEMODOCUS. Going back.
PHILOCTETES. Don't be a fool, Demodocus; stay here. Odysseus is waiting to pounce on you. You're a traitor to Greece. Congratulations!
DEMODOCUS. I think otherwise. Odysseus, for once let a younger man persuade you. My tongue is cleansed. Allow me to plead with him. He trusts me now.
ODYSSEUS. Suit yourself, my lad.
[DEMODOCUS *advances toward the Greeks*]
PHILOCTETES. Don't be a fool!
ODYSSEUS. Take him! [*The soldiers leap at* DEMODOCUS. MEDON, *ready to rush to his help, is restrained by* PHILOCTETES]
DEMODOCUS. Scum!
ODYSSEUS. Hold the boy. From behind. Lock his arms. Bind his wrists. Now then, that's one.

DEMODOCUS. Fool, fool, fool.

PHILOCTETES [*to* MEDON]. The other opening must be guarded. Didn't
you see? A few of them slunk away. Go in and keep watch. [MEDON
obeys] Is that how you'll tempt me to return to Troy? Demodocus,
keep heart. The game isn't finished yet. Bandits! Leap at me! Leap!
Take my corpse to Troy! Manacle my corpse this time!

ODYSSEUS. Philoctetes! Once more! Return with us! How easily we
could capture you!

PHILOCTETES. You don't know what my bow can do. Go back without
me, rascals!

DEMODOCUS. They can't, Philoctetes! They must kill you if necessary!
They are afraid you'll cross to the Trojans!

[*The soldier guarding him forces* DEMODOCUS *to his knees.* DEMODOCUS *cries
out with pain*]

PHILOCTETES. The Trojans are coming too! Of course! Let Hector have
the bow! I'll make my home with them!

ODYSSEUS. Poor Hector. Hector is dead! But you are right, the Trojans
are coming. You are more than right: the Trojans have come! [*He
claps his hands*] I was about to mention them when Demodocus spoke
for me. I thank him.

FIRST SOLDIER. When did they land?

ODYSSEUS. Bring in the Trojans! Now my children, watch carefully.
Surprise Odysseus? Where is the man? There will be no Trojans to
traffic with, Philoctetes; I am going to teach you an unforgettable les-
son. [*Enter the four soldiers carrying two litters, each with a dead man on it*]
Look at your Trojan saviors. They are the last ones you will ever see.
Demodocus is wrong. You'll rot alone in this place.

FIRST SOLDIER. Odysseus, we are all amazed. What happened?

ODYSSEUS. One of our patrols found a small Trojan craft, and some
twenty men ashore. We took them by surprise and killed them all.

FIRST SOLDIER. With losses on our side?

ODYSSEUS. Not a man. Come, Philoctetes, come and look.

PHILOCTETES [*without moving*]. Odysseus, I tell you once again, take
yourself and your henchmen away. My bow is hungry for you. Beware.

ODYSSEUS. I understand. And I give up. If I take you alive, you will kill
yourself.

PHILOCTETES. Like a fly.

ODYSSEUS. Well, what matters in the end is that we shall have no com-
petitors. There they lie. You can even keep Demodocus. [*He seizes*
DEMODOCUS *and pushes him toward* PHILOCTETES, *who moves farther back*]
He's yours. [*He throws* DEMODOCUS *down with a blow*]

PHILOCTETES. Coward!

[PHILOCTETES *has left the opening of the cave unguarded. At a signal from*
ODYSSEUS, *the* FIFTH SOLDIER *rushes into the cave.* PHILOCTETES *utters a
cry but hesitates*]
MEDON [*within*]. Master!
ODYSSEUS [*shouting*]. Kill him!
PHILOCTETES. No!
MEDON [*within*]. Master!
PHILOCTETES. Don't kill him!
CHORUS. Kill!
DEMODOCUS. Kill Odysseus! [ODYSSEUS *catches hold of* DEMODOCUS *and
uses him as a shield*]
PHILOCTETES. I can't.
ODYSSEUS. Bring Medon out!
[*The* FIFTH SOLDIER *carries* MEDON's *body out. With a mighty effort* PHILOC-
TETES *breaks his bow in two. He flings himself over the body.* ODYSSEUS
surrenders DEMODOCUS, *still bound, to one of the soldiers*]
SIXTH SOLDIER. He broke the bow!
FOURTH SOLDIER. He broke the bow!
PHILOCTETES. In my brain too, the bow is broken. Force me back if you
    like. My dead body is yours. Oh Heracles, let them perish before
    Troy all of them, and you, Odysseus, may your corpse be left to the
    dogs, let them devour you and make you their excrement.
ODYSSEUS. Why do you rail at me, Philoctetes? It is you who killed
    Medon, not I. Your hatred for us has made you insane. We came
    here, Greek to Greek, brother to brother, offering you and Medon
    immortal glory, love and reverence. You raved at us as if we, and not
    the serpent, had bitten your ankle that foul day in the grove of
    Chryse. Yet still we offer you the haven of our friendship, still we
    clamor for your help, still we look upon you as our teacher. And such
    is our awe for a man marked by the Gods that we will not compel you
    even now. I now abandon you to your wrath and your misery. I shall
    report you mysteriously dead amidst a crowd of Trojan corpses, and
    exhibit these poor victims for proof. The Trojans will not come
    again. Neither shall we. Never, never will you see a human being
    again. Soldiers! Sack the cave. Destroy everything.
[*Several soldiers enter the cave*]
THIRD SOLDIER [*low*]. Alone . . .
SIXTH SOLDIER [*low*]. Alone . . .
DEMODOCUS. Philoctetes . . .
PHILOCTETES. What?
DEMODOCUS. I pity you.
PHILOCTETES [*to* ODYSSEUS]. Release the boy, Odysseus. What does it

matter to you now? Let him stay here.
ODYSSEUS. Break everything, men. Break!
CHORUS. Alone. . . .
[*The soldiers appear*]
SECOND SOLDIER. Everything is smashed.
ODYSSEUS. Drag the body inside—throw it on the heap. It will be
   stinking soon, stronger than Philoctetes himself. [*To the* CHORUS]
   Back to the ship, my friends.
FIRST SOLDIER. Without him?
ODYSSEUS. Without him. He will never give us his secret.
SECOND SOLDIER. No pity for us?
THIRD SOLDIER. For us who have to do the fighting?
FOURTH SOLDIER. For us who only obey orders?
FIFTH SOLDIER. We never meant you any harm.
SIXTH SOLDIER. Harm? We wanted to fall at your feet.
THIRD SOLDIER. The common soldier was always your friend.
SIXTH SOLDIER. What have we got to do with oracles, higher strategy,
   new weapons, headquarters, military policy?
FIFTH SOLDIER. It is us you punish, not Odysseus, not Agamemnon.
FOURTH SOLDIER. And our wives, our children, who don't even know
   you.
ODYSSEUS. Away, soldiers. No tears. The bow doesn't matter if no one
   has it.
[*The* CHORUS *slowly leaves*]
PHILOCTETES. Leave me Demodocus! I beg you!
[DEMODOCUS *is carried off. The litters with the dead men are taken away too.
   Only* ODYSSEUS *and* PHILOCTETES *are left.* PHILOCTETES *is trembling*]
ODYSSEUS. How quiet it is. Nothing but my voice remains. And after me,
   nothing. [*He draws a dagger, rises and advances toward* PHILOCTETES]
PHILOCTETES. You'll murder me? [*But* ODYSSEUS *throws the dagger at*
   PHILOCTETES' *feet*]
ODYSSEUS. When you are sick of the silence, oh my brother, my
   brother. . . .
[*He turns and leaves.* PHILOCTETES *is alone. He seems bewildered. He enters
   the cave, and comes out again, a broken man, holding a few scraps. Total
   silence. A long time passes. The silence continues. Suddenly he flings himself
   toward the far end of the stage, where the Greeks left, and utters a wild cry*]
PHILOCTETES. Take me! Odysseus! Take me! [*The drum beats hard. The*
   FOURTH SOLDIER *appears*] Take me! Take me! Take me! [*He is sobbing*]
FOURTH SOLDIER. Odysseus! Come back! Take him!
A VOICE [*in the distance*]. Take him!
[PHILOCTETES *lies on the ground. His sobs diminish.* HERACLES *appears*]

HERACLES. Philoctetes, rise, rise! Heracles calls you. Be reconciled. Rise! The serpent and the eagle shall unite. Troy shall fall. Glory to Greece. Glory to man!

[*Reenter* ODYSSEUS, DEMODOCUS, *and the* FIRST *to* SIXTH *soldiers. All except* DEMODOCUS *fall prostrate before* HERACLES]

HERACLES. Rise, Greeks, rise most noble Odysseus. I give you this man, sundered from you so that he might, unknowing, devise your salvation. Take his hand. Honor him. You have mastered him, but now acknowledge him your master. He cowers; he is small and weak; his eyes are filmed with grief and fear; yet he is like a God among you; his thought shall break the citadels. Troy shall fall. And Troy shall be torn out of the earth like a cankered tree.

ODYSSEUS. Humbly, with reverence unutterable, I take back to our thousands, and to Agamemnon the tower above the host, the promise, the certainty, the signature of Zeus.

[*The drum rolls.* HERACLES *vanishes*]

ODYSSEUS. Soldiers, conduct noble Philoctetes to our ship. The bitter words and the cruel acts are erased. The King of Malis is our commander now. Treat him with fear and veneration.

[*The* FIFTH *and* SIXTH *soldiers escort* PHILOCTETES *out*]

ODYSSEUS. Friends, our mission is accomplished; not without difficulties, not, alas, without bloodshed, but accomplished, I believe, in a manner which must satisfy the supreme command. Demodocus, you are pardoned. Unbind him. I will leave you to the private obscurity of your shame, your petty emotions, your pampered self-concern, and not curb you to the prosecution you deserve. Philoctetes is ours, body and soul. Now let the Trojans land and look for him!

FIRST SOLDIER. The Trojans? But you killed them!

ODYSSEUS. No, my children. Sooner or later you must know. Harden yourselves against the inevitable. These two men were sailors on our craft. [*The* CHORUS *cries out in grief*] Their lives were demanded of them, two for ten thousand. Alas. . . .

FIRST SOLDIER. Odysseus!

DEMODOCUS. You murdered two of our men?

ODYSSEUS. When you failed us, Demodocus, when your conscience became petulant, you forced me to give the terrible command. With the bow in his fist, Philoctetes was intractable. I made an inhuman desert about him. I destroyed his nest. I showed him the face of silence. I broke him.

FIRST SOLDIER. But then, surely, master, you never meant to leave Philoctetes behind, with the Trojans on their way even now! What if he had not cried out for us in the end?

ODYSSEUS. He did cry out for us in the end.

FIRST SOLDIER. I shudder at your cunning, Odysseus. Always in control, even when you are surprised. I will never admit that Philoctetes is an intelligent man, in spite of his inventions.

ODYSSEUS. The intelligent man is not always the clever man. No gloating. Let us be soberly satisfied.

FIRST SOLDIER. Not you, Odysseus. Wherever you go, it seems to us that a shimmer of divinity surrounds you.

ODYSSEUS. Wherever I go, I am knee-high in dung and blood. Come, children, away. Demodocus, are you ready?

DEMODOCUS. Leave me here.

ODYSSEUS. Leave you here?

DEMODOCUS. Yes.

ODYSSEUS. Alone?

DEMODOCUS. Yes.

SECOND SOLDIER. Don't be a fool, Demodocus. Come with us.

THIRD SOLDIER. No one will remind you of anything.

FOURTH SOLDIER. Your place in the field is still your place.

THIRD SOLDIER. Do we speak for you, Odysseus?

ODYSSEUS. You do.

DEMODOCUS. Leave me here. Give me some clothes, a few knives, tools, anything you can or will.

ODYSSEUS. What shall we do, my friends? For myself, I don't care. Let him do as he pleases. Demodocus, we set off when the wind blows into our sails. Come if you wish, stay if you wish. You are too small for my concern. [*He leaves*]

[*The* CHORUS *speaks with harp*]

FIRST SOLDIER. As a man older than you and more experienced by far, I will address you freely, Demodocus, and call you a coward. You will tell us that you despise the world, that you abhor mankind, that you condemn life—

SECOND SOLDIER. All of which are words suitable to a poet.

FIRST SOLDIER. But in reality you fear the world.

SECOND SOLDIER. Your decision is not strength, but spite; not courage, but shame.

THIRD SOLDIER. And the cheering fire in the house? The open door, the embrace? "You've come back to us," they cry. They take off your cloak, they bathe your feet, they offer you wine and honey, they cry and fuss over you.

FOURTH SOLDIER. Human beings.

SECOND SOLDIER. Others.

THIRD SOLDIER. Yet yours, your own.

FOURTH SOLDIER. Invisible strings between you and them.

SECOND SOLDIER. Once long ago I quarreled bitterly with my father because he loved my brothers, but me he neglected and even starved; sometimes he beat me; he called me a vagabond. And I left the house; I went to Corinth; I lived alone among strangers. At night I heard the voices next door to mine; during the day I saw people in the street: families, lovers, friends, or polite acquaintances—I envied them all, even the man who patted a dog; and now and then I saw a man alone, like myself, and that man wore the same expression as mine, a studied air of indifference to conceal his despair. He looks around and seems to say, "Me? I am alone only for the moment! I am expecting a happy crowd of friends. Don't worry about me, I beg you." But inside he cries. He goes home and stares at the wall opposite his chair. He eats an apple. He writes a letter. He washes his face. And he sits again and stares. Presently he begins to talk to himself. Then he stops, because he is ashamed. What will he do? He is not tired. What can he do? He paces the floor, lifts a vase from a shelf, places it on a table, he doesn't know why, and sits down again. All he wants now is to see a human being. He knows one at the far end of the city. But this man has a wife and two small children, and it would be a disturbance to knock at his door. What excuse would he have for the visit? He could say, "Excuse me, but I came to borrow the hand-saw you promised me." Perhaps the wife would ask him to come in and share their meal. But if she did, he would reply, "Thank you, but I must hurry, I have an appointment," lest they ridicule him with pity; and he would go home again, and sit, stare, and suffer. Oh Demodocus, believe me, I returned to my birthplace, I kissed the first friend I met in the street; he thought I was mad.

FOURTH SOLDIER. And the war, for that matter, is that so bad after all?

SECOND SOLDIER. No! Better this war all my life, and to lose both my arms, than another month of loneliness.

THIRD SOLDIER. A comrade keeps you warm too.

SECOND SOLDIER. In the heat of battle you hear and see your platoon.

THIRD SOLDIER. At night you roar out a song together.

FOURTH SOLDIER. You share a bottle.

SECOND SOLDIER. A story.

THIRD SOLDIER. A woman.

FOURTH SOLDIER. Show me a good brawler and I'll show you a reliable friend.

SECOND SOLDIER. The worst kind is the man who has no enemies. He has no friends either.

THIRD SOLDIER. Cold blood.

SECOND SOLDIER. Sitting in a corner.

FOURTH SOLDIER. He doesn't know it, but if you left him alone on an island, he would clamor for you, though he acted as if he didn't even know your name.

SECOND SOLDIER. Yes, it's easy to look self-sufficient when you're in good company.

THIRD SOLDIER. For whom will you sing? How will you fare without us who are the listeners? When you sang, we sat still and yet we traveled; we were ourselves and yet we became other men; our lives multiplied; wisdoms not our own became ours. Such was your power over us. But without us, where is your power?

FIRST SOLDIER. Come with us, Demodocus. This is too horrible. You will babble at random and finally lose your language. You will crouch on all fours like a beast. Who knows? You will fornicate with an animal, and beget a monster. Demodocus, live among men. Even hate is better than solitude. The universe is morose, the Gods condemn us; everywhere you look the stars drive insanely in the dense cavern, and we, we few, we poor few, should huddle here and hold each others' hands and say goodbye to the dying, and kiss their lips with a last warmth. But you will die alone, growling vacantly, your head on a stone, and the wild pigs will eat you.

[*Silence*]

FOURTH SOLDIER. He won't say a word.

A VOICE [*in the distance*]. Men! The wind is rising, hurry, hurry!

FIRST SOLDIER. Demodocus. If you came running after us, and caught the rope-ladder while the ship moved away, you might cut a shabby or laughable figure. Many a fool will die rather than cut a shabby or laughable figure. Don't be a fool.

[*The* CHORUS *slowly leaves. A long silence follows*]

DEMODOCUS. Erased from the records of the city and the temple, I now become free and innocent, not rising, not sinking, dumb as the laurel, still as a comet, clean as a drop of rain, patient as a rock, peaceful as the dust. I will stop singing, being perfect. I will be reticent. I will listen to the sea's liquid speech, not one hypocrite among all its syllable waves. Philoctetes, I see Troy in torment to the end of time, to the end of time I hear the scurrilous mirth of the conqueror, the unjust and the just; but to me the seagull will report only the fish dancing in the sea, innocently devouring, innocently devoured. Now my peace begins. And to begin it, Demodocus must bury a man.

Heiner Müller

PHILOCTETES
(1965)

Translated by Oscar Mandel, in collaboration with Maria
Kelsen Feder, from *Philoktet*

An East German writer heavily marked by the ideological preoccupations of the Communist world, Heiner Müller—born in Saxony in 1929—has nevertheless imposed himself throughout the German-speaking zone of Europe as one of its foremost playwrights.[1]

Philoctetes is the fifth of a long series of plays and translations, and the first of several in which Müller turned to classical mythology for his parable. It was published for the first time in *Sinn und Form,* an East German periodical, in 1965 (vol. 17, no. 5), and has since been reprinted in book form four times in West Germany and twice in East Germany. The most recent reprint is in the sixth volume of Müller's plays, issued by Rotbuch Verlag in West Berlin. *Philoctetes* has also become one of his most frequently performed plays, even though it was not staged professionally in his homeland until 1977. Indeed, Müller's relations with the authorities and critics of the German Democratic Republic have long been uneasy, after the all too familiar pattern.

The world premiere of *Philoctetes* took place in Munich, at the Residenz Theater, in 1968 under Hans Lietzau's direction. The same

---

1. I am indebted for the factual material in this headnote to a generous communication by Professor Marc Silberman, and another by Sigrid Kupsch-Losereit.

Three of Müller's dramatic works have been translated so far into English, all by Marc Silberman and Helen Fehervary: The *Horatian* (*Minnesota Review,* Spring 1976); *Mauser* (*New German Critique,* Spring 1976); and *Cement* (*New German Critique,* Winter 1979). *Cement* was produced at the Berkeley Stage in 1979.

A sound introduction to Müller's work can be found in Wolfgang Schivelbusch's *Sozialistisches Drama nach Brecht* (Darmstadt: Luchterhand, 1974). The section pertaining to Müller has been translated as "Optimistic Tragedies: The Plays of Heiner Müller" in *New German Critique* (Spring 1974). Several other articles on Müller have appeared in this journal since that date. Discussions in German are by this time voluminous. The yearly bibliographies of the Modern Language Association should be consulted; but a great deal of additional material is to be found in German, Austrian, and Swiss newspapers.

director mounted a production in Hamburg, West Berlin, and Venice in 1970. A student production took place in Leipzig at the Karl-Marx University in 1974. Later notable productions occurred in Ulm in 1975, in Posnan and Torun (Poland) in 1976, and at the Deutches Theater in East Berlin in 1977. The play has also been staged in Hanover, Mainz, Bern, Vienna, Belgrade, and Paris, and for West German television (WDR-TV network). In January 1980—a few weeks before the present words were written—it was produced in Kaiserslautern, one reviewer calling it "one of the most beautiful and at the same time most difficult works of art of the German post-war theater," and its author "the most significant living writer of the German Democratic Republic."

In the plays we have considered so far, ethical affirmation is not hard to find; and the clashes dramatized in these texts are on the whole quarrels between positive and positive. Müller's play is far more refractory. Indeed, at the first shock of contact, the reader may feel that the playwright endorses nothing whatsoever. His three characters seem *entheroisiert*—"de-heroized"—as one East German critic complained. Is Müller by any chance a surreptitious Absurdist? Did his *Philoctetes* anticipate Ionesco's *Macbett*?

Such a reading would at any rate explain the Communists' distrust of the play. In his earlier works Müller had not been so morally tightfisted. There too grim work needed to be done for the Cause, but as it was a Cause worth doing grim work for—so the texts explained—the orthodox were not excessively jolted. In *Philoctetes*, however, he seemed to have gone too far. The grimness was still present; but where now was the Cause? Odysseus himself characterizes it as a butchery. Since he is a willing butcher, the suspicion arises that Müller is intent on exhibiting, not perhaps a tale told by an idiot, but an idiotic tale signifying nothing; and Odysseus becomes that familiar figure, the genius with respect to means and idiot with respect to ends: the military man blindly obeying murderous orders.

Müller himself has let it be known to his countrymen that his Trojan War represents a conflict under pre-Communist conditions, that is to say of wolf against wolf. But no one has swallowed the bait. In Communist art, an author who depicts a war among feudal lords or industrialists is expected to give strong expression to the underdogs who suffer no matter whose side wins; who are, abjectly or heroically, cannon-fodder for their masters; who ought to take the war into their own hands; whose voice, though suppressed, is heard in the wings; and so forth. Nothing of the sort transpires in Müller's craggy text.

All the same, he is not an Absurdist, and I think it can be shown that his play does obey the orthodox pattern, though it obeys with so little ethical enthusiasm, it is so very reticent, its voice is so uniformly grim, that one must sympathize with the suspicions of his orthodox critics.

Müller has boldly reversed Sophocles. For what is Philoctetes if not the regressive individualist so immersed in his private grievances that he cannot see anything beyond and above them? He may be right in his limited way, but limited ways are wrong. The Chorus in *Mauser* (1970) speak words appropriate to him, if we substitute Troy for Vitebsk:

> Nicht eh die Revolution gesiegt hat endgultig
> In der Stadt Witebsk wie in andern Städten
> Bist du dein Eigentum.

(Not until the Revolution has won its final victory in the city of Vitebsk as in other cities do you belong to yourself.)

The same words can be thrown in the face of Neoptolemus. All he can see is the supposed affront to his private honor. He fails to understand that this affront—Odysseus's seizure of the dead Achilles' weapons—was dictated by policy; was meant for the public good. He lives only for his private vendetta. Like Philoctetes, he is the self-absorbed individualist; and like Philoctetes, he is destined for the scrap heap of history.

His attempt to return the bow to Philoctetes is again made under the emblem of private honor. The text forbids us to call this gesture a moral victory. Odysseus is right: this compassion of Neoptolemus is misplaced, subversive, irresponsible, blind to the needs of the Cause. Here is the very subject Brecht had treated in *The Measure Taken*. Furthermore, if he deserves to be praised for shielding Odysseus from Philoctetes' arrow, we must bear in mind that it was his mistaken "bourgeois" compassion which gave Philoctetes the arrow in the first place. Now, in order to repair his mistake, he is compelled to kill Philoctetes, and thus—as far as he knows—jeopardize the whole Greek enterprise. In short, Philoctetes is a whiner, and Neoptolemus a blunderer. Both are duly defeated, and history marches on, headed by Odysseus.

Gradually, therefore, Odysseus emerges as an authentic hero, though a difficult one. Consider some of his qualities. He alone places the Cause above private considerations. We absolutely believe him when he offers to die for it. His clearheadedness is remarkable. So is his honesty: he calls cheating cheating, a massacre a massacre. He is anything but bloodthirsty. He will kill if he must, but he will try not to. He alone of the three men has a sense of the horror of the war: the others are too selfish to notice. His words of despair over the body of Philoctetes are immensely noble, but despair is only a passing phase with a great leader, and he returns to the task. He does not waste time in recriminations against Neoptolemus. And finally he proves himself the man of the future by deciding not to allow "fate" to beat him. Making the best of a very bad thing, he disinters Philoctetes in order to produce the corpse to the Greeks. That too will help. In short, Odysseus is adaptable. He moves with the circumstances. Somehow the war will be won even without Philoctetes.

Incidentally, Müller has introduced several changes of mind or direction in the play, chief among them this last new angle. He is a good Brechtian here, and Odysseus an excellent Marxist. Nothing is foredoomed; everything can be altered by men who use their reason. As for the harshly humorous finale, it allows Odysseus the satisfaction, for one permissible moment, of getting even with the incompetent Neoptolemus; but it also displays one last time his supreme mastery.

Still, the question remains, What of the Cause? I repeat that Communist critics have every reason to worry about its failure to do what might facetiously be called a song and dance before our eyes. But for the rational critic this reticence is hardly a problem. In the West, for example, everyone agreed that World War II was fought in a good cause, yet few expressed themselves in the lyrical and discredited mode of World War I. I think that Müller has taken this same sophisticated approach in *Philoctetes*. There is work to be done. It *must* be done. The work is dirty. Let us get on with it. But let us not pretend it is clean. We might call this a Western approach. And it is the approach rather than the thesis which disconcerts Communist critics.

It may be that the finest thesis hidden in the text was succinctly expressed by Müller in *The Horatian* (written in 1968–69):

> Die Worte müssen rein bleiben.
>
> (The words must be kept clean.)

At the heart of *Philoctetes* is a desperate longing for incorruptible honesty—for an end to propaganda and sentimentalities. Again: not the Cause, but the approach to the Cause is contested, to the chagrin of the orthodox.

The reversal of Sophocles is completed. Odysseus is right. The good of the state is supreme. The return of the bow to Philoctetes is blameworthy. Müller has in effect reasserted the pre-Sophoclean thesis. Reasserted it, in fact, with superb Greek candor; for the Greeks had been perfectly capable of recognizing, in their most public poetry, that the state, though it should be served, can be a dark-hearted master. Müller's subversively tragic vision is the revival of an Homeric insight.

CHARACTERS

PHILOCTETES
ODYSSEUS
NEOPTOLEMUS

PROLOGUE

[*Spoken in a clown's mask by the actor who portrays* PHILOCTETES]

Dear audience, the play we are about to show
Will waft you from today to long ago
When man was foe to man, when life was tough,
And every month another bloody war came off.
Our spectacle is grim—let me be plain—
It lacks a Message to take home and frame,
Or useful lesson for a cloudy day.
If you're alarmed—the exit lies that way.
[*The doors fly open*]
You've had your chance.
[*The doors close. The clown unmasks and reveals a death's head*]
              Our business hereafter
Is meant for something else than laughter.

[SHORE]
[ODYSSEUS. NEOPTOLEMUS]
ODYSSEUS. This is the place, Lemnos. Here, son of Achilles,
    Is where I beached the man from Melos[1]
    Philoctetes, wounded in our service
    And unserviceable since. Puss oozed
    Stinking from his wound. His shrieks broke our sleep,
    Broke too the silence prescribed at sacrifice.

---

1. Müller has the island Melos instead of the usual mainland Malis. Here and throughout I have remained passably faithful to the author's highly personal punctuation. (All notes are by the editor).

223

This hill's his home, not his tomb I hope.
His cave, a hole ground out by slow water
Ages ago when fish swam where our heels
Tread the dry soil. A spring nearby, unless
Ten years have blotted it. Go. Find his dwelling.
This done, hear my plan and learn your part in it.
NEOPTOLEMUS. The place is quickly found.
ODYSSEUS.   Empty?
NEOPTOLEMUS.   A bed
Of leaves. A cup made of raw wood. Flints. Rags
Soaked in black blood and hung to dry in the wind.
ODYSSEUS. The old wound. He must be close, grubbing
For nourishment or herbs to deaden pain.
Let him not take us by surprise. Me
More than anyone he'd love to kill.
NEOPTOLEMUS. Because you were the knife that cut him off.
ODYSSEUS. You be the net in which I'll pluck him back.
NEOPTOLEMUS. Your words leave wide meshes. What must I do?
ODYSSEUS. Help us. Give unsparingly of yourself.
NEOPTOLEMUS. I do not live to keep myself alive.
ODYSSEUS. Nor must you live to keep your honor safe.
Cheat the bow out of his hand. Were *I* to speak,
Arrows would rush the words back to my mouth.
You he cannot blame for his misfortune.
You did not sail with us. So fork your tongue,
Disarm and make him helpless. Easy work.
And easy work to drag him to our ship.
NEOPTOLEMUS. I came with you to help and not to lie.
ODYSSEUS. Here it happens that the lie will help.
NEOPTOLEMUS. Truth may do more.
ODYSSEUS.   Not ours. Not with him.
NEOPTOLEMUS. How can he harm two men on his one foot?
ODYSSEUS. He can do that and more armed with his bow.
NEOPTOLEMUS. But why not cross our arrows with his own?
ODYSSEUS. Who follows a dead leader into battle?
NEOPTOLEMUS. I think he'll hold his arrows in their quiver
Seeing ours poised on their string.
ODYSSEUS.   He loves our deaths
Better than his life. Furthermore, no life
On Lemnos can be spared, war needs them all.
NEOPTOLEMUS [*throwing down his spear*].
I'll drag him to the ship with my bare hands.

ODYSSEUS [*picks up the spear*].
  Play the hero anywhere but here. Here
  Be shrewd. I cannot use a dead man's cunning.
  Learn from me, before his arrows teach you,
  Fool, that this would be your final errand,
  If I failed to stop you.
NEOPTOLEMUS.   Leave me my errand,
  You keep your fear.
ODYSSEUS. Stop, or else with your own spear
  I'll nail you to this island. Heracles
  Will not appear to you as once he did
  To Prometheus the thief whom Zeus
  Flung for eternal playmate to his birds.
  Your flesh is not the kind that grows again.
  You on your rock the vultures shall pick clean.
NEOPTOLEMUS. Bold words to a defenseless man.
ODYSSEUS.   To teach
  A fool how hollow is defenselessness.
NEOPTOLEMUS. Yes, with *my* spear. And not for the first time
  You hold what's mine, ever competent
  In theft, and best of all at robbing me.
  Flouting justice and wronging me you grasp
  The famous sword, the much-scarred oxhide
  That were my father's when he still had hands
  To use them. Both spears are mine. Give me one.
  I'll show you what a single spear can do.
ODYSSEUS. Show me another time, another place.
  I have seen your spear blood-red
  And do not doubt you slaughter like a man.
  But alive is how I need you, alive
  You too you need me for the moment.
  I command a thousand spears by chance of birth;
  You another thousand; and he disposes
  Of a thousand more—all lost to us
  If you demur. Because I need these arms
  I sailed to Skyros, hauled you off to Troy
  Before you'd tasted life—your father dead,
  Too soon dead for us, his regiments
  Refusing battle, swilling his wine
  And playing dice over his female slaves—
  They had done without too long battling
  To serve Achilles' fame, increase his loot,

And hang the mighty Hector on his spear.
We needed you to club them back to battle
As now we need the king of Melos for his men.
Useless your single hand, untrained for war,
Useless his single hand, one man alone,
But men march willingly in their own blood
Under a leader's boot whose leather
Smells of home. I took your legacy but not
To nurse my fame. Too many men of mine
Had died over Achilles when the fight
Broke out over your father's corpse. Their scars
Cried out but cry no more now that his shield
His sword, his spear, earned by their blood, are mine.
If Philoctetes swims out of our net
His soldiers turn their backs, shrug off our war,
The Trojan washes in our blood and feeds
Our carrion to his native vultures. Come,
You are no thief, no liar. This I know.
But sweet, son of Achilles, sweet is victory.
So coat your tongue with dirt one single day,
One day, we need no more, the rest of life
While life is yours be filled with virtue.
The dirty grave awaits us all if you refuse.
NEOPTOLEMUS. Nothing good grows out of rotten soil.
ODYSSEUS. Soil is one thing, the tree another.
NEOPTOLEMUS. The storm asks of the tree: "Will your roots hold?"
ODYSSEUS. It does not ask the forest.
NEOPTOLEMUS.   Which fire consumes.
ODYSSEUS. Or water, when a flood churns up the soil.
    Something else kills something else, what comes goes,
    And we'll philosophize on Ilium's ruins.
NEOPTOLEMUS. I wish I had no ear or tongue for you.
    Tell me the lies that I must tell.
ODYSSEUS.   Your spear.
    You need not lie in all particulars.
    You are and shall be son of Achilles,
    Best of all our fighters until Paris,
    Expert thief of women, shot him dead.
    Then lie: a wind of hatred blows you home,
    Hatred for the Greeks, hatred above all
    For me. We had summoned you to Troy
    And fame before your father's ashes cooled

Because his soldiers, sunk in mourning,
Would not fight, the war stood still. You came,
But came to grief, your legacy denied, your claim
Denied, and it was I who most deceived you,
I stole the weapons, your inheritance.
NEOPTOLEMUS. Be still if safe return is what you crave.
ODYSSEUS. Slash your own arm if greedy taste for blood
Got from your mother's milk now plagues you
Or I shall beat you back to our alliance,
Beat you with the handle of your father's spear.
NEOPTOLEMUS. I owe my hatred to the enemy,
Such is my duty till the day Troy falls.
That day in my own cause I'll give my spear
Another blood to drink. But do not taunt,
Odysseus, do not cut short your days.
ODYSSEUS. Save your rancor for your mission. Heap mud
Upon my name, do, to your heart's content.
Nothing that helps the cause hurts me. You'll blear
His eyes for your attack till artlessly
He thrusts the arrows and the deadly bow
Into your hands, believing yours, like his,
Yearn to press the blood out of my flesh.
I chose you as the partner in my plan
Because to tell this lie you need not lie,
I have in you a foe to net a foe.
He will mistake your blush of shame for rage
And rage it is perhaps and you yourself
Question whether the blood that rushes
To your temples is the blood of shame
Because you lie, or rage because you don't,
And so your truth will grow more credible
The more your face is painted by your lie.
NEOPTOLEMUS. Be your own partner in this dirty game.
ODYSSEUS. You're not the first man in our war to act
Against his will. Others once shirked like you.
Your father shirked in women's clothes. But I,
Playing the merchant, stripped them off his back,
Offering household wares for sale and tools
Of war. The women of the palace bought
What women buy, but one did not, one shrank
From household wares and grasped the weaponry:
Brave Achilles was the spurious lady!

Me too the princes tricked into their war.
I played the madman then; called my oxen
Generals; threw salt into the furrows;
Pretended not to know my old companions.
They tore my son out of his mother's arms,
They threw him down before my plow; barely
Barely I stopped two times four hooves moving
And hard to stop in motion, terrified
Lest my dear son's dear blood revive the soil
That I had filled with salt to save my life.
They found me sane in short and I was forced
To do my duty. Stories! What next?
Will falling on my knees content you?
[*He kneels*]
NEOPTOLEMUS. Were I a Trojan, sweet would be my duty now.
Well-trained in kissing dust are your two knees.
My father saw you thus. Saw the heroes
Likewise making curtseys in his presence
When his lasting wrath held up your war
Because you would bejewel your poor selves
With his first victory and crop his fame.
ODYSSEUS. More than loss of glory division
Of the booty made him mad. Yet shrewder
Was the father than his son. Well he knew,
While in the dust we counted stones, our death
Was his if he surrendered to his wrath
And let the rust devour sword and shield.
It is your life I ask for on my knees.
[*Rises*]
Your fish is coming, net. His foot still drags.
Farewell for now, for seen with me you die
Before you've stilled your craving for my blood.
NEOPTOLEMUS. He seems more animal than man.
Black vultures swarm above his head.
ODYSSEUS. Beware his bow while he retains it.
And, till bound or free he follows us
To Ilium, where Asclepius heals his foot
And he can stanch for us the greater wound
From which two nations' blood has poured too long—
Until that stinking man can help us
From the stench of war, fear his pain, it is
More dangerous than his deadly arrow.

You heal his wound if you are blind to it.
You still his groans if you are deaf to them.
The work that's to be done is yours alone.
My part, to beg of Hermes, god of wiles,
To add a portion to your store of wiles;
And may Athena, she whom Zeus severed
From his head, help you to victory.
[*Off.* PHILOCTETES *appears*]
PHILOCTETES. Life in my dead land. A thing that walks erect
As I did once elsewhere on two firm legs.
Who are you, biped? Man, beast, or Greek?
If Greek, you die.
[NEOPTOLEMUS *makes a move as if to take cover*]
                              Fly on a thousand feet:
My dart flies faster.
[NEOPTOLEMUS *stops*]
                              Throw down your spear.
[NEOPTOLEMUS *obeys*]
In what language, dog, did you learn to lie?
What bitch threw you into the world, boy,
And what good wind or foul has thrown your ship
Against this stony shore of mine no sail
Has visited no not in all the years
My aging eyes have grazed the sea in vain
For an approaching ship, I alone
Standing on my rock I and my vultures,
A cloud of wings between the sky and me
Biding their time to pick my rotting flesh;
Or after any spar or plank to save me
Swimming, or my remains from the hungry fish.
You wear the Greek dress that once I wore.
A Greek may wear Greek clothes, or did you, friend,
Murder a Greek? Friend is what I call you
If you killed a Greek. I need no reasons.
Say he was Greek: that reason is enough.
I myself am Greek. Reason enough
To kill me if you can, as I shall kill you
If your garments do not lie and you are Greek.
For they were Greeks who threw me on this rock,
Me so wounded in their service my wound
Made me unfit to serve them. Greeks saw it.
Greeks turned their heads away. Look, look at me.

These rags flap in the weather of my exile.
My grave feeds my corpse. But my grave has room
For two. My arrow wants to know, even
Before you utter your last sound: are you Greek?
Your silence says you are and bends the bow.
Die and feed the vultures that I feed on,
And give those beaks a foretaste of my flesh.
NEOPTOLEMUS. You greet your guest with a rough tongue and bid
The hungry weary sailor with drawn bow
To a rough meal. The vultures' belly
Is a narrow bed. Had I known that here
The guest eats arrows and birds get live flesh,
I should have turned my prow towards the salt sea,
More hospitable to its guest than you—
Left you your island, and your island you.
PHILOCTETES. O sound that I loved. O speech I have missed
So long, language of my earliest words,
Tongue I used to spur my thousand oarsmen
And lead a thousand spears to battle.
Yet hated as long as missed. And longer.
Long long I heard it solely from my mouth
When pain dug the cries out of my throat.
Unfeeling rocks returned my cries to me.
My ears crave another voice. Live then, live
Because you have a voice. Speak up, you Greek.
Malign me, praise my enemies. Whatever.
Lie, you Greek. Long, long I have heard no lies.
Where is your ship? Whence did you sail? Whereto?
What is your mission? Have you a mission?
Do you know who stands before you, alien
To himself; stands on his single foot,
The other nothing but foul stinking flesh?
No. You were not among my enemies.
A boy who has borne arms a shorter time
Than I have dragged my bloodied foot about.
And yet their tongues could blacken deeper black
The shadow of my shadow, to make me
Hateful to the very unborn and the dead.
To what misdeed are you lending your hand?
Have I lived too long for my murderers?
Are you the bloodhound on the bloody track
Sent to cut down the suffering beast at last

Before it turns to rip apart their dogs?
I'll give you breathing time to speak the truth.
Time for three more words and then you die. Speak.
NEOPTOLEMUS. I do not know you. Nor, stranger, do I know
Your grievance. You would kill a guiltless man.
PHILOCTETES. Silence, Greek. If this island's known to you
So is my name. They name us in one breath.
Stone after stone breathes out my name who am
This island's ruler and its slave, bound fast
By the salt sea's unbreakable blue chain
I, Philoctetes and Lemnos, my island.
NEOPTOLEMUS. I have heard of Lemnos; of you, never.
As for lying, in Skyros we do not lie.
PHILOCTETES. Yet it may be a certain liar come
From Ithaca, who stole your father's kine,
Paid his due bestriding your own mother,
And that liar it may be begot
A Skyrian liar: you. Hands off your spear.
Be what you will: liar, thief, murderer—
You have a ship and that is all I need,
Grant me a place upon your rowing bench
Or under it. But have you still a ship?
Rid me of this exile, drive from my eyes
The shadows of those vultures, unless
The storm has wrecked your ship and I must share
These fowl with you, double hunger, scant food,
And two men rotting on the open sand.
NEOPTOLEMUS. I am Achilles' son: Neoptolemus.
Dishonored I sail homeward to Skyros,
Troy behind me. Save your shaft for my foe
Who is your foe, the dog from Ithaca.
PHILOCTETES. Welcome, son of Achilles. One fool
Welcomes another. Did you serve the Greeks?
They are just, they punished you for it.
It takes a Greek to be the fool who lifts
A hand to help a Greek. But let that be.
Tell me how long the war for Priam's city
Lasted and of those we love and hated
Who lies in the rubble. For I set out
With the first fleet and was vanquished before
The first onset. No tree helps count the years,
The sun moves in one same circle, the moon

Runs on its black road under the marching stars
So distant as to seem immovable.
After a thousand risings and settings
I grew weary and ceased to count. Tell me,
How long then have I been my enemy
In my own war? That enemy struck home
With weapons far more terrible than those
Troy's hard-bitten soldiers could have wielded.
Yet the sick foot that ground me in the dust
Gave me less pain than one great terror:
Where is my enemy? He has no face.
If only I could see into my eyes
Nail with an arrow wind to sun to still
The waves that fleck the sea the mirror.
Or shall I find my face reflected
In the vulture's glare? But him I must shoot down
To bring him close enough and then his eye
Goes blind to mine. Not till I perish
Do I see my face one second then no more:
Long dying, and to see myself that long,
For that long second gladly I'd have died,
The last to see myself before I vanished
In the hunger of my guests. What's left,
Bones without shape, becomes a lightweight dust
In every weather for the wind to scatter.
Then nothing's left. But you with your two eyes,
Show me my face. Your eyes take in my face.
Turn them away, Greek, they lie. Turn them
Before my nails dig out my image there.
Or am I just a dream of Philoctetes?
No: you hold your breath and so I know
My stench is real. Tell me the dead. Tell me
How many years ago, aflame with fever,
I saw the ships leave unrecallable,
Myself sunk from their sight, unheard my cries,
Already at my ears the sound of wings
Of double wings that plow the pathless blue
Making invisible furrows as they go.
Answer me without haste. A hundred years
Or ten, no god rolls them back, nor do tears
Change dust into flesh again. Besides,
For whom do I care to weep? One only,

One corpse only can draw tears from me,
Many-headed many-tongued Odysseus's
If some chance sword has cut him down—because
I cannot kill what's dead, not kill it once,
Not twice and not a thousand times again
Its whole life long my whole life long.
NEOPTOLEMUS. The city stands unconquered, the war
Is ten years old, the generals live, hateful
To you and me, Odysseus lives, your foe
And mine, dead lies Achilles whom Paris
Pierced, dead by his own hand Ajax who brought
Achilles' body from the battlefield.
The chiefs had promised to the man who'd wrest
That body from the enemy the spear,
The armor, sword and shield—my heritage!—
Hoping such power would stir to win his corpse
The walls of Troy would crack at last and thus
The dead man help them to their victory.
At the butt end of the wall, under stones
And spittle of the shrieking widows his sword
Had made he lay. Ajax, bleeding, groaning
Bore him off—so that the hated Ithacan
Might reap unharmed the fruit of his travail.
The chiefs approved and bartered for the breasts
Of a slave girl what was neither theirs nor his.
When the dupe cried out his wrong, displaying
Empty hands, and showing at the tents
Of his deceivers the blood paid out,
Derision was his prize, the thief's quick tongue
Proved wrong right, and Ajax that night raving
After much wine drunk to quell his fury
Struck, beheaded, slaughtered the cattle
He mistook for Odysseus and the chiefs.
At dawn he saw himself as they saw him
Bedizened with the blood of beasts, his hands
Filled with cows' flesh and still unassuaged
His thirst for other blood. Both armies laughed.
In alien waves he washed his sword and self,
Planted the sword's hilt into the alien soil,
Drenched the shore in his own blood and went home
The long way by his sword into the night.
All this happened and more not worth my telling

While I at Skyros looked after my horses.
There, to make me fill the hole left in their ranks,
The generals dispatched the Ithacan.
With prayers he caught me and sweet words, concealed
The theft of shield and sword and spear, all mine,
Netted me and brought me to unvanquished
Troy, the rimless sea behind me, knowing,
Oh they counted shrewdly on my knowing
That should I raise the sword in my own cause
Before the stones of Troy roll in the dust
The enemy will rise and break our cities.
To keep my anger in its splint was hard
Enough. I left the front. I cannot march
Shoulder to shoulder to the war with him
Who'd torn the spear from the dead fist, the sword
Out of the back, and from the chest the shield
That was my father's, the dust that bore me
When it was flesh. One hope is mine—the same
As yours: may the foe spare me my foe.
PHILOCTETES. Your hatred clutches at my enemy
My hatred clutches at your enemy
And Achilles whom we loved lies in the dust.
Away then. To the beach. To your ship.
Take me to Melos. Let us query, you
From your island, I from mine, with rested eye
Query the sea each day about our foe.
May the tide be kind to him, and smoothly
Bear him to our twin embrace.
[*He cries out*]
                                        Your sword!
Hack off my foot! Child! Take your sword and hack!
My pain returns, the huge bird claws again
A circle through my flesh, my guest rises
From his short sleep to entertain his host
With horrid cries. Your sword! Hack off my foot!
Who placed that stone inside your chest? Your sword!
Give it! My foot has left my own hand free.
NEOPTOLEMUS. Lean on my shoulder, let me take the bow
Until your poisoned foot bears you again.
Give me the arrows too lest they wound you
When agony twists you against yourself.
PHILOCTETES. Greek, don't touch my bow. Until my foot

Bears me again, speak to me of Melos,
Most beautiful to me among all islands.
How long have I not seen the sweet, green boughs
From which we fashioned our black ships. How long
Have I not cursed the man who first bestrode
The seas shod in ships, blamed him for my exile,
But homebound now I praise him longer than I cursed.
How long have I been to myself
Both man and wife, sex-torn, that other wound,
And from the fetters of my body no release
While birds mated high over the foam
Of the salt sea that kisses wave by wave
The red rock which is my brutal bed.
Take me to Melos, help me carry my foot.
It will not bear me where I long to go.
And hold my bow till steady once again
I grasp my steady weapon. My weapon,
My hunger's wings, that gave my teeth the sky,
My grip the clouds. No one but you before this
Has had it from my hand since Heracles
Into my hand remitted it, reward
For the last service done him when I thrust
The torch into the piled-up wood, his son
Unwilling, and reft him of the hated earth,
Sky, children, and wife, burning the hero
Scalded by his wife in Nessus' shirt:
The bow that barely served to lengthen out
My death until you came to raise me up
From my long perishing into the life
That shall not suffer death before its end.
NEOPTOLEMUS [*taking the bow*]. O had I never set eyes on Lemnos,
Nor on Troy. O had I never taken
The step that rends me from my own being
Like an axe, and worse, never to be healed.
Soon you will rue the way that I must go.
PHILOCTETES. Your many words condense into one word.
Revolted by the stench that long since
Gave me to the vultures, to the vultures
You wish to return me a second time.
So be it. Give the bow again and go.
Spare your ship the uncomfortable freight
And your ear my ugly cries of pain.

Let me forget I ever saw you.
The shadow of a shadow passed me by
A phantasm the lewd sun bred from a stone
At midday; perhaps the surf spoke to me
With a human voice, or else a vulture
Who had devoured a Greek at Troy vomited
Greek babble. The bow, babbler, while you live.
I have had ten years away from you
To learn your lessons. Ten were not enough.
Leave me, let me dwell with my vultures again.

NEOPTOLEMUS. And let me speak the truth. Troy cannot fall
Without your soldiers. Your soldiers will not fight
Unless you lead them. I have plowed the sea
To fetch you back to Troy where you shall rise
From long despair to endless glory.
Myself a dupe, reluctantly I duped
The victim of too many lies. Duty
Made me lie: there was no honest way.
Man of Lemnos, hear the whole hateful truth:
On the beach Odysseus waits, your foe
And mine. For this much was no lie: he dies
Dies by my hand, by ours if you choose
After Troy falls. Help us speed its destruction
And therefore his. We need your arm, your voice,
Your thousand men. Asclepius waits for you
To heal your wound. Come, Philoctetes, come,
Your bow, which I too cunningly extorted
From your weakness, is burning through my hand.

PHILOCTETES. Conqueror, is it shame that makes you blush?
Why shame? Cleverly the net was woven:
The best I ever saw. Decoy, you toiled
And did your duty with the best of wills.
Your tutor in deceit, who cheated you
Before, the thief who taught you how to steal,
Your foe and mine, will praise you handsomely.
Conqueror, set your foot upon my neck
Teach the loser what you learned before him
In your defeat, the sweets of subjection,
Groveler teach me how to lick his spittle
Teach me to belly the earth before him
Who leaning on his army trampled me
When racked with fever on the earth I lay.

Foe of my foes, teach me your delights.
O the bliss of being kicked. Another kick.
O joy of being dust under his heel
Like others crushed before me. Dog-hearted
Liar, stinking dog sprung of a satyr
And a boar: a stable-wench threw you
Into a pigsty where a drunken king
Vomited upon you and stood you up
Crowned with swine's dung and anointed with gall.
Take your face out of my eyes, take your lies
Out of my ears back in your craw, the lies
I believed because the voice rose sweetly
From its pool of lies. Spit out your tongue,
Breathe elsewhere: you foul my air. Choke in dung.
O sea. O heaven. O sightless stone.
Chained to the earth with my own foot, disarmed
By my own idiocy while at close range
Stands on two healthy legs the villain
I should have liked to tread under my heels—
Sent to haul into new service the servant
Dropped long ago and snatch from the vultures
The meat he² had spread out for them before.
Now he waits: will his bait hook in the fish
The stinking fish good for the vultures once
But now begrudged them, summoned now to meet
More vultures, stinking on yet sweet of smell
For those who'd soon be stinking but for him.
The foulest-smelling carrion is one's own:
Add one kindness to your other mercies,
Son of Achilles, or, if in this too
You lied, son of No one. Into my breast
Thrust one of my stolen arrows the length
A sword goes from a man's skin to his heart
Then pull it out again, cast shame away,
A dead man tells no tales, then go proclaiming
To your friends the Greeks but first of all
To him of Ithaca, closest to your heart
Because he robbed you of your legacy,
And to your children, if the war keeps trim

2. In this especially difficult passage, it would appear that the "he" has shifted from Neoptolemus to Odysseus.

Your seed, and peace gives leisure-time to sow it,
Proclaim that Philoctetes died a fool
Of fools, since he believed a Greek. He died:
Quiver of his own arrow, that flew
From his own bow, that was stretched at his own
Command by the first fool that came to Lemnos
After him, island of fools, where folly
Had tossed him, island of vultures, red rock
Where fools eat vultures and are eaten by
The meat they ate. And do not bury me
In alien country or familiar ground
Lest my dust meet yours in the stream of stone
Beneath. Nor burn my corpse and spread my ashes
In the seeming void lest a chance wind mix
Your dust with mine. And do not leave me
To the vultures: dead men mingle in their gut.
And do not throw me to the fish: my flesh
Might well become your harbor. Nor to the salt
The bottom salt that could be shortly
Entertaining you as well with lips
That wash and wash until your bones resemble
Salt, resemble me who sank before you
Resembling salt and for as long as salt
Resembles salt we would be like to like.
But lift me to the crater, where smoke flies up
From a sun under our feet that neither
Rises nor sets and drop me so I fall
Of my own weight swifter my one foot than
A thousand hurrying feet down through the smoke
Down to the undivided fire. With this
My last is said, send the arrow on its way.
NEOPTOLEMUS. I wish the war could end another way
    Than by our enemy conquering
    Our enemy, another way to glory
    For you and me than this: my walking
    In a net of shame down to the seashore
    To bring tidings of my conquering lie,
    Delivering my shameful catch, red-faced,
    Black-handed, to my enemy and yours
    Then to return with him to bind you fast
    And drag you to our ship: it must be done.
    Your neck must bear the yoke of duty.

So must mine, though sooner than deprive you
Of your bow I'd have your arrow pierce my breast.
[*Exits with the bow*]
PHILOCTETES. If I could turn myself into a shaft
That kills, and feels the killing that it does!
If I could hurl this island on his head,
Die in the deed but see him drown and taste
His salty death before I took my own.
But he who made me made me half a thing.
My hand that tackled spear and bow lacks strength
To fling myself the distance of an arrow,
My foot that trampled nations when it marched
In union with my men, my foot needs earth:
Earth thrives without me, but I need earth
And treading it something is left to me.
Hear me Philoctetes, man of Lemnos,
My ear has gorged on your complaints: enough!
Muzzle your shouts, your wait is over now,
Bend your neck, horse put on the harness,
Learn to live again and join the butchery.
[*He stands up*]
They need you. You are worth netting again.
Run fish, take your place in the meshes.
And if the stench you make poisons the air,
Rest easy, their noses are on duty,
You do not stink. What, my foot, not moving?
After ten years you'd like a different ship?
There is no other ship, the chain is strong.
Your enemy's your only friend. Swallow
Your hatred. You chewed it long. It fed you
It and the vultures. Thank the Greeks for it.
Keep it warm until you are avenged.
You lived for his death. Wait a little longer.
Fair prospects open. Let a thousand shafts
Protect your prey for the thousand and first.
So you would act were you another man
Crying and stinking as you did. But mine
Was the wound mine the flesh that cried after
The fleet and after the humming sails.
I was the man who tore at the vultures
Bitten by the years. I and I and I.
Mine is the hate I bought at such a price.

Keenly now my foot takes the promise
to be whole again next to its brother.
Its leaden weight of pain are wings to it
A mighty lure drags off my rotten flesh.
Go, there's room for you under his heel.
Live for his next kick. Sweet life among men,
Guzzling blood together once again!
Human touch: a fist. Bread: their spittle.
Run with your single leg into the mud
That heals all injuries, the old, the new,
And let the stench of battle blot my own.[3]
[*He begins to leave*]
Who goes there?
[*Enter* ODYSSEUS *and* NEOPTOLEMUS]

ODYSSEUS.   You know him, Philoctetes.

PHILOCTETES. Whose unforgotten voice calls out my name?

ODYSSEUS. That of a man who remembers yours
    Since, serving Greece, he threw you to the vultures.

PHILOCTETES. Threw the soldier wounded in that service.

ODYSSEUS. And by that wound become unfit to serve.

PHILOCTETES. Philoctetes.

ODYSSEUS.   You.

PHILOCTETES.   Who am I? Who are you?

ODYSSEUS. Odysseus, whom you know. Don't play the fool.

PHILOCTETES. Odysseus was a liar. If you are
    Odysseus and call me Philoctetes
    Then I am not he.

ODYSSEUS.   Perhaps Odysseus
    Lies so well he makes himself believe
    He is Odysseus, and lies again,
    Is someone else, therefore is no liar,
    And calls you Philoctetes in full truth.
    So much for chatter. Stand up and come.

PHILOCTETES [*to* NEOPTOLEMUS].
    Give me my bow, friend, give me one arrow.

ODYSSEUS. Come willingly or manacled. But come
    You must, to serve yourself and us.
[*to* PHILOCTETES]
                                          The rope.

---

3. This deceptive submission seems to echo ll. 666–83 of Sophocles' *Ajax*.
There are several other apparent echoes from *Ajax* in Müller's play.

PHILOCTETES. The bow! Scrub this blot that mars your name.
Undo that which you did against your will.
A liar made a liar of you, a thief
Made you a thief. Wash clean your name.
Return the bow, take back your name again.
ODYSSEUS [*to* NEOPTOLEMUS]. You hurt him if you do his bidding.
And every minute lost on Lemnos dooms
Another soldier in our distant war.
PHILOCTETES. Then will I stand stock-still till the last Greek
Lies on a mountain of Greek corpses piled
Upon a wasted city, call it Troy
Or give it a Greek name; lies closer to
The seat of thunder than to earth; his sword
Broken and his shield smashed and his helmet
Dented by the stars making their rounds;
Butchered by the same last Trojan that he
Butchered on the mountain of Troy's corpses
And nothing's left but corpses battling
For a place to rot. A minute's cheap
And every minute kills another Greek.
Precious minute! Keep the bow. My weapon
Will be time. I stand idle. One Greek dies.
Idle again. Another Greek. Oh Time,
Murderous and ageless, whom I cursed
Ten years as hour by hour you gave the rope
Another twist to bind me to this rock,
Praised be your course from which is no escape
From which is no abstention, where you go
I go, our dwelling place above the gods.
ODYSSEUS. Bind him.
NEOPTOLEMUS.   My heart aches that I must help him
And deny you your own bow. I must bind you
To set you free. There is no other way.
PHILOCTETES. Take one more step and you will tie your rope
About the void while I go plummeting
From rock to lower rock of my own weight
And will, worth less to you each time I strike
Where living man can never follow me.
Then you can scrape the pieces of my flesh
Clean off the cliff and wrap my carcass
In your sails to lay it putrid at the feet
Of those you serve, useful to keep their flesh
And yours safe for an hour from Trojan dogs.

There, turned dog myself, I'll lie in ambush
For you dogs. When Trojan dogs rip up
Your flesh, it will be Philoctetes
Biting, Philoctetes who eluded you
And in a dog's gut held your place for you.

ODYSSEUS [*to* NEOPTOLEMUS].
Take up his bow again and come away.
He'll be needing neither it nor us.
[*To* PHILOCTETES]
The wind your fall will make may stiffen
Priam's wall against our storm. And brief may be
Your headstart in the dust if Zeus lends us
No lightning-bolt against Troy's citadel.
But dying soon or late neck in the yoke
Willing or unwilling, we shall die, I think,
Not all forgotten by the sons who grow
Out of the dust that was our flesh.
While you commander of a thousand spears
Fall headlong in the emptiness you made
And sooner will a god lend us his fire
Than any living mouth pronounce your name.

PHILOCTETES. Stay. Do not leave me to the vultures
A second time.

NEOPTOLEMUS.   Forget the vultures.
Join us and away. Your bow.

ODYSSEUS.   Give me the bow.
Rage does not turn so soon to smoke
Rage fed so long and with such food.
Help him walk. My arm won't make his going
Smooth, and time is short.

PHILOCTETES [*to* NEOPTOLEMUS].
                    Now the second time
You take my bow, which I had rather see
In fragments in your hand than held in his.

ODYSSEUS. You deny yourself more than your weapon.
If nothing else will serve, think of your vengeance.

PHILOCTETES. Is it yourself you throw at me for bait?
It smells of corpse: the corpse you will soon be.
Go your ways, yet there is no return for you,
For you to Ithaca, for you to Skyros.
Go with the bow, which I no longer need.
Leave me. I will not let you use me.

Give me a sword, and axe, a knife. Hack off
My legs lest they run after you against
My will. Sever my head lest with my eyes
I follow you and track your moving sails,
And lest my voice louder than breaking waves
Pursues you to the strand and out to sea.
Hack off my hands, besides, lest voicelessly
They beg you for a place upon your deck
Or at the front. And lest my stumps beg on
Against my will, tear from my trunk both arms.
My trunk will acquiesce at last and fall
Senseless on senseless stone: such is my will.
NEOPTOLEMUS. Leave him to himself and to his final peace
    If life with us seems worse to him than death.
ODYSSEUS. One life is granted you, me and him alike.
    Come. He'll rave till he can rave no more.
    When he is dumb we shall take stock again.
[ODYSSEUS *and* NEOPTOLEMUS *leave*]
[*Pause*]⁴
[NEOPTOLEMUS *enters with the bow*]
PHILOCTETES. Do you come bearing new lies and stronger rope?
NEOPTOLEMUS. Take back your bow. Then follow us to Troy
    Or stay on Lemnos as you choose but take
    What I so wrongly won abusing
    Your weakness. Let me be clean, as he is not.
PHILOCTETES. You break too late with them. Your change of mind
    Changes nothing. Philoctetes is nothing
    To himself nothing to you Greeks nothing
    Will tear and break when my flesh tears falling
    And my bones break falling from rock to rock
    Nothing shall keep the Trojan dogs from you
    Nothing live on Lemnos but its vultures
    And between them and you small difference.
    I am nothing now that to elude you
    I hound myself out of my nothing life.
    Keep the bow, break it, throw it to the winds.
[*Enter* ODYSSEUS]
ODYSSEUS. Why here? What are you plotting with the bow?
NEOPTOLEMUS. The bow you stole from him using my hand

---

4. Müller suggests an optional intermission here.

My hand returns to him, one of your preys
Saves the other.
ODYSSEUS.   Give me the bow.
NEOPTOLEMUS.
Not you will hinder me from being just.
ODYSSEUS. You give away your life and mine.
NEOPTOLEMUS.   Let me
Not owe my life to dirty victories.
ODYSSEUS. Perish Greece, and he, and you, and I!
NEOPTOLEMUS. Not dying is for gods. Men must not lie.
ODYSSEUS. You should have borne with lies a little longer.
Under our keel is water in abundance
To wash away the spot, neither your blood
Nor ours was needed, and the sick wretch there
Would have been journeying to recovery.
I should have asked a stone to stand by me
Deaf to the voice which years of silence made
Too siren-sweet and stone-blind to the face
His foot wrenched to a mask in years of exile.
Why did I leave you eye and ear? Before
His wound opens your fist, give me his bow—
His other weapon—then hurry to our ship,
There rock the waves in your two arms, there cry
If you have tears because the gods gave fish
No wings or from our bark no leaf can sprout—
There wait until he loves his life again.
We two have gone so far that we must follow
To the end. Spit out compassion, it tastes
Of blood, we lack the time and room for virtue.
Learn from the gods another day. Today
You are a man and live with other men.
NEOPTOLEMUS [*to* PHILOCTETES]. Take it before his tongue twists me
again.
ODYSSEUS. Step back or else the vultures get your arm.
NEOPTOLEMUS. Or the fish your tongue.
[*He drops the bow. Swordfight with* ODYSSEUS. PHILOCTETES *picks up the
bow*]
PHILOCTETES.   Stop.
[*To* NEOPTOLEMUS]   Throw down your sword.
I want him to live.
[*To* ODYSSEUS] Him you may cut to shreds.
I do not hate him; why should I weep

For him? Now drop your sword as well: at once!
It must not nick your skin. I want you whole.
Your death is my allotted task. Alas
That we are mortal and cannot kill now
And now and forever.
NEOPTOLEMUS.   Your hatred proves
You loved your life. Duty compelled Odysseus
To take it from you: now he returns it.
PHILOCTETES. Smooth words learnt by rote. The man you speak of
Is no longer me. Go see if a stone
Will listen to your complaints till I shut off
That irksome noise your voice.
NEOPTOLEMUS.   Using the bow
I returned to you, trusting the man you were.
PHILOCTETES. Yes, using the bow.
ODYSSEUS.   Listen, Nobody,
Let me tell you who you were: Our rescue
From the sea storm, our way to Troy,
When the sea god rocked our fleet greedy
For a swimming wood not of his making
Hungry for us, beasts not of his making.
Waves raised us to the clouds, the clouds struck back
With rain, each vessel was each vessel's foe,
Mast cut down mast and plank crashed plank
As the god took the helm, spinning, swirling—
Himself, though firmer than firm upon the foam,
Driven by wanton winds and the land
So coveted before now deadly close.
Yet his prey eluded the violent god:
The snake lay curled around the altar.
Each man pointed to each man: you alone
Took the bite and opened Troy for us.
And once again the god saw us sail on
And held his breath to prison us. No-wind
Accomplished what the wind had failed to break.
Thirty sails drooped. You whom we had thanked before
Now foiled our sacrifice roaring with pain
Where silence was prescribed. Your blackened foot
Led you to Lemnos. I shall lead you now
From weary years of exile to final
Merited glory. Kill me and you kill
Three thousand. Three thousand killed, Troy stands safe

And if it does our cities die. Your foot
Treading my neck walks towards death. Without me
All living green dies for you, I am your tree
I am your grass. Without me they are not.
PHILOCTETES. Is your mouth still open, does your tongue wag
  Obediently still to prolong your time?
  Watch how silence will shatter your talk.
  What are cities to me? I see none here.
  They are nothing. Fantasies. Images
  Made by words, dream habitations, traps
  Blind eyes have set in empty air, branches
  Out of rotten heads where lie mates with lie.
  They do not exist. Green does not exist.
  Bald is my spot of earth. Let yours be so.
  This Lemnos is a thing which idle gods
  Stretched without purpose between one nothing
  And another; razed and scabbed and possessed
  By a fire in its bowels stolen
  From the gods; and bare it shall remain
  Till it reconquers nothing from its scabs
  Emptied once and for all when Night takes back
  The stars it lent. Pluck out your eyes. They lie.
  Their sockets will speak truth. As for my life,
  It knows one single truth, which is your death.
ODYSSEUS. Take another way out of your wretchedness.
  He and I have failed. Let you and him succeed.
  Dead men do not taste the laurel's berries.
  I speak of my own death: in the shadow
  Of your bow death brands my words. My name
  Already tastes of blood. Follow the boy
  Over my corpse to Troy. He had no share
  In your old hurt and in the new one shared
  Unwillingly. Devise me a good death,
  Some lie that keeps my soldiers in their harness.
  Tell them my corpse cannot be found: either
  A fish, envious of my eloquence,
  Ate me—or else a sea god did because
  I spat into the waves.
NEOPTOLEMUS.   I gave away
  The bow. Now I become your shield.
  [*To* PHILOCTETES]
                                    Take my life

For his.
[*To* ODYSSEUS]
      Mine is worth less to Greece than yours.
ODYSSEUS. Out of my way till you regain your senses.
PHILOCTETES. Do as he says. Besides, your face must serve
  As a mirror now to show me how he dies
  Before you do. Why did God deny me
  Sight to see my seeing eyes; why forbid
  This point of time to linger? If only
  I could pry the picture of his death
  Out of your eyes, his cry of agony
  Out of your ears.
  [*To* ODYSSEUS]
              Learn your task from me.
  Learn what you must do to serve the chieftains.
  I shall pierce your foot. Stinking it shall drive you
  Crawling to and fro upon this rock
  Three-footed, running from the stinking fourth
  To no avail, running from your screams
  To no avail, screaming louder as you run,
  And louder in you if you stop your ears,
  Drunk with your own stench, carrion for vultures,
  Shrivelled inside vultures, dung for vultures,
  Dung presently of vultures; crawl and race
  Your own rottenness; but it crawls faster
  Than you, it reaches your foot, you it reaches,
  Crawl, crawl, crawl faster. Have you learned to scream?
  Lemnos will teach you. Can you eat vulture?
  Lemnos will show you how. Eat what you reap,
  Here's tree, here's grass, here's green for you before
  I rip you root and all out of yourself.
  [*He shoots a vulture and throws it to* ODYSSEUS]
  Your vulture. Learn from him that which you taught.
  Eat; he has eaten your kind before;
  Soon he will dine on you; eat, eat your grave
  So you can feed your grave after you die.
  What, friend, you shudder, you do not relish
  Your work?
NEOPTOLEMUS. Nor I mine.
  [*He picks up his sword and runs* PHILOCTETES *through the back*]
              The first of my dead
  Are you whose gate to hell gapes at his back.

I wish another man had opened it.
Pitiful glory, killing a dead man.
His blood flows from the belly of his death,
But long ago it dribbled from his foot.
I have ended both his injury and ours.

ODYSSEUS. You proved yourself my quick apprentice.

NEOPTOLEMUS. What shadow blackens the day?

ODYSSEUS.   The nation
Of vultures gathers for its final work.
Your own good deed demands another. Stones.

[NEOPTOLEMUS *brings stones*]
Let not his corruptible remains pass
Through the guts of vultures: that way is strange
To flesh, where what was rent is heaped together,
Breast covers neck and foot covers skull. With stones
I cover what I threw upon the stone.

[*They throw stones*]
Save the bow. He requires it no more.
Nor do the vultures want it. It irks me
That I owe my life to such a death.

NEOPTOLEMUS. And me, that I bestowed it upon you.
Though not for long. His hand holds nothing now.
Time was it held a thousand spears.

ODYSSEUS.   What is
Is. Take up his bow.

NEOPTOLEMUS.   Did you not tell me
Troy will crush us if we lose this man?

ODYSSEUS. So I said. And now I unsay it.
Lost for good, down the stones on two sound feet,
He must become superfluous to us
Who long ago was indispensable
In many a storm. Our war must close
Without him. Take his quiver too.
One arrow, one Trojan. I wish a god
Would pull me down into his sleep. Thunder,
Roll the sky out of my eyes. Tear, lightning,
Tear from me the ground on which I stand.
Nothing. And so we leave, to trade again
This less than steady ground for one that roils,
And this half-buried man for corpses
Burying a soil become too scarce to hold
So many dead so quickly killed. Many

But not enough, quickly yet too slowly,
For Troy will not be ours until the dead
Shall mount higher than its walls. Come, hurry,
For God might note my prayer and strike me dead
With his black wing before my time, and then
One butcher less returns to slop in blood.
[*He goes, then stops*]
Though we failed to catch our fish alive
The corpse might serve as bait and serve, who knows,
Better than before: he cannot keep us now
From honing spears and swords upon his wound.
Remove the stones and lift the corpse. Load it
On my back. I shall lend it my two feet.
[ODYSSEUS *carries the body*]
Alive and wretched on this rock you weighed
Heavier on me than now, emaciated
Feather-light after ten years of fasting.
[*To* NEOPTOLEMUS]
Alas the Trojans came ashore before us
To turn this man against his fellow Greeks.
But he staunch Greek kept faith with us, not gold
Nor eloquence nor threats could shake his truth,
For which they murdered him. We saw him perish
Saw him from the sea while wrestling for our lives
With the wild waters: beset upon his rock
By seven Trojans, till the eighth slew him
From behind and louder than the breakers
Rang his cry. Unforgettable the sight
For us, sent too late and all but vanquished
By the sea. Aghast, you dropped the oar,
Was it not so? A mighty wave threw us
Just past the rock, then sucked us back again,
And on that very wave the enemy
Flew past our spears upon his speedy ship
While yet we grappled with the tide and so
We forfeited our vengeance too. Fleeing
In all haste, they left the bow to us.
The sword thrust in his back confirms my tale.
NEOPTOLEMUS. If Philoctetes can be spared, so can you.
You showed me how to trample underfoot
What's best in me. I, thief, liar, killer,
I saw the Trojans murder not one man but

Two.
ODYSSEUS [*Turning about, the corpse still on his back*].
  Here's my dead back. Shoot. Give the lie
Another useful twist. Yet think of this:
If I was butchered by the Trojans too
My testimony's gone. Three thousand Greeks
Will disbelieve you, knowing from your mouth
And mine the hatred that you bear me
For carrying your father's arms. Return
To Troy: the bow is yours: you won it
With your sword; and so the string is stretched
Against yourself, the shaft bounds back on you,
Besides the weight of stones which your own men
Will hurl at you. The borrowed oxhide
Is a handy shield. A better one's
The dead man on my back. But your hatred
Clothes me all in iron.
[*He turns again.* NEOPTOLEMUS *puts away the arrow*]
NEOPTOLEMUS.   Would it were otherwise.
ODYSSEUS. Trade your load with mine and walk before me.
  [ODYSSEUS *takes the bow,* NEOPTOLEMUS *the corpse*]
At Troy I shall be telling to you the lie
That could have washed your hand if you had spilled
My blood on Lemnos here and now. Move on.
Faster. Let not your rage evaporate.
The table's set for you at Troy. Move on.

Bibliography

Adams, S. M. *Sophocles the Playwright*. Toronto: University of Toronto Press, 1957.

Alt, Karin. "Schicksal und Physis im Philoktet des Sophokles." *Hermes* 89 (1961): 141–74.

Avery, H. C. "Heracles, Philoctetes, Neoptolemus." *Hermes* 93 (1965): 279–97.

Bowra, C. M. *Sophoclean Tragedy*. Oxford: Oxford University Press, 1944.

Calder, W. M., III. "Aeschylus' *Philoctetes*." *Greek, Roman, and Byzantine Studies* 11 (1970): 171–79.

———. "A Reconstruction of Euripides, *Philoctetes*." In *Greek Numismatics and Archaeology: Essays in Honor of M. Thompson*, edited by Otto Mörkholm & N. M. Waggoner, pp. 53–62. Wetteren, Belgium: Editions NR, 1979.

———. "Sophoclean Apologia: *Philoctetes*." *Greek, Roman, and Byzantine Studies* 12 (1971): 153–74.

———. "Die Technik der Sophokleischen Komposition im Philoktetes." In *Hellenische Poleis*, edited by E. C. Welskopf, pp. 1382–88. Berlin: Akademie-Verlag, 1974.

Dalfen, Joachim. "Philoktetes und Oedipos auf Kolonos: Das Spätwerk des Sophokles und sein zeitgeschichtlicher Hintergrund." *Studia Humanitatis: Ernesto Grassi zum siebzigsten Geburtstag*, edited by Eginhard Hora and Eckhard Kessler, pp. 43–62. Munich: Fink, 1973.

Erbse, Hartmut. "Neoptolemos und Philoktet bei Sophokles." *Hermes* 94 (1966): 177–201.

Errandonea, Ignacio. "Filoctetes." *Emerita* 23 (1955): 122–64; 24 (1956): 72–107.

251

Faguet, Émile. "Sophocle: *Philoctète*, par André Gide." *Propos de Théâtre*. Paris: Société française d'imprimerie et de librairie, 1903.

Fuqua, Charles. "Studies in the use of myth in Sophocles' *Philoctetes* and the *Orestes* of Euripides." *Traditio* 32 (1976): 29–95.

Gellie, G. H. *Sophocles: A Reading*. Carlton, Victoria: Melbourne University Press, 1972.

Grosjean, Jean, ed. *Les tragiques grecs*. Bibliothèque de la Pléiade. Paris: Gallimard, 1967.

Hamilton, Richard. "Neoptolemus' Story in the Philoctetes." *American Journal of Philology* 96 (1975): 131–37.

Harsh, P. W. "The Role of the Bow in the *Philoctetes* of Sophocles." *American Journal of Philology* 81 (1960): 408–14.

Hester, D. A. "Very Much the Safest Plan; or, Last Words of Sophocles." *Antichthon* 7 (1973): 8–13.

Hinds, A. E. "The Prophecy of Helenus in Sophocles' *Philoctetes*." *Classical Quarterly*, n.s. 17 (1967): 169–80.

Jameson, M. H. "Politics and the *Philoctetes*." *Classical Philology* 51 (1956): 217–27.

Jebb, R. C., ed. and trans. *Sophocles: The Plays and Fragments, pt. 4, The Philoctetes*. Cambridge, 1890.

Jouan, François. *Euripide et les légendes des chants cypriens*. Paris: Belles Lettres, 1966.

———. "Le Tennès(?) d'Eschyle et la légende de Philoctète." *Etudes classiques* 32 (1964): 3–9.

Kamerbeek, J. C. *The Plays of Sophocles: Commentaries, Part 6, The Philoctetes*. Leiden: E. J. Brill, 1980.

Kieffer, J. S. "Philoctetes and Arete." *Classical Philology* 37 (1942): 38–50.

Kirkwood, G. M. *A Study in Sophoclean Drama*. Ithaca, N. Y.: Cornell University Press, 1958.

Kitto, H. D. F. *Form and Meaning in Drama*. New York: Barnes and Noble, [1957].

———. *Greek Tragedy*. 2d ed. London: Methuen, 1950. 3d ed. London: Methuen, 1961.

Knox, B. M. W. *The Heroic Temper: Studies in Sophoclean Tragedy*. Berkeley: University of California Press, 1964.

Kott, Jan. *The Eating of the Gods: An Interpretation of Greek Tragedy*. New York: Random House, 1973.

Lesky, Albin. *Die Tragische Dichtung der Hellenen*. 3d ed. Göttingen: Vandenhoeck & Ruprecht, 1972.

———. *A History of Greek Literature*. New York: Crowell, 1966.

Lessing, G. E. *Laocoon; or, On the Limits of Painting and Poetry*. Trans. E. C. Beasley, rev. for Bohn's Library. London, 1914.

Letters, F. J. H. *The Life and Works of Sophocles*. London: Sheed & Ward, 1953.

Lida, Maria Rosa. *Introducción al teatro de Sofocles*. Buenos Aires: Paidos, 1971.

Linforth, Ivan M. *Philoctetes: The Play and the Man*. Berkeley: University of California Press, 1956.

Looy, Herman van. "Les fragments d'Euripide." *L'antiquité classique* 32 (1963): 162–99.

Mandel, Oscar. *A Definition of Tragedy*. New York: New York University Press, 1961.

Marx, Friedrich. "Philoktet-Hephaistos." *Neue Jahrbücher für das klassische Altertum* 13 (1904): 673–85.

Masaracchia, Agostino. "La scena dell'*emporos* nel Filottete di Sofocle." *Maia* 16 (1964): 79–98.

Milani, L. A. *Il mito di Filottete nella letteratura classica e nell'arte figurata*. Florence, 1879.

———. *Nuovi monumenti di Filottete*. Rome, 1882.

Murray, Gilbert. *Euripides*. The Athenian Drama Series, vol. 3. New York, 1902.

Muth, Robert. "Gottheit und Mensch im Philoktet." In *Studi in onore di Luigi Castiglioni, 2: 641–58*. Florence: Sansoni, 1960.

Norwood, Gilbert. *Greek Tragedy*. 4th ed. London: Methuen, 1948.

Nussbaum, Martha. "Consequences and Character in Sophocles' *Philoctetes*." *Philosophy and Literature* 1 (1976–7): 25–53.

Pauly, A. F. "Philoktetes." In *Paulys Real-Encyclopädie der klassichen Altertumwissenschaft*, vol. 19, cols. 2500–2509. Stuttgart, 1894–1963.

Perrotta, Gennaro. *Sofocle*. Messina and Milan: G. Principato, 1935.

Pestalozza, Uberto. *L'éternel féminin dans la région méditerranée—ne*. Translated by Marcel De Corte. *Latomus*, vol. 79 (1965). Translation of *L'eterno femminino mediterraneo*. Venice: Neri Pozza, 1954.

Poe, Joe Park. *Heroism and Divine Justice in Sophocles' Philoctetes*. *Mnemosyne*, supp. vol. 34 (1974).

Pohlenz, Max. *Die griechische Tragödie: Erläuterungen*. 2d ed. Göttingen: Vanderhoeck & Ruprecht, 1954.

Pratt, Norman T. "Sophocles' 'Orthodoxy' in the *Philoctetes*." *American Journal of Philology* 70 (1949): 273–89.

Reinhardt, Karl. *Sophocles*. 3d ed. Translated by Hazel Harvey and David Harvey. Oxford: Blackwell, 1979.

Robinson, D. B. "Topics in Sophocles' *Philoctetes*." *Classical Quarterly* 63 (1969): 34–56.

Roscher, W. H. *Ausführliches Lexikon der griechischen und römischen Mythologie*. Leipzig, 1884–1937.

Rose, Peter W. "Sophocles' *Philoctetes* and the Teachings of the

Sophists." *Harvard Studies in Classical Mythology* 80 (1976): 49–105.

Schlesinger, Eilhard. "Die Intrige im Aufbau um Sophokles Philoktet." *Rheinisches Museum für Philologie* 111 (1968): 97–156.

Schmidt, Jens U. *Sophokles Philoktet: Eine Strukturanalyse.* Heidelberg: Carl Winter, 1973.

Seale, David. "The Element of Surprise in Sophocles' *Philoctetes.*" *Bulletin of the Institute of Classical Studies of the University of London* 19 (1972): 94–102.

Stumbo, Beniamino. "Il Filottete di Sofocle." *Dioniso* 19 (1956): 89–110.

Taplin, Oliver. *Greek Tragedy in Action.* Berkeley: University of California Press, 1978.

―――. "Significant Action in Sophocles' *Philoctetes.*" *Greek, Roman, and Byzantine Studies* 12 (1971): 25–44.

Untersteiner, Mario. *Gli 'Eraclidi' e il 'Filottete' di Eschilo.* Florence: Sansoni, 1942.

―――. *Sofocle.* 2d. ed. Florence: Nuova Italia, 1974.

Valgimigli, Manara. *Poeti e filosofi di Grecia.* 3d ed. Bari: Laterza, 1951.

Vidal-Naquet, Pierre. "Le *Philoctète* de Sophocle et l'éphébie." In *Mythe et tragédie en Grèce ancienne,* ed. J.-P. Vernant and Pierre Vidal-Naquet. Paris: Maspero, 1977.

Wace, A. J. B. and F. H. Stubbings. *A Companion to Homer.* London: Macmillan, 1963.

Waldock, A. J. A. *Sophocles the Dramatist.* Cambridge: Cambridge University Press, 1951.

Webster, T. B. L. *Athenian Culture and Society.* Berkeley: University of California Press, 1973.

―――, ed. *Philoctetes.* Cambridge Greek and Latin Classics. Cambridge: Cambridge University Press, 1970.

Weinstock, Heinrich. *Sophokles.* 3d ed. Wuppertal: Marées-Verlag, 1948.

Whitman, C. H. *Sophocles: A Study of Heroic Humanism.* Cambridge, Mass.: Harvard University Press, 1951.

Wilamowitz-Moellendorff, T. J. W. von. *Die dramatische Technik des Sophokles.* Berlin: Weidmann, 1917.

Wilson, Edmund. *The Wound and the Bow.* London: W. H. Allen, 1952.

Acknowledgments

I acknowledge with thanks the kindness of the following persons and publishers for granting permission to reprint or translate copyrighted material:

Alfred A. Knopf, Inc. for permission to reprint *Philoctetes; or, The Treatise on Three Ethics* from *My Theater*, André Gide, translated by Jackson Mathews. Copyright © 1951 by Alfred A. Knopf, Inc.

Robert Torrance and Houghton Mifflin Company for permission to reprint *Philoctetes* from *The Women of Trachis and Philoctetes*, by Sophocles, translated by Robert Torrance. Copyright © 1961 by Robert Torrance.

Heiner Müller and Suhrkamp Verlag for permission to translate *Philoktet*, by Heiner Müller. Copyright © Suhrkamp Verlag, Frankfurt on the Main, 1966.

Indiana University Press for permission to reprint a selection from *The Trojan War: The Chronicles of Dictys of Crete and Dares the Phrygian*, by R. M. Frazer.

Cassell Ltd. for permission to reprint a selection from *The Pharsalia*, by Lucan, translated by Robert Graves.

Columbia University Press for permission to reprint a selection from *The New Columbia Encyclopedia*, New York, Columbia University Press, 1975, p. 2133.

Loeb Classical Library and its publishers, Harvard University Press, for permission to reprint selections from: *Roman History*, by Appian, translated by Horace White; *The Library*, by Apollodorus, translated

255

by J. G. Frazer; *Minor Works,* by Aristotle, translated by W. S. Hett; *Tusculan Disputations,* by Cicero, translated by J. E. King; *Discourses,* by Dio Chrysostom, translated by J. W. Cohoon; *The Library of History,* by Diodorus Siculus, translated by C. H. Oldfather; *Metamorphoses,* by Ovid, translated by F. J. Miller; *Description of Greece,* by Pausanias, translated by W. H. S. Jones; *Imagines; Callistratus; Descriptions,* by Philostratus, translated by Arthur Fairbanks; *Moralia,* by Plutarch, translated by F. C. Babbitt and H. North-Fowler; *Tragedies,* by Seneca, translated by F. J. Miller; *The Geography,* by Strabo, translated by Horace L. Jones; *The Argonautica,* by Valerius Flaccus, translated by J. H. Mozley.

Also by Oscar Mandel

Drama

The Fatal French Dentist (1967)
The Collected Plays, in 2 volumes (1970–71)
The Patriots of Nantucket: A Romantic Comedy of the American Revolution (1976)
Amphitryon, after Molière (1977)

Fiction

Chi Po and the Sorcerer (1964)
The Gobble-Up Stories (1967)

Poetry

Simplicities (1974)
Collected Lyrics and Epigrams (1981)

Criticism

Definition of Tragedy (1961)
Annotations to "Vanity Fair" (1981)

Commented Translations and Critical Anthologies

The Theater of Don Juan: A Collection of Plays and Views, 1630–1963 (1963)
Seven Comedies by Marivaux (1968)
Five Comedies of Medieval France (1970)
Three Classic Don Juan Plays (1971)
The Land of Upside Down by Ludwig Tieck (1978)
The Adriadne of Thomas Corneille (1981)